To Mike —
renowned gustatory anarchist

From Andy —
leading radiogenic charlatan

With warmest wishes.

May 7th, 1990.

STUDIES IN COMMUNICATION

General Editor: John Fiske

UNDERSTANDING
RADIO

IN THE SAME SERIES

Introduction to Communication Studies   *John Fiske*
Understanding News   *John Hartley*
Advertising as Communication   *Gillian Dyer*
Case Studies and Projects in Communication
                                    Neil McKeown
Key Concepts in Communication   *Tim O'Sullivan,*
            John Hartley, Danny Saunders and John Fiske
An Introduction to Language and Society
                                    Martin Montgomery
Popular Culture: The metropolitan experience
                                    Iain Chambers

UNDERSTANDING RADIO

Andrew Crisell

METHUEN   LONDON AND NEW YORK

First published in 1986 by
Methuen & Co. Ltd
11 New Fetter Lane, London EC4P 4EE

Published in the USA by
Methuen & Co.
in association with Methuen, Inc.
29 West 35th Street, New York NY 10001

Printed in Great Britain by Richard Clay
(The Chaucer Press), Bungay, Suffolk

British Library Cataloguing in Publication Data

Crisell, Andrew
Understanding radio.
— (Studies in communication)
1. Radio broadcasting
I. Title   II. Series
384.54   PN1991.5

ISBN 0–416–38330–0
ISBN 0–416–38340–8 Pbk

Library of Congress Cataloging-in-Publication Data

Crisell, Andrew.
Understanding radio.
(Studies in communication)
Bibliography: p.
Includes index.
1. Radio broadcasting—Great Britain.
I. Title   II. Series.
PN1991.3.G7C75   1986   384.54'0941   86–12562

ISBN 0–416–38330–0
ISBN 0–416–38340–8 (pbk.)

CONTENTS

GENERAL EDITOR'S PREFACE

This series of books on different aspects of communication is designed to meet the needs of the growing number of students coming to study this subject for the first time. The authors are experienced teachers or lecturers who are committed to bridging the gap between the huge body of research available to the more advanced student, and what the new student actually needs to get him started on his studies.

Probably the most characteristic feature of communication is its diversity: it ranges from the mass media and popular culture, through language to individual and social behaviour. But it identifies links and a coherence within this diversity. The series will reflect the structure of its subject. Some books will be general, basic works that seek to establish theories and methods of study applicable to a wide range of material; others will apply these theories and methods to the study of one particular topic. But even these topic-centred books will relate to each other, as well as to the more general ones. One particular topic, such as advertising or news or language, can only be understood as an example of communication when it is related to, and differentiated from, all the other topics that go to make up this diverse subject.

The series, then, has two main aims, both closely connected. The first is to introduce readers to the most important results of contemporary research into communication together with the theories that seek to explain it. The second is to equip them with appropriate methods of study and investigation which they will be able to apply directly to their everyday experience of communication.

If readers can write better essays, produce better projects and pass more exams as a result of reading these books I shall be very satisfied; but if they gain a new insight into how communication shapes and informs our social life, how it articulates and creates our experience of industrial society, then I shall be delighted. Communication is too often taken for granted when it should be taken to pieces.

John Fiske

ACKNOWLEDGEMENTS

My first and general debt is to the editor of the Studies in Communication series, John Fiske, who has been supportive and enthusiastic throughout the genesis of this book. Among my colleagues I must express my gratitude to Patricia Waugh, who made many useful suggestions and though often subjected to my own half-formed thoughts on radio was still ready to brush aside my occasional misgivings about the book's worth. I must also acknowledge the help of Michael Pickering, who directed me to some valuable sources of information about broadcasting history, and John Christopher, whose knowledge of linguistics gave me much food for thought about the nature of radio language. I am grateful to Sunderland Polytechnic for granting me a term's leave during which much of this book was written.

For such practical knowledge of radio production as I possess I am indebted to Virtue Jones and John Lavis, who made my year with BBC Radio Newcastle such a pleasant and rewarding one. I must also express my warm thanks to both Ken Stephinson of the BBC Network Centre, Manchester, and Marjorie Lofthouse of the BBC Network Centre at Birmingham for all the information they have given me on broadcasting and production techniques, audience behaviour, and media organizations in general. Jock Gallagher of the BBC Network Centre at Birmingham was a mine of information on phone-ins, for which I am grateful.

Certain material which appears in this book has occasioned three important debts. I wish to thank Messrs B. A. Robertson and Alan Tarney and the publishers Bar Music Ltd /ATV Music Ltd for permission to reproduce an extract of the lyrics from 'Wired for Sound'; the BBC for their generous permission to reproduce part of the news bulletins from *The World at One* and *Newsbeat*; and Mr John Arlott and the BBC for kindly allowing me to quote from some broadcast cricket commentary. To Mr Arlott I owe a further debt for the pains he took to provide corrections to the transcript of the broadcast. Having acknowledged all these debts I must however add that in making any mistakes or omissions which occur in the following pages I have needed help from no one: casting modesty aside, but not regret, I claim them as all my own.

Finally I must express my deep gratitude to my wife and two daughters, who throughout the writing of this book have given help, support and encouragement and borne my absences of mind, person and good humour without one word of complaint. It is for them – Margaret, Ellen Jane and Harriet Daisy – that I wrote it.

INTRODUCTION

This book is intended for students on media and communications courses in higher and further education and would, it is hoped, be of equal benefit to those with an academic interest in radio and those with a practical interest in programme production. Its purposes can be stated with deceptive modesty. The first is to determine the distinctive characteristics of the radio medium. This is attempted by locating radio among other modes of communication, individual and collective, literary and visual, by examining the historical development of British radio institutions, and by developing a theory of the signs, codes and conventions by which the medium conveys its messages. But in this latter endeavour I am not so much concerned with particular messages or texts and the deeper cultural meanings or 'dominant ideologies' they may enshrine as with how radio conveys or mediates messages of any kind. The second purpose is to explore the significance of its characteristics for such of its users as the journalist, the teacher, the dramatist and, not least, the listener; to examine the potentialities of radio as a medium of information, culture and entertainment for both broadcasters and audience.

The apparently arbitrary and disparate nature of my chapter headings requires some explanation. 'Commentary' is clearly not a programme category in the sense that 'News and Current Affairs' is and ought, perhaps, to have been subsumed under it. But as anyone who has worked in radio production will concede, programmes are notoriously difficult to categorize, or even to distinguish from individual broadcasting techniques. Drama, for instance, could be regarded as a programme category in its own right or as a technique in some other programme category such as educational radio or light entertainment. Indeed it could be argued that in a covert way drama often informs all other kinds of output by moulding them into its own format of confrontation, crisis and conclusion (Higgins and Moss, 1982). But given that there are at least titular differences between programme categories, it will be apparent that I have not included them all. Encouraged by the fact that the audience does not so much attend to individual programmes as simply listen to 'the radio' – to a general flow or sequence of programmes (Williams, 1974, 86–94) – the approach I have adopted is pragmatic: the omission of certain categories and a switching from one category or technique to another as each seemed to afford some particular insight into radio's character or potentialities. I would hope, therefore, that while the kinds of programmes I discuss may be inadequate as a catalogue of what it is possible to broadcast on the medium, they are at least as illuminating about radio as those I have omitted, and broadly representative of them.

Two final points. First I have made reference to BBC programmes and not to those of Independent Local Radio simply because the former are broadcast nationally and therefore more widely known. Secondly I have been anxious to acknowledge that both sexes are amply represented within such broadcasting roles as 'the presenter', 'listener' or 'producer', yet have wished to avoid such tiresome duplications as 'her/ his', 'herself/ himself', and so on. Hence while I have been fairly consistent in my attribution of pronouns within a single chapter, I have not hesitated to refer to the listener or broadcaster as 'she' in one chapter and 'he' in another. However, if I describe the listener to cricket commentary as 'he' and the phone-in presenter as 'she', I hope I shall not be understood to suggest that there are no female cricket enthusiasts or that no male broadcaster ever chairs a phone-in: nor should my other partial descriptions be taken only at their face-value.

PART ONE
THE MEDIUM

1 CHARACTERISTICS OF RADIO

Into the car, go to work and I'm cruisin'
I never think that I'll blow all my fuses
Traffic flows – into the breakfast show . . .
AM–FM, I feel so ecstatic now
It's music I've found
And I'm wired for sound.

           ('Wired for Sound' sung by Cliff Richard)

What strikes everyone, broadcasters and listeners alike, as significant about radio is that it is a *blind* medium. We cannot see its messages, they consist only of noise and silence, and it is from the sole fact of its blindness that all radio's other distinctive qualities – the nature of its language, its jokes, the way in which its audiences use it – ultimately derive. We can get a clearer idea of radio's characteristics by comparing it with other modes of communication.

The commonest, most basic mode can be described as *interpersonal*, in which the sender of the message and the receiver of it are physically close to and within sight of each other. The *contact* between them is oral and visual, perhaps even tactile. The primary *code*, or system of signs by which they communicate, is linguistic, that of *speech*, but likely to be aided by various 'presentational codes' of a paralinguistic nature – facial expressions, gestures, bodily movements and postures, and so on (Fiske, 1982, 71–4). The *context* to which the message refers and which enables it to 'make sense' is likely to be understood by both sender and receiver because of its physical proximity or because of their shared background or experience. But in addition lots of 'phatic' remarks are possible to check that the contact is working ('How are you?', and so on), and lots of 'metalingual' remarks to

3

check that the code is being understood ('Understand?'). And both kinds of remark prompt *feedback* – the (in this mode) easily possible transmission of the receiver's reaction to the sender. Hence the message has every chance of being accurately 'decoded', or made sense of.

The obvious advantages of modes of *mass* communication are that the sender can communicate with multitudes of receivers at the same time and at distances beyond that achievable by interpersonal communication. But the contact becomes impersonal and the risk of ambiguity and misunderstanding much greater. Feedback is an impossibility because thousands or millions of receivers cannot simultaneously transmit their varying reactions back to the sender: and because the sender cannot simultaneously present herself in person to each member of the audience she must send a representative of herself – an independent, often visible message in the form of a *text* (as in books and newspapers) or an *image* (as in film and television). But since the sender and receivers are remote from each other this message has to carry a heavy freight. In varying degrees it has to create the context to which it refers; the sender herself, who is present only within the message, does not effectively exist outside it; and the receivers for whom the message is intended. On the other hand since, as we have seen, feedback is an impossibility in mass communication there is no genuine facility of metalingual or phatic communication: the sender cannot check that the code or contact is working. For all these reasons it is of considerable advantage that the message should in some way or other be visual.

The oldest mode of mass communication is that of written characters – *literature* in its widest sense of 'writing, written language'. The code, a printed text, may be supplemented by other codes – numbers, drawings, photographs, diagrams: but the permanence of the contact compensates for its impersonality. Bereft of the presence of the sender, the receivers may read and re-read her message at leisure: decoding does not have to be instantaneous. In film and television, modes of mass communication whose message is in the form of an image, decoding does have to be instantaneous. There is no single, static text which can be perused at leisure. But this is offset by the fact that in film and television the conditions of interpersonal communication are partly re-created. The receivers can see and hear the sender: the primary code in which she communicates – speech – is supplemented by 'various presentational codes. And/or they can hear her while seeing by means of other images, which may include an image of writing, the context to which her message refers.

How, then, is radio distinguishable from these other modes of mass communication? Very largely in ways which seem to redound to its disadvantage. There is no image and no text. The contact, or *medium* as I will now term it, is utterly non-visual: the receivers, who are *listeners*, or collectively an *audience*, cannot see the sender or *broadcaster* as they can on television or film; nor are they offered the compensation of a visible and lasting message as they are in literature. Its codes are purely auditory, consisting of speech, music, sounds and silence, and since – as we shall see – the ear is not the most 'intelligent' of our sense organs their deployment has to be relatively simple. The risks of ambiguity or complete communication failure are high, and so in all kinds of radio much effort is expended on overcoming the limitations of the medium, on establishing the different kinds of contexts which we would generally be able to see for ourselves. First there is the context to which the message refers – a context which most interpersonal communication can take for granted. Physical objects or processes which are normally self-evident have to be described: 'Tell the listeners what you are doing.' 'Can you describe this object to us?' Second and more literally, there is the context of the message itself – the surrounding 'messages' (items or programmes) which also help the listener to make sense of what he hears. The description of the object may reveal that it is a fire-dog, but he will have no idea why a fire-dog is being described to him unless he has gleaned from the other messages he has heard that the programme is about antiques. One way of conveying context on the radio is by what is sometimes known as 'signposting', for example, 'Later in the programme we'll be talking about the Budget to the Leader of the Opposition'. By indicating the programme's shape or structure, signposting enables the listener to know whether he wishes to keep listening. In purely visual media such as books and newspapers – media whose messages exist in *space* rather than in time – this kind of context is immediately apparent. In a newspaper we can see at a glance what paragraphs or stories surround the one we are presently reading, and in a book or magazine we can flick through the adjacent pages or turn to the table of contents. But of course not all visual media exist purely in space: television, film and theatre are partly characterized by movement and (in common with radio) sound, which exist primarily in *time*. In film and theatre, however, the need to establish this kind of context is much less since their messages normally consist of a single plot which the spectators have been following throughout, rather than a number of discrete items which they are at liberty to dip into and out of. Like radio, television often solves the problem of context by signposting, but being a visual medium it has other resources, too: images of programmes or items which will be shown later, split-screen techniques, captions superimposed upon images, even images consisting only of printed words. Radio has nothing but different kinds of *sounds*, some of which it uses to establish the beginnings and ends of programmes for us by what are variously described as 'frame' conventions (Goffman, 1980, 162–5) or 'boundary rituals' (Fiske and Hartley, 1978, 166–7) – ways of telling us that what we are about to hear is a play and not a continuation of the news bulletin we have just been listening to. This is sometimes done by a silence (which in these circumstances is a sort of negative form of sound) or by a signature- or theme-tune and/or an announcement: 'And now *The Archers*. Mike Tucker's milk-round hasn't got off to a very good start' (two contexts are established here: that of the programme itself, a drama serial which is following the seven o'clock news, and that of the point in the story which the serial has reached). But messages in radio consist primarily of speech, and speech consists not just of words, as writing does, but always and indissolubly of words expressed in *voices*. Hence a third kind of context which often needs to be established is the reality of the radio station and the broadcasters themselves, even when they are not the subject of the programme. In a discussion programme like *Start the Week* the presenter might, for example, introduce one of his guests with some such remark as 'Glad you managed to beat that hold-up on the M4 and get here on time!' Remarks of this kind are seldom heard on the television, where we can see the presenter, the guests and the studio that surrounds them; but they are common on the radio where their purpose is to locate the station within the solid, workaday world of motorways and indicate that the broadcasters are not just 'voices in the ether' but people like us who are liable to get stuck in traffic jams and miss their appointments.

Hence the constraints imposed by radio's blindness are severe and were underlined by television, which with its growth in popularity during the 1950s was thought to be about to supersede radio altogether. I shall return shortly to the problems which the blindness of the medium can create, but want first to stress that blindness is also the source of some real advantages which it possesses over other media. The most famous of these is, of course, its appeal to the imagination. Because it offers sound-only instead of sound and vision the listener is compelled to 'supply' the visual data for himself. The details are described, or they may suggest themselves through sound, but they are not 'pictured' for him, he must picture them for himself – and he may, indeed, use them as a basis for picturing *further* details which are *not* described. Moreover as we all know, the scope of the imagination is virtually limitless: we may picture not only lifelike objects but the fantastical, impossible scenes of an experimental play.

This appeal to the imagination gives radio an evident advantage over film and television, but it could be objected that the advantage depends upon a partial notion of the imagination, that in point of fact it is more than a purely visual faculty. When watching a film of bacon and eggs cooking in a pan we imagine the *smell* they give off; when we read a description of a fairground we imagine among other things the *noise* of the crowds and the blare of the roundabout organ. The workings of the imagination are various and obscure, but we might make the preliminary suggestion that it is the faculty by which we re-create for ourselves any impressions which we would experience at first hand through one, some or all of our five senses. Since the greatest number of senses through which any of the mass media can communicate to us is two, sight and hearing, it follows that *all* the media, and not just radio, will invoke the imagination to compensate for their various deficiencies. Nevertheless it would seem that the primary and dominant function of the imagination *is* visual, as its derivation from 'image' suggests; for in replicating the functions of our senses it seems also to replicate the hierarchy into which they appear to arrange themselves, with sight at the top – in our ordinary deployment of our sensory faculties our primary means of understanding or interpreting the world seems to be visual. We may hear, smell or touch an object, but it is not until we have *seen* it that we feel we really 'know' it. The faculty of sight, then, seems to be a kind of epistemological yardstick which determines how we make sense of the outside world and what credence we attach to our other sensory faculties. Once we have seen the filmic image of the bacon and eggs we can imagine their smell, and once we have pictured our fairground we can imagine the noise of the crowds and the organ. But for most of us at least, it would seem to be extremely hard to imagine even that unique and wonderful aroma without some previous or accompanying image, whether literal or figurative and however momentary, of the bacon and eggs themselves or of the situation (for example, the breakfast table) in which they would be encountered in ordinary life. In other words, the first impulse of the imagination seems to be to visualize, even in the case of non-visual sensations such as sounds or smells: but once we have an actual or figurative picture of what approximates to the source or habitation of these sounds or smells our imagination will be able to move down the sensory hierarchy and replicate the subordinate impressions of sound, smell, taste, and so on.

Yet even though we may be prepared to agree that the imagination is predominantly visual in its replication of sensory experience, we may still regard this as a rather partial way of defining the imagination since it can do much more than this. It can replicate abstractions, qualities which cannot be seen or tasted, as when a film or television audience imagines a character's inner thoughts or feelings from the expression on her face. At this point I must emphasize that the workings not only of the imagination but also of all our mental faculties are highly mysterious: they have teased philosophers and psychologists for centuries, and it is difficult to make claims about them which are more than merely subjective or intuitive. However it is at least arguable that a visualizing tendency attaches not only to the imagination but to other mental faculties such as thought, memory and feeling. Since much (some philosophers would say all) of the material on which these faculties operate is derived through the senses, it is not surprising that something of its original manifestation seems to accompany it, nor is it the case that this manifestation is merely an irrelevant left-over; in the abstract processes of thinking, feeling or remembering, the mind seems to need frequent inspiration from the visible phenomena of the external world – a need which is suggested by the presence of certain metaphors in our language. We speak, for instance, of 'grasping' an idea as though it were before our eyes, of 'throwing light' on a problem in order to 'see' (that is, understand) it better. It could be argued, then, that some visualization, however dim, fleeting and emblematic, is present in other mental faculties than the imagination, and so since these faculties also deal in sense-impressions (even though these may be somewhat attenuated) we might now extend our definition of the imagination by saying that it replicates not only the sense-impressions but those other mental faculties which incorporate them. Hence when we see our film character's facial expression we can also imagine her thoughts or feelings without difficulty, most probably in terms of the images already provided by the film (of the other characters, the events which have befallen her, and so on) but possibly in terms of images drawn from our own experience. The mystery lies in the fact that although the abstraction, the character's thought or feeling, is apparently unknowable except in terms of these visualizations we are never in danger of confusing the latter with the former, the image with the inner activity which it represents. But the point of relevance to us here is that even though the imagination may be a predominantly visual faculty we do not have to close our eyes to use it. Not only are we capable of watching and visualizing simultaneously, we do it all the time; but when we have the power of vision it is less obvious to us that we visualize. This means that our imagination is much more active when we watch plays, films or television programmes than the champions of radio claim, for not everything which they deal with is visible. Some of it is physically suggested, as by our character's facial expression, some of it is merely described – and when it is we imagine that, too. When, for instance, a comedian tells a funny story we watch him, but even as we do so we picture – or *imagine* – the characters and events of his story. And even at the level of external reality not everything can be seen, for the setting which is displayed to us implies a contextual world which is off-stage or 'outside the picture' and which we will also have to imagine – a fact often exploited by horror films in which the menace lurks just off the screen, so that all we can see is the terrified expression of the character who is being menaced! Nevertheless it seems undeniable that radio will invoke the audience's imagination much more than film, theatre or television, since *nothing* that it deals with is visible. We must imagine not only our character's thoughts and feelings but her expression, total appearance, physical situation, and so on. However, two other important points must be made about the role of the imagination. The first is that radio is not the only medium which makes such extensive use of it. It is every bit as active when we read a book, and indeed reading and listening are rather similar in the sense that within the broad limits set by language both reader and listener can form a mental picture of what is being described. But whereas literature's 'pictures' are entirely an effect of language, radio's are also suggested by the sound of voices and of other phenomena which imply the existence of a material world we cannot find in books but can see in theatre, film and television. Hence the distinctiveness of radio is not that it involves the imagination while the other media do not, but that it involves it to a different *extent*. In literature *everything* must be imagined since nothing can be seen except printed words, nor can anything be heard. In the visual media many things can be seen and heard and proportionately less is left to the imagination. In radio many things can be heard, and this direct intimation of the material world is perhaps why, in its drama productions at least, its verbal descriptions of a physical setting or of a person's thoughts or appearance are generally much more economical than those of literature and closer to those of theatre, film and television. Moreover the fact that its codes are auditory and therefore exist in time explains the greater sense of 'liveness' that we get from radio (and the visual media) than we do from literature; for when we start to read a book we know that the last page has already been written. But radio, even when its programmes are pre-recorded, seems to be a 'present-tense' medium, offering experiences whose outcome lies in an unknown future. Like theatre and television, then, it seems to be an account of what *is* happening rather than a record of what *has* happened. Nevertheless the fact that *nothing* can be seen on the medium means that the demands which it makes upon the imagination are much greater than those made by the visual media and virtually as great as those made by literature.

The second important point which we must keep in mind is that the imagination is not confined to matters of fiction or make-believe. When listening to the radio we are obliged to imagine not only the world of a play or story but also the *real* world of news, weather reports and current affairs. Indeed, although it is dangerous to be dogmatic in these matters, it seems likely that codes in any medium which refer to anything which we cannot actually see – whether they be words, sounds or other kinds of symbols and whether they refer to listeners' requests, hobgoblins or stocks and shares – will automatically create pictures in our minds, that we cannot actually 'make sense' of these codes without at some stage and in some measure forming images of what they refer to. (One possible exception is music, since it is somewhat uncertain how far music 'refers to' or 'represents' anything in the conventional sense. But even music carries imaginative associations, as when one hears a Bach organ recital and tends to picture the organ itself or the inside of a cathedral.)

It is largely upon the listener's ability to imagine matters of fact that radio's distinctive and much vaunted sense of personal companionship seems to depend, for we hear not only the descriptions and sounds of real or imaginary worlds but the voice of the person who is describing them and we therefore form a picture of her, too. As is the case with readers of books and viewers of films or television, the pleasure the listener gains from the company of those whom he 'meets' on the medium is bound up with the sense of his own anonymity, of freedom from the obligations imposed by 'real life' relationships. He is not obliged to talk back to his radio companion, or to continue listening if he is bored. But the role of the imagination is much more crucial to the listener or the reader than to the viewer, because it is with the person *as imagined* from the words and sounds of radio or from the words of books that he forms his relationship, not with a person who is so largely pre-realized for him. And this role of the imagination transcends the conventional distinction between fact and fiction because in books and radio people and things are 'imaginary' whether they actually exist or not. In the visual media there is a general tendency towards the factual: a character in a play may be 'fictional', but she is still physically and visibly 'real'. But in books and radio there is a general tendency towards the fictional. Jimmy Young presenting his morning show on Radio 2 may be an actual person, but since we can know him on the radio only by picturing, *imagining*, him he is in a sense a 'fiction'. Two further points illustrate this fictional tendency of radio. The first is that within the broad limits set by the language and sounds of the medium any listener who has not seen Jimmy Young on television or elsewhere may imagine him to be quite unlike he is without in any way 'misunderstanding' his broadcast or failing to absorb its full impact. And the second point is that since imagining is an individual act there is unlikely to be any uniformity among the 'pictures' of Jimmy Young which the listeners form – even those listeners who know what he looks like. Indeed it is very probable that there will be as many pictures as there are listeners. Hence there is the paradox that while radio is a long-distance mode of communication it is also an inward, *intimate* medium, and so integral does the imagination seem to be to the way in which we decode virtually all its messages, whether factual or fictional, that when we speak of its 'appeal to the imagination' we mean in effect its basic ability to communicate.

Another advantageous effect of radio's blindness, and one which can reinforce its appeal to the imagination, is its *flexibility* – the fact that it can leave the listener free to perform other activities while he is listening. These characteristics have been enhanced by the technological developments of the last thirty years or so. The first radios were crystal sets, and since reception was generally poor and took place via headphones listening was a solitary activity which allowed the listener little scope to do anything else. But by the mid-1920s the crystal set had been largely replaced by the valve wireless, which incorporated a loudspeaker and remained in general use until the end of the 1950s. By modern standards its reception was of somewhat primitive quality, it was heavy and attached to an outdoor aerial so that it could not easily be moved about, and it was expensive. Even in the 1930s its price ranged from £8 to £30 (S. Briggs, 1981b, 33). Not surprisingly, then, very few households could boast more than one set, and since there was no television to provide an alternative attraction it was common practice for the members of the household to sit down and listen as a *group* (McLuhan, 1967, 327; Pegg, 1983, 197; S. Briggs, 1981a, 15). The replacement of headphones by a loudspeaker also meant that it was now possible to do other things while listening and the wireless was often used as mere 'background'; but these things could only be activities which could be performed within earshot of the loudspeaker. Portable wirelesses existed but it was the replacement of valves by transistors at the beginning of the 1960s which revolutionized radio listening. The development of VHF, FM and stereo had already made vast improvements in the *quality* of reception, but the transistor enabled radio sets to be built which consumed much less power and were much cheaper to buy. When the government abolished the radio licence fee in 1971 the cost of buying and listening to the radio was reduced yet further. So cheap had radio become by the end of the 1970s that there were 2.53 sets to each household (Paulu, 1981, 350), or virtually one set for every man, woman and child in the United Kingdom. This means that as in the days of the crystal set, listening has once again become a mostly *solitary* activity, which presents us with another paradox about radio – although its audiences may be counted in millions the medium addresses itself very much to the *individual*. The change in broadcasting styles which has occurred over the years is illuminating. In the days of wireless, the indifferent quality of the reception and the group nature of the audience tended to encourage a somewhat declamatory style of delivery. Now that the broadcaster may, if she wishes, whisper into the ear of the isolated listener delivery has become much less formal, more intimate. Indeed it may not be too fanciful to see this change of style reflected in a change in terminology. Am I alone in sensing that outside formal contexts or fixed collocations such as 'the British Broadcasting Corporation' the word 'broadcast' sounds faintly archaic – aimed, like broadsides and broadsheets, at a vast, passive audience and with little sense of the individuals who comprise it? Whereas its synonym 'transmit', literally 'to send across', seems rather more concerned for the recipient and hence, when a choice between the words is possible, more often used.

But the cheapness of radio means not only that listening is once again a mainly solitary pursuit, but that the range of things the listener can do *while* listening has been greatly extended, for he is no longer restricted to what he can do within earshot of a set which he must share with several others. He can now afford his own set in his own location. Moreover it is not a *fixed* location, for quite the most important consequence of the transistor was that it enabled radios to be made which were lighter, more compact, and which were therefore easily portable or at the very least movable. Thus if the owner wishes to listen to his radio he is not confined to his own room or even his own house, he can take his radio with him and listen in at his place of work or while picnicking, watching a soccer match, or whatever. Sets soon became small enough to be carried round like a book and even slipped into a pocket, and thanks to tiny lightweight headphones the listener can now gain excellent reception while threading his way through noisy crowds and thunderous traffic. Similarly if he wishes to listen while driving, radios are fitted in most cars as standard equipment. By the end of the 1970s nearly 70 per cent of all radio sets in the United Kingdom were either portable or 'mobile' in the sense of being fitted in motor vehicles (Paulu, 1981, 350). Hence radio is an 'intimate' mode of communication not simply because its messages can be fully 'realized' only inside the listener's head, but because they frequently reach him in circumstances of solitude and privacy and can accompany him in an unprecedented range of places and activities. This means that it can be, and is, assimilated to his daily existence much more than are the other media, and to a much greater extent than ever before.

This use of radio as what is sometimes termed a 'secondary' medium can never be emulated by television, even though the latter has also become smaller and cheaper in recent years: for while it too may be carried round its message cannot be absorbed in the same way. It makes a larger and more rigid claim on our attention, so that if it is treated as secondary (and such treatment is not unknown) we can say that most of its message is being missed since the visual codes which make up so much of that message are being ignored. The radio listener, on the other hand, can be driving along a remote Highland glen and without taking his eyes from the road be instantaneously apprised of an earthquake in the Far East. Neither newspapers nor television can match radio in terms of this immediacy as a purveyor of news and information. Nor in order to demonstrate such immediacy is it necessary to instance news which originates from the far side of the globe. What is happening in the near neighbourhood may be of much more practical importance to the listener, and on an awareness of this fact rest the greatest achievements of local radio. While driving to work the motorist can be warned about an accident which has blocked the road a few miles ahead of him, and local appeals can also reach people who are unable to stop work and attend to any of the other media – the drama club's appeal for a suit of armour for tonight's play, the soccer club's request for help in clearing a snowbound pitch for tomorrow's match. Such items are too numerous and trivial for network radio to broadcast but they are vital to small communities and, quite apart from the numbers of 'secondary' listeners they reach, can be publicized much more cheaply and quickly than in the local press. Indeed, in the time they would take to appear in the press they would cease to be 'news' at all.

The point has often been made that radio's enduring power as a mass medium derives from its unique combination of suggestiveness and flexibility – from the effect of its messages, whether factual or fictional, upon the listener's imagination together with the fact that it can accompany him in a range of other activities he may wish to perform. But the flexibility may also work *against* its suggestiveness in a way not possible in the visual media: for the freedom that radio affords us to pursue other activities while listening can, and frequently does, detract from our full understanding of what it purveys. Listening is a good deal easier than ever before but by the same token often a good deal less attentive – much of the message can be ignored. Radio communicates through only one of our five senses and beyond the bounds of this communication is a kind of no-man's land where it must constantly fight for the listener's attention against the other sense impressions which make up the situation in which he presently finds himself – driving the car, washing the dishes, and so on. This perhaps explains why there is now so much music on the radio; for while music may *allow* us to use our imagination it does not 'refer' to anything in the way that speech does and so does not *require* us to use it: it therefore makes ideal background listening. These partly complementary, partly conflicting characteristics of radio – its suggestiveness and imaginative appeal on the one hand and its flexibility on the other – have led some observers to discern two categories of listener. A former head of audience research at the BBC distinguishes between the medium's 'predominant role – as a source of entertainment' and its 'subordinate role – as an accompaniment to other activities' (Silvey, 1974, 209); while a former Director-General distinguishes between those who regard it 'as an art form on its own merits' and those for whom radio is mere background, a 'service element' (Trethowan, 1970, 7). These variations in the audience pose a considerable problem for the programme producer: for if she wishes to create an 'art form' for the listener as distinct from mere background for 'hearers', how far is she at liberty to do so? Her constant dilemma, acute in education programmes but present in other kinds such as dramas and documentaries, is how far to develop a theme which will become increasingly esoteric and how far to preserve its accessibility for the hearer, who pays less attention to radio's messages but who is always, potentially, a listener. Of course this distinction between listener and hearer, or between the predominant and 'background' functions of radio, is useful provided that we do not exaggerate it; for while there is no doubt that the opportunities to treat radio as a 'service element' have increased greatly in recent years it is highly likely, even before the advent of television, that a great many people have *always* done something else while listening to the radio –

even if only knitting or smoking. This does not mean to say that the greater part of their attention may not be focused on the radio, and in my own use of the term 'secondary medium' I do not wish to suggest that of the probable 98 per cent or so of the audience who treat it in this way hardly anyone is paying much attention to its messages. Indeed such terms as 'predominant' and 'secondary' tend to obscure the fact that much more than in any other medium a whole *range* of attention is possible, from hearing through 'overhearing' to listening, from those who want unobtrusive background noise – 'acoustic wallpaper' – to those who seek an object of concentration. But this poses as big a problem for the audience researcher as for the programme producer because the former is always in some doubt as to who the radio audience actually is and whether there is any correlation between the amount of attention which is paid to radio's messages and the extent of its effects or influences, a subject we shall return to in Chapter 10. In Chapters 2 and 10 we shall also look at the extent to which actual listening varies between 'popular' and 'quality' networks, at how far the sorts of distinctions between types of listeners which were made by Silvey and Trethowan still hold good – and at what implications this behaviour has for modern programme planning.

My purpose in the following chapters is first to give some historical account of the technological and institutional development of radio and then to explore the characteristics of the medium from the varying perspectives afforded by different kinds of programmes. But in discussing those characteristics which certain kinds of programmes seem to me to illuminate I do not wish to suggest that they are not present in other kinds. In treating the multi-levelled, ambivalent relationship between broadcaster and listener under 'Commentary', for instance, I do not wish to imply that this relationship does not exist in varying degrees in *all* radio involving personal presentation; nor do I wish to suggest by discussing the distinctive nature of radio language under 'News and Current Affairs' that this language is of any less fundamental a significance in other kinds of programmes. As I have already remarked, the distinctions between programme categories are in any case uncertain: it was many years before the BBC was able to disentangle radio drama from its Features Department; drama is often used in educational broadcasts, many of which are closely akin to documentaries; and documentary can often shade into news and current affairs. My hope is merely that by looking at radio's attempts to do different things we might gradually form a composite picture of its nature and possibilities.

2 THE HISTORY AND DEVELOPMENT OF RADIO IN BRITAIN

> the isle is full of noises,
> Sounds and sweet airs, that give delight, and hurt not.
> (Shakespeare, *The Tempest*, III, ii)

Many histories of British broadcasting have been written, ranging from the detailed and scholarly (A. Briggs, 1961–79; Paulu, 1956, 1961, 1981; Pegg, 1983) through the potted (Golding, 1974; A. Briggs, 1985) to the subjective and anecdotal (Black, 1972; Snagge and Barsley, 1972). This historical sketch, and it can be no more, will focus on the technological development of radio itself and the possibilities therein which technology has opened up rather than on the social and political contexts of broadcasting. Of course these contexts must not, and will not, be ignored, for technological developments cannot be fully understood without them and, indeed, are themselves social and political events. Nevertheless in a book of this nature and in a history of such brevity the emphasis must generally dwell upon what has happened to the medium itself.

Throughout the nineteenth and early twentieth centuries scientists of many nationalities, notably the Italian Guglielmo Marconi, were attempting to transmit messages over distances, first by means of wireless telegraphy and then by wireless telephony. But it is important to realize that these were primarily envisaged as means of *point-to-point* communication, for example ship to shore, and that when radio (or 'wireless' as it was known in the early days) was developed it was largely thought of in these terms. In Britain the Postmaster-General had been empowered to control wireless telegraphy by an Act of Parliament in 1904, and he regarded wireless telephony, whether directed at individuals or at all and sundry, as a natural extension thereof, and therefore as also subject to his control. In fact, for most members of the political establishment it was not only the case that radio was a mere by-product of point-to-point modes of communication; there was even a suggestion of primitiveness, of a lack of refinement, about a medium which *broad*cast – addressed the world at large rather than maintained confidentiality by addressing private individuals (A. Briggs, 1961, 34). In February 1920, when the Post Office gave permission to the Marconi Company to begin broadcasts to wireless enthusiasts from a transmitter in Chelmsford, it did so with a sense of unease that they would interfere with point-to-point services (Paulu, 1956, 8). This unease was fuelled by the armed forces, who for a long time resisted the encroachment of broadcasting on their wavelengths on the grounds that their secret messages would be overheard (Williams, 1974, 32). Thus, apart from the wireless manufacturers and the few home enthusiasts with receivers, there was little appreciation of the medium's *social* possibilities. Not until 1922 did the Post Office draw a distinction between technology which addressed individuals and that which addressed all and sundry (A. Briggs, 1961, 96). In that year the Marconi Company was allowed to make regular broadcasts from Writtle and shortly afterwards their London station, 2LO, was opened. Nevertheless the Post Office still feared chaos and congestion on the wavelengths and declined to license other wireless manufacturers who wished, like Marconi, to conduct broadcasts as a way of stimulating the sale of their receivers. On the other hand it was equally reluctant to allow one manufacturer to hold a broadcasting monopoly. It therefore proposed that the leading manufacturers form a broadcasting syndicate or consortium, and as a result the British Broadcasting Company was licensed by the Post Office as a *de facto* (though not *de jure*) monopoly and began transmissions in November 1922. Its funds came from three sources – the original stock, royalties on the receivers which its member companies sold, and a portion of the revenue from broadcast receiving licences. In return for the financial risk of setting up the service the manufacturers were guaranteed protection against foreign competition.

The first general manager, later managing director, of the British Broadcasting Company was J. C. W. (later Lord) Reith, whose Scottish Calvinist upbringing led him to see broadcasting as a high moral responsibility. Through its programmes he therefore sought to provide a comprehensive public service and quickly turned the company from a commercial enterprise into a respected national institution. Its output embraced a wide range of music, drama and comedy, a children's hour, and with the help of external advisory committees, religious and schools broadcasts. Within three years a national network had been established, and with the opening of the long-wave transmitter at Daventry in 1925 reception was available to 85 per cent of the population, many with a choice of national or regional programmes. The population reacted to the new medium with prodigious enthusiasm. In 1923 the Post Office issued 80,000 licences, but probably four or five times as many sets were in use: in 1924 1 million licences were issued, but up to 5 million sets were in use (Black, 1972, 23). In three more years the number of licences doubled, and by 1939 9 million sets existed under licence (A. Briggs, 1965, 6). By 1928 radio audiences were never less than 1 million and often as high as 15 million (Black, 1972, 26).

The first radio receivers were crystal sets, which were easy and cheap to make but could also be bought from the BBC, complete with two pairs of headphones, for between £2 and £4 (ibid., 20–1). They soon gave way to valve receivers with loudspeakers which enabled people to listen in groups and were virtually universal by the early 1930s. It has been calculated that the average price of the cheaper radio sets – £1 to £2 in the 1920s and £5 to £6 in the 1930s – was still quite expensive for the working classes, who were slightly under-represented in the national audience until the arrival of cheap 'utility' sets in 1944 (Pegg, 1983, 47–9). But open to them were the relay exchanges, basically central radio receivers which in return for a rental could be wired to loudspeakers in individual homes. It is also significant that as the new technology improved and the demand for sets grew, their prices fell. Two-valve sets which cost

21

£17 10s. in 1923 were retailing for 5 guineas in 1925 (A. Briggs, 1961, 231) – though this was still a price which was well beyond anything the working classes could afford.

Despite its range and popularity the programme diet suffered from an important deficiency imposed by a body which was a good deal more prescient about radio's potential than many others of the time: the Newspaper Proprietors' Association. The BBC was forbidden to broadcast any news bulletins before 7 pm and any commentary on public events. Nor could it broadcast news other than that which was bought from the main agencies. These restrictions were not finally thrown off until the European crisis of 1938 (Paulu, 1956, 156). Nevertheless there were some isolated portents of radio's possibilities as a news medium. In 1926 occurred the General Strike. There were virtually no newspapers and so the NPA lifted its restrictions on the way in which the BBC gathered and broadcast the news. But the BBC's reportage of the strike was compromised by the delicacy of its own position. Its Charter had not yet been granted and the government had the authority to turn it into a mouthpiece and even to requisition it altogether. Not surprisingly, then, the BBC's perspective on the events was broadly pro-government. It did not report everything, but nor did it distort, and it was never wholly associated with the government (A. Briggs, 1961, 360–73). Some strikers denounced it, but many came to rely on it, and what the strike did in terms of radio was to establish it in the nation's life as a vital channel for the rapid dissemination of news and information.

A second event, much less important in itself yet an even more dramatic portent of radio's news potential, was the Crystal Palace fire of 1936. It occurred after the evening papers had shut down and before the morning papers appeared, and was the BBC's first 'scoop'. From the scene of the fire a young reporter named Richard Dimbleby broadcast a live telephone report against a background of shouts, firebells and the crackle of flames (Black, 1972, 73; Herbert, 1976, 14–15), and demonstrated that as a news medium radio is not only quicker than newspapers but more 'concrete' in the sense that it can convey the *sound* of what it reports.

But to return to the problems which faced the British

Broadcasting Company. Not only did it suffer from restrictions on its news output, but the evident popularity of its other programmes did not protect it from financial difficulties. Anomalies and loopholes in its royalty and licensing arrangements left it seriously short of revenue, and so in 1925 the government set up the Crawford Committee to consider the whole future of broadcasting. In fact the situation suited Reith, who wanted the BBC to become a public institution free from commercial pressures on the one side and political interference on the other. The committee was of like mind and as a result of its recommendations the British Broadcasting Corporation was set up by Royal Charter on 1 January 1927, with Reith as its first Director-General. Since then its constitution and statutory obligations as a publicly funded yet quasi-autonomous institution have remained largely unchanged. It is obliged to inform, educate and entertain; to report the proceedings of Parliament; to preserve a balance between political points of view; and in a national emergency to broadcast government messages, the source of which it is at liberty to name. It is also happy to accept two prohibitions: it may neither advertise nor editorialize. Under the terms of its Charter (conferred by the Crown) and its Licence and Agreement (its title to broadcast conferred by the government), it has a guaranteed income from receiving licences and maintains full editorial independence. Of course, as Scannell and Cardiff point out (1982, 162), it is subject to state pressures in a number of indirect ways. The Charter is renewable, and only the state can increase the licence fee. It also appoints the Board of Governors.

Soon after its foundation the Corporation underwent a rapid expansion, enhancing its output and its reputation. In 1932 it moved its headquarters into the purpose-built Broadcasting House, an act which symbolized its coming-of-age as a national institution, and in the same year began its Empire Service, the first of an interlocking range of external services whose illustrious history cannot, alas, find room here. Meanwhile it had also recognized the need for a choice of domestic networks and established the National Programme, which mainly originated from London, and the Regional Programme, which drew its material primarily from six regional services and was also fed by a London key service. Both were 'mixed programme' networks and not markedly different in tone or content:

> Mixed programming offered a wide and diverse range of programme materials over the course of each day and week. Typically it included news, drama, sport, religion, music (light to classical), variety or light entertainment. Not only did it cater for different social needs (education, information, entertainment), but for different sectional interests within the listening public (children, women, businessmen, farmers, fishermen, etc.). (Scannell and Cardiff, 1982, 167–8)

Reith's aim was to vary the output in such a way that the listener might be 'surprised into' an interest in a subject which she had not previously enjoyed or even known about: the intention was always to give her 'something a little better than she thought she wanted'. Such paternalism may seem somewhat objectionable today and it did not go unchallenged even in the 1930s. One manifestation of the BBC's broadcasting philosophy was the 'Reith Sunday', the one day when a large majority of people had the leisure to listen to the radio and craved relaxing fare. What they got, however, was a transmission which did not begin until 12.30 pm and consisted only of religious services, talks and classical music. But two continental-based commercial radio stations were set up in order to take advantage of the situation. The first was Radio Normandie (founded by someone with the wonderfully apposite name of Captain Plugge), which began broadcasting from the north coast of France in 1931 and offered the southern areas of Britain a diet of American-style programmes including soap-operas. The second was Radio Luxembourg, which opened on an unauthorized wavelength in 1933 and whose programme of mainly light music could be heard all over Britain. On Sundays the number of listeners to these stations exceeded those who stayed tuned to the BBC: it was the first sign of discontentment with the latter's domestic monopoly.

The second challenge to Reith's broadcasting philosophy came mainly from within the BBC itself, although it was doubtless strengthened by the threat from commercial radio – the demand for regular and systematic research into audience behaviour and tastes, about which virtually nothing was known other than through casual letters from listeners. Reith feared that such research would inevitably influence and even dictate broadcasting policy, that worthwhile minority programmes would be sacrificed to the popularity ratings. Nevertheless its advocates won the day and an Audience Research Department was set up in 1936. By 1938, the year of Reith's resignation, it had gathered much information about the British radio audience, including reassuring evidence of its very broad social composition.

With the outbreak of war in 1939 the BBC combined its National and Regional Programmes into a single Home Service, but in order to maintain the morale of the troops forming the British Expeditionary Force in France it introduced in 1940 the Forces Programme, predominantly an entertainment service of dance-music, sport and variety which foreshadowed the Light Programme. The Forces Programme was seen merely as a temporary expedient (Scannell and Cardiff, 1982, 187): what was not appreciated at the time was that its uniformly 'light' output was the beginning of the end of Reith's mixed programming policy, which would finally disappear with the formation of Radios 1 to 4 in 1967 (Pegg, 1983, 207–8). Within two years the Forces Programme was being listened to by more civilians than servicemen and attracting an audience 50 per cent larger than that of the Home Service (A. Briggs, 1970, 47).

It is widely agreed that the BBC's performance during the Second World War was impressive. At home it was a means of social cohesion, and abroad was generally regarded as an island of truthfulness amid a sea of rumour and propaganda. But to the media student the war is of greater interest as a time when radio at last came into its own as a rapid news medium, a role it has maintained even in an age of television. The BBC's 9 pm news bulletin commanded huge and avid audiences and it was under pressure of the war that the techniques of news broadcasting evolved from the early days of straight bulletin delivery to something like the blend of reading, correspondents' reports and sound actuality that we are familiar with today. The gathering of news became better organized and from 1944 the BBC began to employ its own foreign correspondents. Bulletins were supplemented by extended news programmes such as *Radio Newsreel*, which began in 1940, and new production techniques were adopted such as the association of comment with fact and the insertion of actuality into news broadcasts. But the catalyst to all this was technology: sound recording was vastly improved during the war. As Asa Briggs points out (1970, 325–6) the recording of news and talks acquired a special importance from about 1941 onwards. It removed the need to bring broadcasters into studios which were at risk from air raids, provided reserve material, allowed more outside reporting, made programme exports easier, served the needs of the monitoring service and enabled producers to anticipate any problems of censorship which might arise with the War Office. Ironically it was the Germans who pioneered the developments in recording technology, but they made much less imaginative use of it on the air than did the British. BBC reporters like Richard Dimbleby were given the same battle training as the soldiers and sent back front-line dispatches using portable disc-recorders and skilful editing to bring commentary and actuality closer together. The news programme *War Report*, which began on D-Day, 6 June 1944, made extensive use of recorded actuality and commanded regular audiences of between 10 and 15 million in Britain alone (A. Briggs, 1970, 662). Such actuality has remained an integral part of radio news, a way of guaranteeing its immediacy and truth to life.

Well before the war ended the popularity of the Forces Programme made it clear that there could be no simple reversion to the peacetime system of two substantially similar mixed programme networks. Consequently in 1945 the Director-General of the BBC, William Haley, announced the plan of a new tripartite system which had long been in preparation. The Home Service was to continue as a basic London service which a federation of regional services – Scottish, Northern, Midland, Welsh, West and Northern Irish – could draw upon; the Forces Programme was to be superseded by the very similar Light Programme which replaced it without a break on 29 July 1945; and the Third Programme, an unashamedly 'highbrow' network devoted to the arts, serious discussion and experiment, began broadcasting on 29 September 1946. Taken as a whole, the three networks represented an ingenious reconciliation of popular demand and the old Reithian seriousness of purpose, a compromise of streamed and mixed programming which was to work fairly well for the next ten or fifteen years. As Haley pointed out, the old mixed programme concept had presented the listener with certain problems:

> Before the war the system was to confront him with the necessity for pendulum-like leaps. The listener was deliberately plunged from one extreme to the other. The devotees of Berlin (Irving) were suddenly confronted with Bach. Many listeners were won for higher things in this way, but many were irretrievably lost. For the weakness of the process was that so many intolerances were set up.
>
> (cit. Smith, 1974, 83)

Hence although mixed programming was not to be abandoned (in an age without television many people still found it desirable as well as possible to *listen*), within each network the *range* of programmes was narrowed and a certain uniformity of tone created. Moreover a complementary relationship was established between the Light and the Home and between the Home and the Third which gave the plan an edifying cultural purpose.

> It rests on the conception of the community as a broadly based pyramid slowly aspiring upwards. This pyramid is served by three main Programmes, differentiated but broadly overlapping in levels and interest, each Programme leading on to the other, the listener being induced through the years increasingly to discriminate in favour of the things that are more worth-while. Each Programme at any given moment must be ahead of its public, but not so much as to lose their confidence. The listener must be led from good to better by curiosity, liking, and a growth of understanding. As the standards of the education and culture of the community rise so should the programme pyramid rise as a whole.
>
> (cit. Smith, 1974, 83)

It was during the war and for the ten years or so after it that radio enjoyed its heyday, providing programmes of distinction in every genre to audiences of many millions. This was the period of what were regarded as radiogenic 'features' programmes – programmes of a factual, often documentary, nature but partly created through imaginative scripting which blended narration, actuality, dramatic dialogue and sound effects. It was also the period of *Children's Hour* and *Radio Newsreel*, of discussions and debates such as *The Brains Trust* and *Any Questions*, of drama – not only 'classical' plays but popular serials like *Dick Barton* and *The Archers* – of light entertainment such as *ITMA* and *Workers' Playtime*, and of a vast output of classical and popular music both on record and performed by innumerable orchestras including the BBC's own.

What was to end radio's pre-eminence was, of course, television, which had been pioneered by John Logie Baird and others during the 1920s. The BBC began test transmissions in 1930 and six years later opened a regular service for a few thousand viewers in the London area, using both the Baird and EMI systems. The service was stopped by the war, but even when it resumed in 1946 television was commonly thought of as 'radio with added vision' rather than as a medium which was fundamentally different. Before the war Reith had thought of 'integrating' radio and television (A. Briggs, 1965, 608) and in 1949 Haley wrote in the *BBC Quarterly*: 'television is an extension of [radio] broadcasting. That is the crucial point . . . [television and radio] are complementary expressions within the same medium. They are part of one whole' (cit. Paulu, 1981, 54). This naïve misconception was to have prolonged and negative effects on certain aspects of television production:

> When BBC Television began it was inevitable, if not very appropriate, that one of its departments should be called Television Talks. This department dealt, in effect, with anything that was not drama, light entertainment, sport or news. The name continued in use for a long time and is an indication of how difficult the BBC found it to come to terms with the fundamental difference between radio and television, how many of the concepts of radio were taken over and imposed on television and how little the top echelons of the television service understood the new medium.
>
> (Hood, 1975, 40)

This insistence on seeing television in terms of radio not only provoked sensational resignations among the more perceptive members of the television service, but also dominated the presentation of television news until 1955, when the BBC was finally forced to make changes by the competition from ITN (Smith, 1976, 148–9). Nevertheless the post-war rise of television was inexorable and two major events of the 1950s were seen, accurately, as marking its arrival as the major mass medium and less accurately as portending the very extinction of radio, whose blindness was regarded by many as an unequivocal disadvantage. The first event was the coronation of Elizabeth II in 1953. The way in which it was covered by television would be impressive even today. Over 20 million people (56 per cent of the population) watched the service in Westminster Abbey, far outnumbering listeners in almost every part of the country (A. Briggs, 1979, 466–7). The second major event, which followed a prolonged public debate about the BBC's broadcasting monopoly, was the establishment in 1955 of a second, commercial, television network under the regulation of the Independent Television Authority. The debate centred on television but was ultimately of relevance to radio, too. Those who favoured the continuance of the BBC's monopoly argued that competition would force down standards and indeed threaten its very existence as a public service. When ITV came on the air the BBC's Director-General, Ian Jacob, complained:

It may be argued that the BBC is in a position to ignore the relative size of its audience and that it is not obliged to compete with Independent Television. But, to some extent, it must compete for its audiences, or its audiences will diminish beyond that level at which the Corporation could continue to claim that it is the national broadcasting authority. This is the situation into which the Corporation has been placed by competition.   (cit. Paulu, 1981, 42)

In being forced to compete for large audiences the BBC might neglect its duty to provide programmes for minorities. But the arguments against monopoly were also powerful and most tellingly summarized by Sir Frederick Ogilvie, a former Director-General of the BBC: 'Freedom is choice. And monopoly of broadcasting is inevitably the negation of freedom, no matter how efficiently it is run' (cit. Smith, 1974, 85).

Still, faced with competition from first one and then two television networks, radio went into a long decline that some thought would prove terminal. Between 1949 and 1958 the BBC's average evening radio audience dropped from nearly 9 million to less than 3.5 million, three-quarters of whom were people without television sets (Paulu, 1961, 155). Though television was clearly the major cause, there were problems within radio's tripartite progamme network. First the element of overlap was too broad, especially between the Home and the Light. *ITMA*, for instance, was broadcast on the Home (A. Briggs, 1979, 58). This meant that in so far as each network lacked a separate identity its hold on listener loyalty was weakened. In search of a particular kind of programme, a listener might find herself scanning the schedules of at least two of the three networks. One consequence of the overlap was that the Light was too serious for some listeners, for whom Radio Luxembourg was again becoming a more attractive alternative. At the other extreme, the Third Programme was regarded by many as absurdly recherché, an exclusive club for highbrows and intellectuals. During the first fifteen years of its existence it averaged only 2 per cent of the total radio audience (Paulu, 1961, 156). But from time to time attempts were made to mend matters. In 1957 its output was cut from five and a half hours per day to three and a half hours, the two-hour space it cleared being given over to an educational concept known as 'Network Three'. In tones at once funny and sad one retired features producer remembered Network Three as merely a part of radio's twilight gimmickry. 'This emerged as specialist listening for every kind of minority interest from Buchmanism to bee-keeping: it soon became known as the Fretwork Network and attracted even fewer listeners than the Third Programme itself' (Bridson, 1971, 232).

The year 1964, when pirate broadcasters came on the air and television provided yet more competition in the form of BBC 2, marked BBC radio's lowest ebb. The Third Programme was again dismembered, becoming the Music Programme during the daytime, Study Session between 6 and 7.30 pm on weekdays, the Sports Service on Saturday afternoons, and a truncation of its former self during the evenings. But more significant was the end of two radio 'institutions', both made redundant by the visual appeal of television – the Features Department (Bridson, 1971, 288–304; Snagge and Barsley, 1972, 177) and *Children's Hour*. Nevertheless three developments in broadcasting technology had already taken place and although two of these were to guarantee radio's future, in the case of the most important one it was not the BBC which was the first to exploit its potential. Perhaps the least important, although aesthetically very satisfying, was the development of stereophonic sound. The first test transmissions in stereo took place in 1958, the first regular broadcasts in 1966, and stereo is now a commonplace but vital feature of radio, particularly in 'radiovision' broadcasts during which an orchestra or group is televised while its music can be simultaneously, and more richly, heard on the radio. Rather more important was the opening in 1955 of the first two VHF transmitters at Wrotham in Kent. One of the transmitters also used frequency modulation (FM), which provided listeners with freedom from all kinds of interference; 'but the future role of VHF was to reintroduce low-power programming for very specific audiences, a return in an age of television to the first broadcasting patterns of 1922' (A. Briggs, 1979, 561–2). In other words, it is VHF which has made possible the extensive development of local radio – a fact which underlay one of the first policy decisions taken by the IBA in 1973 (Baron, 1975, 76).

But the most important development in broadcasting technology occurred much earlier – in 1947 – and applied not to radio transmitters but to receivers: the manufacture of the first transistor (Goldhamer, 1971, 901). By replacing the old wireless valve, which was large, costly and consumed much primary power, the transistor allowed radios to be constructed which used less power, were more reliable, and most important of all, were much cheaper and smaller – small enough to be carried around in a hand or a pocket. In a word, what the transistor would achieve was a revolution in the way radio was used, something which was recognized by Frank Gillard of the BBC:

The transistor has made the radio into the truly ubiquitous mass medium. Radio is no longer something to which you necessarily have to go. Radio goes with you. So it becomes a

31

personal service. You come to count on it . . . to give you a certain service at a certain hour, wherever you might happen to be. Consequently the usefulness of the medium is enormously enhanced, and those in charge of sound in the years ahead must increasingly take this service function into account . . . in planning their programme output.　　　　　(Gillard, 1964, 8)

Not only did the transistor allow the listener to take her radio anywhere, for it was no longer a fixture of the home or factory but could go with her to the seaside or out into the country, it greatly extended the number of things she could do *while* listening, such as working out in the garden or even driving her car. At the beginning of the 1960s only 4 per cent of all British cars carried radios (Paulu, 1961, 155), but the 1970s saw an enormous growth in the number of car radios, which began to be fitted as standard equipment. By 1978 68 per cent of Britain's radio sets were either portable or mobile (Paulu, 1981, 350), and recently the Chairman of the BBC calculated that 10 million, nearly 60 per cent, of Britain's 17 million vehicles have radios (Hewson, 1984, 8). But it was at the beginning of the 1960s that the transistor revolution began, so that at the very time when radio had lost its pre-eminence and seemed, indeed, to be facing extinction it discovered a new and apparently irreducible advantage in its very limitation. As a secondary medium it could be carried around and its messages absorbed in a way not possible even with portable television.

It is, of course, important to realize that while the transistor greatly *extended* radio's role as a secondary medium it did not *create* it. Listeners had always been able to use radio as an accompaniment to other activities, but they had come to use it almost exclusively in this way as a consequence of television, for television had replaced radio as the main leisure medium. Previously, the husband in the factory and the wife back home in the kitchen may well have done their jobs while accompanied by *Music While You Work*, but in the evening they would have sat down to do little or nothing except listen to the radio. Now, their evenings would be spent watching television. This meant that in so far as radio continued to be heard it was seldom heard as anything *other* than an accompaniment to other activities; and it is highly likely that among the vast majority who used the radio in this way was a substantial number for whom it became little more than a background noise. In these circumstances, then, Haley's tripartite cultural pyramid was suspect in theory as well as in practice, for it presupposed *listeners* at a time when the radio audience consisted increasingly of *hearers*. In an age of television, Radio Luxembourg's diet of continuous light music made much more sense, and the evidence suggests that between 1945 and 1955 radio audiences were moving in the opposite direction from that which Haley had hoped for – from the serious and demanding to the light and entertaining (Paulu, 1956, 380; A. Briggs, 1979, 558). By 1955 Radio Luxembourg was claiming an average evening audience larger than the Home's (Paulu, 1956, 360–1), and it is not surprising that during this period Luxembourg was much more in touch with developments in popular music than the BBC was (A. Briggs, 1979, 759).

But Luxembourg was unable to take full advantage of the new lease of life, this time as a mainly secondary medium, which the transistor gave to radio during the 1960s; for Luxembourg was confined to evening transmissions and a weak signal. Instead, the initiative was seized by a number of 'pirate' radio stations which began to broadcast almost round the clock from various ships and forts in British coastal waters. Inspired by Radio Luxembourg and even more by US radio, the pirates were unashamedly commercial operations and informed by a realization almost totally lacking at the BBC – that the transistor, at once radio's salvation and its curse, meant that the listener could take her set almost anywhere and listen to it almost all the time; but that since she would almost certainly be doing something else while she listened she would often treat it as little more than 'background'. Continuous pop music was the ideal form of output. The first of the pirates, Radio Caroline, began broadcasting from a ship off the Essex coast in March 1964, and by 1967 no fewer than nine ships and forts were on the air. Caroline and a nearby ship broadcasting as Radio London were the slickest and most professional and reached the largest population, and their impact was sensational. A Gallup Poll found that in its first three weeks Caroline gained 7 million listeners from a potential audience of only 20 million (Harris, 1970, 8). It was estimated that within a year the total daily audience for pirate radio was between 10 and 15 million (ibid., 31), and by early 1966 the audience for this and for Radio Luxembourg was over 24 million (ibid., 53). The BBC's findings were more sober but no less eloquent. Within its transmission area Caroline commanded an audience about one-third that of the Light Programme; 70 per cent of its listeners were under 30 years old and treated it largely as background listening. Since there was no appreciable decline in the Light Programme's audience it was clear that Caroline and the other pirates were meeting a youthful need for radio that the BBC had neglected (Silvey, 1974, 212–13).

The BBC was not totally to blame for this state of affairs: the amount of recorded music it could play was severely restricted by a long-standing agreement with the Musicians' Union. The pirates, on the other hand, observed no restrictions and paid no royalties on the records they played. But their fundamental act of piracy was their usurpation of frequencies, for which they were finally forced off the air by the government's Marine Broadcasting (Offences) Act in August 1967. Nevertheless their consequences were considerable. The BBC's response to the demand they had identified was to turn one of the two frequencies which the Light Programme had occupied into a continuous pop music network named Radio 1. It began broadcasting in September 1967. Meanwhile the Light, Third and Home continued as mixed programme networks and were renamed Radios 2, 3 and 4 respectively. Audience size was now as important a criterion in moulding the BBC's radio policy as its duty to cater to a wide range of tastes, and Ian Jacob's fears about the threat to its broadcasting monopoly had proved well-founded!

But although the pirates had been sunk, BBC radio's worst enemy remained. In the very same year, 1967, the introduction of colour transmissions on BBC 2 was a reminder, if one were needed, that television was now the major mass medium and that in order to survive radio must seek out, and largely confine itself to, those things it could do best. These things were spelt out in the BBC's pamphlet *Broadcasting in the Seventies* (1969), which announced a radical new plan for network radio. The pamphlet began by acknowledging that radio had yielded to television as the main focus of attention and was now treated by the listener as secondary to her other activities. It therefore echoed Gillard's view of radio's new role as a 'service function', the listener relying upon it to fulfil certain requirements at certain times. Since she may not be listening too closely the old mixed programme pattern, with its sudden changes and pleasant surprises, was inherently unsuited to such a role. What was needed instead was a more uniform and predictable kind of content, an uninterrupted supply of music, perhaps, or of information: 'experience, both in this country and abroad, suggests that many listeners now expect radio to be based on a different principle – that of the specialised network, offering a continuous stream of one particular type of programme, meeting one particular interest' (*Broadcasting in the Seventies*, 1969, 3). Moreover, since the programmes would all be of one type, the divisions between them would become less important and the programme concept itself give way to more extended sequences.

Broadcasting in the Seventies wrote the epitaph on the Reithian principle of tempting the listener to unexpectedly beneficial or pleasurable types of programme. Henceforth, the BBC's duty to provide a comprehensive public service would be fulfilled not in any one network alone but through the networks as a whole – a point conceded in the *BBC Handbook 1978* (1977, 264). In April 1970 Radio 2 became a network for continuous 'middle-of-the-road' music, while Radio 3 lost many of its speech programmes to Radio 4 and devoted a larger share of its output to classical music. Both networks retained some vestiges of mixed programming, notably sport, but only Radio 4 survived in something like its old form. It continued to carry a number of general entertainment programmes, but also specialized to some extent in informational or 'spoken word' output – news and current affairs. It is important to recognize that radio's new role was forced upon it not simply by the ascendancy of television but by its own technological sophistication. So numerous and portable had transistor sets become that the Post Office could no longer keep track of them in order to collect the licence fee. Bowing to the millions of radio owners who evaded it, the government abolished radio-only licences in 1971. But as Smith points out (1974, 128) this weakened the position of radio *vis-à-vis* television in the BBC because there was no longer a sum of money raised specifically for it: it was therefore being 'carried' by its more successful and glamorous partner. However, the largely specialized pattern of network radio has remained ever since and there is no evidence that its audiences wish it otherwise. Between 1980 and 1982 there were some stealthy moves towards mixed programming on Radio 1 (Wade, 1983a, 9). They cost the network three-quarters of a million listeners (Wade, 1983b, 7).

The other major development of the last twenty years has been in local radio. Though the natural heir to the VHF transmitters which had been opened since the 1950s, local radio seems also to have been inspired by the offshore pirates (Harris, 1970, 43, 84). Indeed it may not be too fanciful to suggest that the pirates helped in two ways to awaken the latent demand for a service which had been technically feasible for some ten years. First they were in some sense 'local' themselves. None of them broadcast over an area larger than the Home Counties, many of them publicized local events and aroused local loyalties, and a few, such as Radio London and Radio Essex, took local names. Secondly, although they afforded no broadcasting access to actual members of the public, they broke the BBC's virtual monopoly of radio to fulfil a demand which it had neglected, and so in that sense assumed a public 'voice'. Perhaps, then, they helped to foster what Anthony Smith describes as

the growth of a public demand that radio (and indeed broadcasting in general) should become a means of 'two-way' communication, that it should no longer remain the exclusive platform of the BBC and its invited guests. Local radio seemed to be a means by which some kind of 'right to broadcast' could be created, within the general framework of the BBC. . . . [It] was to become a forum for the whole of the cultural life of a *community*.　　　　　　(Smith, 1974, 151)

After a successful experiment in 1963–4 the BBC opened its first local radio station at Leicester in 1967 and followed up with many others during the 1970s and 1980s, using them ultimately as a replacement for regional radio, which was discontinued in 1983. In the light of Smith's remarks it is not surprising that the phone-in has been a staple of local radio, even though it seems to have been first used on a network in 1969. But it has been a genuinely new broadcasting technique in giving the radio listener his own voice on the air.

Local radio was not a BBC preserve for very long. In 1972 the ITA was renamed the Independent Broadcasting Authority and empowered by the Conservative government to license a national spread of independent local radio (ILR) stations. The IBA is a corporate, government-established body rather like the BBC's Board of Governors. It merely selects and gives contracts to the programme companies, owns and operates the transmission facilities – for which the companies pay a rent – and regulates the balance and advertising-content of their output. The first stations, Capital Radio and the London Broadcasting Company, opened in London in 1973, and there are presently about fifty spread fairly evenly over Britain, broadcasting (some for twenty-four hours a day) a mixture of local news and information, phone-ins and pop music. Capital is among the few stations whose output approaches anything like genuine mixed pro-gramming since it extends to some classical music and drama, while LBC specializes in news and current affairs and provides an international news agency (Independent Radio News) for all the other ILR stations.

What are radio's present circumstances and how will it be affected by future developments both inside and outside sound broadcasting? It has to be conceded that live television was only the first of a number of technological challenges to radio's influence which have intensified over the past ten years or so. Since 1974, 'teletext' – the Ceefax and Oracle systems – has enabled us to get visual updates on the news from our television screens without having to wait for radio bulletins. Video cassettes, video games and home computers provide domestic alternatives to simply 'listening to the radio', and the proliferation of television channels (Channel 4 since 1982 and soon to follow 'direct broadcasting by satellite' – DBS – and cable television) has spread the media audience ever more thinly. The most significant development was breakfast television, which began in 1983 on both BBC and ITV at what has always been one of radio's peak listening-times. In the last quarter of that year it caused a 10 per cent drop in the amount of time per week which the average person spent listening to the radio (*BBC Annual Report and Handbook 1985*, 1984, 45). But perhaps its threat can be contained until such time as the British people can get ready for work and school without taking their eyes from the screen. There is also, however, an 'internal' threat to radio listening – a threat which is literally *inside* many radio receivers: the cassette recorder. Radio-cassetting and 'time-shift' listening mean that programmes can be heard and re-heard which would otherwise have been missed; but the cassette facility also means that many who would formerly have been radio listeners are now listeners to commercial tapes.

A consequence of all this is that the audience which is able and willing to pay close attention to radio output grows ever smaller, along with the number of networks or stations producing a variety of self-contained programmes which require such attention. The only network which still offers something approaching mixed programme fare is Radio 4, nor can the BBC take all the credit for this. Its planners want to stream it into a news and current affairs network and have at least succeeded in making speech its dominant mode: in 1984 only 4 per cent of its ouput was music (*BBC Annual Report and Handbook 1985*, 1984, 145). Their plans have been limited only by the network's faithful adherents, who retain the admirable if old-fashioned belief that radio is there to be listened to and not simply heard. But their numbers dwindle. Often, the attentive housewife of the past is now the professional woman with limited access to the radio, and it was estimated that Radio 4's 1984 audience of 4.5 million had dropped by 6 million over the previous ten years (Wade, 1984a, 12). Even Radio 3, much more arcane but offering an almost unbroken output for lovers of classical music, has more nearly maintained its audience (Moorehead, 1983, 8). Small wonder, then, that Radio 4 has been experimenting with programmes and programme-formats to attract the newer generation of casual listeners. *Rollercoaster* was a three-hour radio magazine whose overall length was intended to discourage listeners from switching off, but whose brief items had the even more important function of *not* discouraging them from switching on. Unlike, say, a play, which has a prolonged structure in which everything is integral, such a programme is full of redundancy. You can switch on without feeling you have missed anything vital, or to change the fairground metaphor from rollercoaster to roundabout, you can get on or off at any of its points. Another experiment is the morning discussion programme *Taking Sides*, which can be simultaneously seen on television and heard on the radio, the object being to enable those who have begun by watching to turn on the radio in the car without losing the thread of the discussion.

For the radio 'purist' who still regards the medium as an art form meriting her fullest attention this may indicate a depressing future. The overall shrinkage of its audience means that even when stations do gain new listeners they do so not at the expense of other media but of other stations. Where ILR stations have been opened, for example, they have taken up to one-third of Radio 2's listeners (Appleyard, 1983, 10). But the portents are by no means entirely bleak. Despite its contraction in recent years Radio 4's regular audience continues to be numbered in millions, which surely suggests that the nation still has room for at least one mixed programme network. And there may be another to follow. Independent national radio (INR), the first countrywide commercial radio station, is expected to come on-air in about 1990, and though the indications are so far few they do point to a programme format which will combine those of Radios 2 and 4. Nor have all the recent developments in technology been inimical to radio. One consequence of VHF, FM and transistorization is that sound broadcasting has become easier and cheaper than ever before. Something of this can be seen in the growing number of 'in-house' radio stations – campus radio in colleges and universities, hospital radio serving one or a whole network of sites. But much sound broadcasting is even less institutional than this and is, in fact, turning into something of a cottage industry – at once 'hi-tech' and semi-domestic. For a few thousand pounds an individual can set up a radio station in his bedroom and transmit to his neighbourhood, and this is already happening with the increasing number of 'community' radio stations (CR) which have been operating piratically on

VHF but which the government is expected to legalize within the next few years. On a local scale this opens up a truly exciting future for radio, pointing to a time when the medium will be subject to fewer technological and political restrictions than ever before. But lest you, the reader, should be horrified at the thought of such a free-for-all, it might be worth reassuring you with a brief look at why radio has been under these restrictions for so long.

It has often been pointed out that throughout their history the broadcasting media have never enjoyed the same freedom of expression and political independence as the press, but have been subject to a high degree of government regulation (McQuail, 1983, 25, 86; Smith, 1976, 61). In democratic societies the fundamental justification for this has been technological – the scarcity of wavelengths – but technological restrictions are ultimately inseparable from political ones. As Anthony Smith puts it:

> Broadcasting, in Britain at any rate, did not have to confront any question of 'censorship' because there was only one centrally licensed 'publisher', the BBC. In a way, broadcasting – with its wavelength problems – brought the issue of press control back into the Tudor age, where a scarce medium was placed under government licence. (Smith, 1976, 54)

Just as publishing had a single source for its messages in the form of the printing press, so the single source of broadcasting's messages is the transmitter, except that before the days of off-air recording the suppression of the broadcasting source would have meant that nothing would have survived of its messages. This is not likely to be the case in publishing since its messages are 'permanent': suppression of the printing press does not include suppression of the copies of the messages it may already have produced – copies which are likely to provoke the suppression only if they are numerous. And the more numerous they are, the more likely it is that some will survive. This means, in effect, that government control over broadcasting has been potentially much more 'total' than its control over the press. But times are changing. Just as printing technology became better and cheaper and made it harder for governments, whatever their intentions, to continue to keep control over what was being published, so broadcasting technology has been developing in much the same way. The pamphleteer was soon able to set up a printing press in his back-yard and then dismantle it before the licensing authorities could find him; and now the radio enthusiast can install a studio and transmitter in his van and drive off before the Department of Trade can locate them. Recently the ILR regulating authority, the IBA, required as a condition of its franchise that Viking Radio in Hull should spend £200,000 to bring its studios and equipment up to a certain standard: meanwhile a pirate station in London was broadcasting success-fully on equipment costing one-twentieth of that sum (Webster, 1984, 1). Since VHF and FM have alleviated the wavelength problem at local level, government control of radio has become not only more difficult but much harder to justify on technological grounds. And as the technological justification disappears, the remaining grounds for control can be seen for what they are – political – and are proportionately less appealing. For a long time Britain has allowed print media which are politically partisan and which represent not a balance or spread of interests but certain *individual* interests to the exclusion of others. Now that there is room for a multiplicity of stations, radio is likely to follow suit. In the days when wavelengths were scarce it was right, in a democracy at least, that the stations which occupied them should be politically balanced, editorially neutral, and attempt to cater for as wide a range of interests as possible. Now there seems little reason why a radio station should show any more political or editorial neutrality than the *Daily Telegraph* or *Morning Star*: and if there are magazines which cater exclusively for vegetarians or Roman Catholics, then why not radio stations? Indeed the arguments for govern-ment control of radio are, if anything, even weaker than those for controlling the press. The fact that radio is not a 'dead' medium but contains living sound has, it is true, worried some, including Lord Reith's first programmes organizer, C. A. Lewis, who in 1922 lamented that 'Many things, harmless-looking enough in print, sound very different read aloud' (cit. Smith, 1974, 43): but unless it is recorded off-air, radio content is of its very nature more ephemeral than print. Faced on the one hand by a large proportion of its own ILR stations which were expensive to set up, must provide a semblance of political neutrality and a balance of information, education and entertainment, and which are showing little or no profit; and on the other by a growing number of pirate stations which are cheap to set up and run and whose freedom to broadcast what they like is subject only to the tastes of their listeners and advertisers; the IBA is bowing to the inevitable and giving its franchisees a much larger measure of financial and editorial freedom (Brooks, 1984b, 7). The government is also taking a realistic view of local radio developments and is expected to legalize the pirate stations, creating a new tier of community radio which may also be regulated by the IBA but much more loosely than it has so far regulated the ILR stations. Whatever the party in power the future looks assured: CR satisfies the Conservative belief in free market competition and the Socialist belief in giving a voice to local and ethnic minorities.

In radio, then, we are soon likely to see a world of almost de-regulated broadcasting – a world much more closely analogous to that of the press. Listeners will have a radio dial which will be something like the acoustic equivalent of a magazine stall. Just as the latter contains political journals which make no claim to editorial neutrality and specialist magazines which cater for tastes and hobbies of all kinds, so the listener may be able to browse among a range of CR stations which will be geared to the sort of minority interests to which the networks and even the local stations can at best give no more than one programme a week, and which at worst they are forced to ignore altogether. Thus CR might include stations for Rastas, London Cypriots, fans of country and western music, old age pensioners. Indeed the analogy with the press ends only when one considers that the costs of running such stations are likely to be rather less than the printing and production costs of newspapers and journals. And in terms of broadcasting techniques, it is also likely that CR will radically revise our present, somewhat hidebound notions of presentation and programme content.

The state of CR in France is in advance of ours and therefore shows us our own future. In 1981 the Mitterand government decided that freedom of the airwaves was preferable to the state broadcasting monopoly, which it ended. Consequently by 1984 there were more CR stations in Paris, eighty-two, than there were LR stations in the whole of Britain – stations which catered to such diverse audiences as Arabs, Jews, anarchists, gays, right-wingers, jazz enthusiasts and culture-buffs (Brooks, 1984a, 54). There is, of course, a possibility of overprovision, a risk that some stations will not survive the competition. But in Britain at any rate, there are already some hints that various stations are competing with one another rather less directly than formerly and looking for separate niches in the market. In view of the vigour with which the BBC proclaimed the demise of regional radio and the dawn of local radio, it is not surprising that the Corporation is currently saying very little: but probably on the grounds of cost it seems to have given its newer stations rather larger transmission areas than had previously been intended and to have made somewhat furtive changes of nomenclature. The recently opened stations at Norwich and Lincoln have taken the names of their counties, not of the towns; and since 1980 Radios Brighton, Medway, Blackburn, Birmingham and Carlisle have become Radios Sussex, Kent, Lancashire, West Midland and Cumbria respectively. It is true that the areas covered by these stations are still very much local rather than regional, but such names do suggest an appeal to larger geographical loyalties than are made by the independent stations and are, perhaps, a way of showing that they are not competing in the same market as ILR but trying to offer a different kind of 'product'.

In the near future, then, the prospective listener may find herself faced with an embarrassment of riches, a choice of up to three levels of sound broadcasting. In her immediate neighbour-hood there could be one or more CR stations, some catering to special interests, some to minority groups, but with a range no bigger than a suburb or an area the size of one or two London boroughs. At urban or county level she will be able to hear a BBC and/or an ILR station with similar ranges but attempting to stimulate rather different loyalties; and at national level the four BBC networks, together with an INR station which as we have seen may even bring something of a revival of mixed programming. If in one sense radio has had its day, it is also proving capable of forging what is in both senses a 'sound' future.

Suggestions for further work

Over a span of several days make a point of listening whenever possible to your local radio station. If you can receive both BBC LR and ILR, and/or if there is a CR station near you (some of which the Home Office has now licensed on an experimental basis), allocate several days to each. How does the 'product' of each station compare in content and quality with the products of its rivals, including the national networks? Can you deduce what programming policy each LR station has and what kind of audience it is trying to reach? (You might, for instance, decide that your ILR station is trying to compete with Radio 1 rather than with its nearest BBC LR station.) Do these LR stations seem to you to have introduced new kinds of programme content or formats? In what ways have they extended the possibilities of the medium beyond what has traditionally been provided by the networks?

3 WORDS, SOUNDS AND MUSIC: RADIO SIGNS AND CODES

Radio is the art of communicating meaning at first hearing.
(Laurence Gilliam, former Head of Features, BBC Radio)

We must now look more closely at the raw material of radio, at the signs which its codes make use of in order to convey messages, and for this purpose I shall borrow some rudimentary distinctions from what is in fact a highly sophisticated classification of signs devised by the American philosopher, C. S. Peirce (1839–1914). Peirce, who is commonly regarded as a founding father of semiotics or semiology, the study of signs, distinguishes between the *icon* – a sign which resembles the object which it represents, such as a photograph; the *index* – a sign which is directly linked to its object, usually in a causal or sequential way: smoke, for instance, is an index of fire; and the *symbol* – a sign which bears no resemblance or connection to its object, for example the Union Jack as a symbol of Great Britain (Peirce, 1960, I, 196; II, 143, 161, 165, 168–9; Hawkes, 1977, 127–30; Fiske, 1982, 50). In radio all the signs are auditory: they consist simply of noises and silence, and therefore use *time*, not space, as their major structuring agent (Hawkes, 1977, 135). The noises of radio can be subdivided into words, sounds and music, and we will look at each of these in turn and also at the nature and functions of silence before attempting some general observations about the codes of radio.

Words

Since words are signs which do not resemble what they represent (we may represent a canine quadruped by the word 'dog' but we may equally refer to it as 'chien', 'hund' or 'cur' or even invent a private word of our own), they are symbolic in character. Their symbolism is the basis of radio's imaginative appeal which I mentioned in Chapter 1, for if the word-sign does not resemble its object the listener must visualize, picture or *imagine* that object. But there is an important difference between words which are written or printed on a page and words on the radio, and that is that words on the radio are always and unavoidably *spoken*. They therefore constitute a binary code in which the words themselves are symbols of what they represent, while the voice in which they are heard is an index of the person or 'character' who is speaking – a fact which was perceived and researched fairly early in the medium's history (Pear, 1931). In other words such factors as accent and stress have semiotic functions, or at least effects (O'Donnell and Todd, 1980, 95). Almost irrespective of what is said in a French accent, for example, the listener may automatically ascribe a romantic personality to its speaker. In fact, voice can be so powerful an expression of personality that merely by virtue of some well-delivered links a presenter or disc jockey can impose a unifying and congenial presence on the most miscellaneous of magazine or record programmes. Moreover, the voice of a continuity announcer is an index not only of herself, whom she may identify by name from time to time, but of the whole station or network. As a matter of deliberate policy she will give a kind of composite unity to its various programmes, set the tone or style of the whole network (Kumar, 1977, 240–1). Indeed an announcement such as 'You're listening to Radio 4' is ambivalent, for its means not only 'The programmes you're presently hearing are the output of Radio 4' but 'Since the network has no other self-conscious means of expression, *I* am Radio 4'. The ambivalence can be seen rather more clearly, and is taken even further, in the name of the USA's world service where at intervals we can hear 'You're listening to the Voice of America' in which the 'voice' is an index not only of the

46

continuity announcer and the radio station, but of the entire nation.

By now it will be clear that signification is not static or rigid, but a highly fluid or elastic process which varies according to context and the preconceptions we bring to it – a fact which is not sufficiently acknowledged by some semioticians. A voice may be interepreted merely as the index of a human presence; or on another level as the index of a personality (a country bumpkin, seductive French woman, and so on); or on yet a third level as the index of a programme, broadcasting institution or entire nation. It might be useful to see the latter two levels as examples of *extended* signification.

Sounds

Unlike words, which are a human invention, sound is 'natural' – a form of signification which exists 'out there' in the real world. It seems never to exist as an isolated phenomenon, always to manifest the presence of something else. Consequently we can say that sounds, whether in the world or on the radio, are generally indexical. We could of course say that recorded sound on the radio is iconic in the elementary sense that it is an icon or image of the original sound or that a sound in a radio play is an icon of a sound in the real world, but if we do we are still faced with the question of what the sound *signifies*, what it is that is *making* the sound. Thus sounds such as the ringing of a door-bell or the grating of a key in a lock are indexical in signifying someone's presence. Shut your eyes for a moment and listen. The chances are that you will become aware of sounds which you have been hearing for some time but which you have not been aware of before. You have not been aware of them because you are reading such a fascinating book that you have ignored the messages coming from your ears. Suppose, however, that your desire for a cup of coffee is almost equal to your absorption in this book and that a friend has agreed to bring one to you about now. You will be quite capable of picking out from the welter of unimportant noises which surround you the keenly awaited sounds of rattling cup and turning door-handle. But the radio medium is such that the listener cannot select his own area of attention in this way: the broadcasters must prioritize sounds for him, foregrounding the most important ones and eliminating the irrelevant ones, or if this is not possible reducing them to the level of the less important ones. This has been illustrated in respect of radio drama by Erving Goffman (1980, 162–5). Taking a conversation at a party as his scenario Goffman points out that whereas in real life we would be able to distinguish the important from the less important strand of sound, this has to be done for us on the radio by certain conventions. Among the possibilities he instances

1 Fading in party chatter then fading it down and holding it under the conversation, or even fading it out altogether.
2 Allowing one or two low sounds to stand for what would actually be a stream of background noise.

What Goffman is concerned to stress about these conventions is their artificiality, which is aptly conveyed in the stock phrase 'sound *effects*': 'the audience is not upset by listening in on a world in which many sounds are not sounded and a few are made to stand out momentarily; yet if these conditions suddenly appeared in the off-stage world, consternation would abound' (ibid., 163). Nevertheless it is important to realize that such conventions are indispensable even in radio which deals with real life. In a location interview, for instance, the interviewer will set the recording-level on her portable tape-machine so that the sound of her voice and that of the person she is interviewing will be foregrounded against all the other noises of the location. Let us imagine an interview which takes place against a background of traffic noise. If the interview is with a superintendent of highways about noise pollution the traffic noise, while of less importance – and therefore less loud – than the interview, will still be of relevance to it. If, however, the interview is with the Chancellor of the Exchequer about his Budget proposals the noise of traffic will be quite irrelevant, an unavoidable evil, and the listener will be fully capable of distinguishing between these positive and negative functions of background noise. This second type of location interview is, of course, a *faute de mieux*: it brings a broadcasting facility to an interviewee who cannot be brought into the studio, for an important function of the studio with its sound-proofing is that it eliminates irrelevant noise altogether. My point, then, is that radio does not seek to reproduce the chaotic, complex and continuous sounds of actual life: it may tolerate them to a degree, but seeks to convey only those sounds which are relevant to its messages and to arrange them in their order of relevance. Nevertheless the ultimate test of relevance is the verbal context: it is the subject under discussion in the interview which will tell us whether we should be paying any attention to the traffic noise.

Yet even when the relevant sounds have been distinguished from the irrelevant, the *level* of that relevance often needs to be determined. Let us imagine a programme which begins with an owl-hoot. The 'relevance' or importance of the sound is not in doubt since we can hear virtually nothing else. But what does that relevance consist in? Are we to take the sound simply as an index of the bird, as we would in a documentary about wild-life or the countryside? Or does it carry what I have termed an extended signification in evoking not merely a solitary owl but an entire setting – an eerie, nocturnal atmosphere, as it would in a radio melodrama or a programme about the occult? In the first place, how do such sounds as owl-hoots acquire an extended signification? A crowing sound, for instance, frequently signifies not only 'a cock' but 'daybreak', while the sound of strumming may suggest not only a guitar but a Spanish setting. Because radio broadcasters seldom walk while broadcasting, the sound of footsteps, frequently heard – and ignored – in real life, acquires a peculiar suggestiveness on the radio. Drama producers will use it sparingly, and to convey not only that a person is moving but also that an atmosphere of tension or solitude is developing. This extended signification seems to be established through a process of custom and habit. It is likely that such sounds were originally chosen as an effective way of reinforcing particular pieces of dialogue or description. But since they *are* effective and part of what is a rather limited range of resources open to the radio producer they were chosen again and again and came to acquire the status of a convention, an acoustic shorthand, in that they could *replace* or absorb much of the adjacent language. In hearing the hoot of the owl the listener would begin to brace himself for darkness and mystery before a word had been uttered. Nevertheless, while such conventions may be useful in replacing *much* of adjacent language they cannot *wholly* replace it, for ultimately it is only the words which follow upon our owl-hoot which will tell us whether what we are listening to is *Sounds Natural* or *Afternoon Theatre*.

But it is not simply the case that radio broadcasters must discriminate between important and unimportant sounds on their listeners' behalf and that they must also make the *level* of that importance clear: in some cases they must clarify the very *nature* of those sounds. Why? Shut your eyes and listen again to the sounds around you. You may be surprised at how few of them you can identify with any precision. The frequency range of most sounds is narrow and what we often overlook about the way in which we normally recognize them are the clues our other senses afford, notably the visual sense. When we do not actually see what is causing them they often mean nothing at all. Moreover studio simulations of sounds can often sound more 'real' on the radio than the actual sounds themselves would. Among the better known and genuine examples of these studio simulations are the clapping together of coconut shells to convey horses' hooves and the rustle of a bunch of recording tape to convey someone walking through undergrowth (McLeish, 1978, 252). These are not straightforwardly indexical, since the sounds made by coconut shells and recording tape have no *direct* connections with horses and people in undergrowth. They are 'images' of the sounds made by horses and people and are therefore best described as iconic indexes. They might also be described as 'non-literal signifiers' analogous to an actor in the theatre who represents a table by kneeling on all fours (Elam, 1980, 8); but in radio such signifiers must approximate rather more closely to that which they signify than signifiers in the visual media. Yet however carefully selected and 'realistic' the sounds may be, the listener may still be unclear as to what aspect of reality they are meant to signify. The rustle of recording tape may sound like someone walking through undergrowth, but it also sounds like the swish of a lady's gown and remarkably like the rustle of recording tape. In a radio play which of these things would it signify?

Accompanied by 'Damn! I don't often hit it off the fairway': a golfer searching for his ball in the rough.

Accompanied by 'Darling, you'll be the belle of the ball tonight': a lady in an evening gown.

Accompanied by 'This studio's a pig-sty. Throw this old tape out': a bunch of recording tape.

In other words, sounds require textual pointing – support from the dialogue or narrative. The ear will believe what it is led to believe. This pointing might be termed 'anchorage', which is how Roland Barthes describes the function of words used as captions for photographs. Visual images, he argues, are polysemous. But so are sounds. Hence words help '*fix* the floating chain of signifieds in such a way as to counter the terror of uncertain signs' (Barthes, 1977, 39).

Music

Music on the radio, as on television, seems to perform two main functions. It is an object of aesthetic pleasure in its own right, in record shows, concerts, recitals, and so on; and either by itself or in combination with words and/or sounds it performs an ancillary function in signifying something outside itself.

As an object of pleasure in its own right, music is quite simply the mainstay of radio's output. Some stations offer little or nothing else. Even on the four BBC networks, one of which – Radio 4 – devotes over three-fifths of its output to news and current affairs, music accounted for 61.3 per cent of total radio output in 1983–4 (*BBC Annual Report and Handbook 1985*, 1984, 145). The difficulty is to define such music in semiotic terms since there is some doubt as to the sense in which music can be said to signify. Broadly speaking, words and images refer to something outside themselves but the assertion cannot be quite so confidently made about music. Music with lyrics seems to present less of a difficulty since we could say that the significance or meaning of the music is expressed in the words; but it might equally be argued that the music means one thing and the lyrics mean another and that they are quite capable of counterpointing as well as complementing each other. Quite apart from this, the question of what meaning (if any) attaches to wordless music is a

51

formidable one. It can of course be seen as an index of the instruments and musicians that are playing it. When we hear a record on the radio but miss the disc jockey's introduction to it, we may still be able to identify which group is playing by the characteristic sound it has evolved. But to leave the matter there is rather like saying that spoken words are signs of nothing but the identity of their speaker. Dictionary definitions of music generally ascribe an emotional significance to it, and some compositions (for example Tchaikovsky's *1812 Overture*) evoke historical events: but while acknowledging this we would have to point out that music does not convey these emotions or events with anything like the precision that words do. Indeed there is room for disagreement about the emotional significance of certain compositions with unrevealing titles like 'Opus No. 3' or 'Study in E Flat' – and who could tell merely from hearing it that Chopin's *Minute Waltz* is about a dog chasing its tail? This means that written commentaries which point to particular features of a piece of music as referring to particular emotional or historical conditions tend to rely consciously or unconsciously on circumstantial evidence – the title of the piece and/or the famous legend which it 'narrates', the situation in which it was composed, the biographical and psychological details of the composer, and so on. Hence our very difficulty in discerning what music refers to means that if it does signify, then apart from its local imitations of 'natural' sounds its mode of signification will be almost entirely symbolic.

This virtual absence, or at any rate imprecision, of meaning in music makes it at once highly suited to the radio medium and somewhat unilluminating as to its nature. It is highly suited because in being largely free of signification it allows us to listen without making strenuous efforts to imagine what is being referred to, but to assimilate it, if we wish, to our own thoughts and moods – a fact which helps to explain why music has become even more popular since radio's rebirth as a secondary medium. But it is unilluminating in the sense that in its fully realized form (that is, not as a written score) it consists almost purely of sound, refers scarcely at all to anything outside itself, and is therefore one code which is not distinctively shaped by radio since radio is itself a purely acoustic medium. This was recognized fairly early in broadcasting history by a features producer who wished to dismiss the idea that there was anything especially 'radiogenic' about music:

> There is no such thing as radio music. Composers go on composing music just as if wireless had never been invented, and the music of all periods is played before microphones in exactly the same way as it has always been played. It does not have to be 'adapted'. (Sieveking, 1934, 24)

Apart from the fact that radio allowed the listener to hear music without visual distractions (and even in this was anticipated by the gramophone), the point is that music is rather less revealing about the nature and possibilities of the medium than, say, news, drama and light entertainment: for whereas we can compare radio versions of the latter with their corresponding forms on the stage, screen or in newspapers and see the distinctive way in which the medium has adapted them, music in its essential form is always and everywhere the same. Not modified by radio, it does not particularly illuminate it.

Nevertheless the broad emotive power of music enables it to be combined with words and/or sounds as a way of signifying something outside itself, and some of these forms of signification are worth considering in detail.

1 Music as a 'framing' or 'boundary' mechanism. Musical jingles (sometimes known as 'IDs') identify or 'frame' radio stations just as signature or theme music frames an individual programme by announcing its beginning and/or end. Station IDs are similar in function to the voice of the continuity announcer, they set the style or tone of the station and could be seen as both index and symbol. It is interesting to speculate why musical IDs are more closely associated with 'popular' and verbal IDs with 'quality' networks; but it is certainly the case that the work done by continuity announcers on Radios 3 and 4 is performed largely by jingles on Radios 1 and 2!

As a way of framing individual items theme music is also common in film and television, but it is of particular significance in radio because of the blindness of the medium. Silence, a pause, can also be used as a framing mechanism, but unlike that of film and television it is *total*, devoid of images. To give the programmes connotations, an overall style or mood, music is therefore an especially useful resource on radio – less bald, more indefinitely suggestive, than mere announcements. Let us take a formal but lively piece of eighteenth-century music played on a harpsichord – a gavotte or bourrée composed by Bach, perhaps – and consider its possibilities for the radio producer. It is highly structured and symmetrical in form and therefore commonly regarded as more cerebral or 'intellectual' than the Romantic compositions of the following century. She might therefore regard it as ideal theme music for a brains trust or quiz programme. But its characteristics have other possibilities. The 'period' quality of both the harpsichord and the music is unmistakable and might lend itself to a programme about history or antiques. Alternatively the 'tinny' tone of the instrument combined with the rhythmic nature of the piece might introduce a children's programme about toys or music boxes or with a faery or fantasy theme. You can doubtless imagine other possibilities for yourself, and I would simply make two further points. The first is that depending on the specific contents of the programmes I have suggested, it would be possible to discern all three modes of signification in such theme music – the symbolic, the indexical and the iconic. Secondly I would stress that these are *extrinsic* meanings of the music: we could not say that it is 'about' cerebration or history or toys. Another way we might describe them is as 'associative' meanings: in a serial, for instance, the theme music will bring to the listener's mind what he already knows about the storyline; even more than this, it is a 'paradigm' of that *genre* of programme (Fiske and Hartley, 1978, 169). This function of music as a framing mechanism and the two following functions are noticed by Goffman (1980, 164–5).

2 Music as a link between the scenes of a radio play or the items of a programme. Such links are analogous to curtain drops in the theatre, since they keep certain aspects of the programme apart and may additionally signal advertising breaks. But as

well as keeping apart they bridge the changes of scene or subject, thus providing a kind of continuity.

3 'Mood' music during a play, a background enhancement which is understood not to be heard by the characters, but is heard by the listeners as a clue to the characters' feelings or thoughts. These last two functions of music could be seen as symbolic, but there is another which Goffman appears to overlook:

4 Music as a kind of stylized replacement for naturalistic sound effects in a play, for example musical simulations of storms or battles. It has an imitative function and is a sort of iconic index. It is heard by the characters in the play, but not in that form.

5 Music in an indexical function, as part of the ordinary sounds of the world which radio portrays. These sounds are usually known collectively as 'actuality'. Here is a typical example from a news programme:

FADE IN SOUND OF BAGPIPES AND DRUMS
Presenter: The Band of the Argyll and Sutherland High-
landers, who were today granted the freedom
of Aldershot.

The semiotic function of the music would be much the same whether it were live actuality from the freedom ceremony, or a recording of the actuality, or simply taken from a gramophone record (radio producers often 'cheat'). In the first instance the music would be indexical and in the other two instances the recordings would simply be acting as icons of the sounds the band was making at the ceremony – sounds which are an index of its presence. They would therefore be iconic indexes.

Silence

Though it is natural for us to speak of radio as a sound medium we should remember that the *absence* of sound can also be heard. It is therefore important to consider silence as a form of signification. It has both negative and positive functions which seem to be indexical. Its negative function is to signify that for

55

the moment at least, nothing is happening on the medium: there is a void, what broadcasters sometimes refer to as 'dead air'. In this function silence can resemble noise (that is, sounds, words and music) in acting as a framing mechanism, for it can signify the integrity of a programme or item by making a space around it. But if the silence persists for more than a few seconds it signifies the dysfunction or non-functioning of the medium: either transmitter or receiver has broken down or been switched off.

The positive function of silence is to signify that something is happening which for one reason or another cannot be expressed in noise. Because radio silence is total (unlike film and theatrical silences, which are visually filled) it can be a potent stimulus to the listener, providing a gap in the noise for his imagination to work: 'Pass me the bottle. Cheers. . . . Ah, that's better!' But such silences or pauses can suggest not only physical actions but abstract, dramatic qualities, generate pathos or irony by confirming or countering the words which surround them. They can also generate humour, as in a famous radio skit which featured Jack Benny, a comedian with a reputation for extreme miserliness:

> The skit consists of a confrontation between Benny and a mugger on the street. Says the mugger: 'Your money or your life'. Prolonged pause: growing laughter; then applause as the audience gradually realises what Benny *must* be thinking, and eventually responds to the information communicated by the silence and to its comic implications.   (Fink, 1981, 202)

How, then, does the listener discriminate among these various negative and positive functions of silence? His guide is clearly the context – in the first instance whether any noise frames the silence and in the second, what that noise signifies.

The primary code of radio

In fact context (as will by now be clear) is the key to the meaning of the sounds, music and silences of radio – and the means by which the context is established is at bottom *verbal*. Sound conventions can indicate the relative importance of the different strands of radio content by means of levels and fades, but they cannot explain the *nature* of that importance. On the other hand we have seen that silence and sounds draw not only their meaning but also in some cases their very identity from the words around them. It is clear too that in its ancillary function music also requires the clarification of words, for music alone will not be able to tell us whether we are about to hear a brains trust or a history programme or a children's fantasy; and even when music is broadcast as a background enhancer it is not clear without the words in the foreground precisely what is being enhanced. But with respect to music which is broadcast for its own sake our case is harder to argue because the peculiar semantic status of music has somewhat contrasting implications. If it is at least agreed that music does not enshrine the kind of meaning that words do, there is an evident need to set it in a verbal context: it is not 'self-sufficient'. But on the other hand it could be argued from the same premise that music is literally inexplicable and therefore entirely self-sufficient: and it is surely true that music is much less parasitic upon context than sounds are. A series of shuffling or clicking noises divorced from their visual or verbal surroundings will leave us totally baffled as to their nature and significance; but a piece of music is instantly recognizable as music and can be fully appreciated as such, even if we have never heard it before and have no inkling as to what it is or who wrote it. Public sound-systems in restaurants, airports and supermarkets pump out continuous 'muzak' with no attempt at verbal contextualization. Nevertheless there seems to be a deep and abiding impulse to explain or identify music – an impulse that no radio station ignores entirely. If we are interested in any kind of music our first desire is to know what it is, even if the answer is an unrevealing 'Symphony in G'. Moreover it is clear that because the inherent meaning of music is elusive the linguistic context can *invest* it with meaning. A particular rock record will seem progressive and 'heavy' when presented by John Peel and sound anodyne and 'middle-of-the-road' when announced by Tony Blackburn. Nor is this peculiar to pop, but common in music traditionally regarded as 'significant' in both senses of the word. We all know about the bright idea of the marketing man who boosted record sales by incorporating the 'Toccata and Fugue in D Minor' into an album entitled 'Bach's Greatest Hits'.

It seems reasonable to suggest, then, that the primary code of radio is linguistic, since words are required to contextualize all the other codes. We must therefore look at this code a little more closely. Since the medium is blind the words cannot be *seen* by the receiver but only *heard* by him: hence the linguistic code of radio approximates much more closely to that of *speech* than writing. But there is an important measure of difference. Much radio talk is first written down – scripted: indeed at one time *all* of it was (Rodger, 1982, 44–5), and to that extent it has a *literary* nature. This means that much radio talk is premeditated rather than spontaneous. It is also more explicit than spontaneous speech in that it creates its own context or situation to a much greater extent (Gregory and Carroll, 1978, 42–3). It is more fluent, precise and orderly, less diffuse and tautological, than ordinary speech. As well as these advantages scripted talk runs to time and ensures that no important information is omitted or presented out of sequence. Hence words on the radio could be regarded as the application of oral language to a situation which normally calls for writing, that is, where what is referred to is not simultaneously apparent to sender and receiver since they are separated – remote from and invisible to each other. These words do not constitute conventional orality but what has been termed 'secondary orality' (Ong, 1982, 3, 136).

But there is a general convention on the radio that scripted speech does not 'admit' to being scripted. Aspiring broadcasters are taught to regard scripts as the 'storage of talk' (McLeish, 1978, 65) and encouraged to work into them expressions which occur less frequently in writing than in speech – 'Well now . . . ', 'Come to think of it . . . ', the latter an implicit denial that anything has been premeditated. The purpose of such colloquialisms is to discourage the flat, expressionless tone of the unskilled broadcaster who concentrates on the *words* of her script rather than on what they refer to – a problem which does not arise in unscripted talk. The secret of much apparently impromptu delivery was revealed many years ago in Professor John Hilton's broadcast on how to give a radio talk:

For, of course, I read every word. If only I could pull it off every time – but you have to be at the top of your form. Yes, of course, every word's on paper even now – this – what I'm saying to you now – it's all here.   (cit. Cardiff, 1980, 31)

Even lectures on Radio 3 are usually described as 'talks' to deflect attention from the fact that they are read.

Why should reading disguise itself as spontaneous talk? The act of reading implies *absence* – the separation of addresser and addressee. The addresser has been replaced by a text, so that if a radio listener is aware that a broadcaster is reading he will assume that she is either relaying the words of somebody else or erecting a barrier between herself and her audience. Hence to avoid creating this impression of absence and impersonality much radio talk which is actually scripted – programme presentation, weather forecasts, continuity, cues, trailers and so forth – is delivered as if it were unscripted and impromptu.

Nevertheless there are certain kinds of radio talk which are not passed off as impromptu but announced as being *read*, notably the news ('This is the six o'clock news *read* by Brian Perkins') and readings from novels and stories ('A *Book* at Bedtime'): and while even within the BBC presentation-styles vary greatly from the rapid and urgent to the solemn and sedate, I would contend that our awareness that they are being read derives much more from these announcements than from any distinctive 'reading tone'. Indeed in the sense of being a mode of expression analogous to a 'speaking tone' it seems doubtful whether such a thing exists. I base this contention on the fact that the differences between orality and literacy seem a good deal less absolute than is commonly supposed. It has recently been shown that writing carries a considerable 'oral residue' (Ong, 1982, 40–1, 115, 149), that writers instinctively and inevitably conceive of the word as primarily a unit of *speech* and their readers as quite literally an *audience*. An obvious but not unique example would be a Churchill or Macaulay, whose oratory was committed to the page but which always addressed the ear rather than the eye. We revere Shakespeare as a giant of literature, but the major part of his work consists of plays – plays whose dialogue, however 'literary', was written to be delivered as if it were spontaneous speech. Such dialogue is also plentifully enshrined in that genre which is pre-eminently the child of print, the novel; and even in works which contain little actual conversation, like *Catcher in the Rye*, there is often a first-person narrator who addresses the reader throughout in what is highly colloquial language – a fact which is bound to be reflected in any broadcast reading of it. It could be objected that such an example is atypical, that much literary language is a good deal more formal than Salinger's and that this would be reflected in the tone in which it was read. But formality is not a preserve of literary language: much unscripted *talk* is formal – the off-the-cuff explanations of a teacher, for instance, or the reprimand she might deliver to a pupil. Conversely, the language of radio news, which is self-evidently written down, is formal too: at least it is not colloquial in the sense that Salinger's is. Yet when the newscaster reaches a tragic or humorous item, her voice-tone becomes suitably grave or light-hearted, even on Radios 3 and 4. (We might notice in passing that just as words when voiced can evoke a sense of the broadcaster's personality, so the personality of the broadcaster can enhance the words; and of course different personalities may produce subtle differences of expression, which is not to say that their various readings may not be *equally* expressive.) Formality, then, is not a *lack* of expression, it is not the same thing as a reading tone – and I would argue that what determines the tone of voice is not so much whether a communication has been written down or is spoken extempore as the *purpose* of that communication and the circumstances in which it is delivered. It seems likely that if a reader gives literary language its full expressive value her tone will not be very different from an ordinary speech tone, and that what we are accustomed to describe as a reading tone is really a flat and expressionless preoccupation with the words on the page rather than with what they mean. Since this tone is common among inexperienced broadcasters the measures prescribed by their instructors are understandable: but I would suggest that the tone of the accomplished news or story reader, whose skill lies in bringing out the full meaning of the words, is virtually indistinguishable from the tone of the ordinary articulate speaker, and is an implicit recognition that writing is merely 'programmed talk' –

not separate from speaking but a technological development of it.

But if it is true that a reading tone is not readily detectable among skilled broadcasters, why should news and stories on the radio *declare* themselves to be read? In each case the text must be accorded a primacy (or 'foregrounded', to re-employ this term, this time in its linguistic sense) – though for rather different reasons. In the news the words must carry an air of definitiveness and accuracy, it must seem to be 'authorless' – originated by the events themselves. The impression that the newscaster is extemporizing it would negate its very purpose. She is therefore cued as a news *reader* and is likely to speak with a 'received pronunciation' (RP) so that her reading will maximize the symbolic function – the meaningfulness – of the words while minimizing her voice's function as an index of her personality. By this means it is suggested that she is the mere mouthpiece of the words and not their originator. In the case of story-readings the text is also foregrounded but for its beauty, not its truth. It is writing which is in one way or another good enough to act as an object of interest in its own right instead of as a barrier between broadcaster and listener – of more interest than the broadcaster's own words. Its literariness is declared as the main justification for the programme and it is the reader's function to express that literariness, or linguistic beauty, in whatever manner seems appropriate.

Yet even when the listener is aware that the words on the radio are being read to him he must still be able to grasp their meaning through the *ear*, an organ which is a good deal less comprehending than the eye, particularly when deprived of the help of the other organs which it receives in most acts of interpersonal communication. The cause of this lack of comprehension has been eloquently defined:

> Sound exists only when it is going out of existence. It is not simply perishable but essentially evanescent, and it is sensed as evanescent. When I pronounce the word 'permanence', by the time I get to the '-nence', the 'perma–' is gone, and has to be gone. (Ong, 1982, 32)

This is another reason why the scripted nature of radio talk is rarely acknowledged, for it is a general truth that much language is written down precisely because its meaning is too complex to be assimilated by ear, and the listener's awareness that it is read is therefore likely to make him feel that he will be unable to follow it. And it is certainly the case that radio language will not be easily followed unless it is syntactically fairly simple or else fairly concrete in subject-matter. The descriptions of physical phenomena which are characteristic of novels, stories and even news items, their preoccupation with personalities, utterances and events – all this lends itself to radio. So, too, do ideas, opinions and arguments when expressed in the syntax of spontaneous speech. But when these ideas and arguments become more abstract and their expression is premeditated, or when they require sustained explanation or specialist knowledge, the radio medium is less effective (McWhinnie, 1959, 49–50). The BBC's Audience Research Department once tested a group of people on how much they could understand of a talk intended for the 'average' Light Programme listener: the average listener in the group could correctly answer only 28 per cent of the questions which were asked about the talk after it was broadcast (Silvey, 1974, 141). Indeed it has been observed that the importance of the radio interviewer is not only as the poser of questions but as the interpreter of answers, the 'plain man' who in brief paraphrases renders the complex or specialist responses of the expert into language intelligible to the lay public (Cardiff, 1980, 38).

It will be helpful to summarize our findings so far. Much radio talk is 'literary' in the sense that it has first been written down, but with certain notable exceptions it suppresses these literary origins and even when it does not its expression must be simple or concrete enough to be comprehended through the ear alone. Its messages will therefore tend to have a high level of *redundancy* (Fiske, 1982, 10–12; Ong, 1982, 39–40) – that is, material which is predictable or conventional; for speech is notoriously evanescent, as are all signs that exist in time. The listener has no chance of retrieval, cannot introduce his own redundancy as a reader can by reading something twice. Radio language is, then, very similar to that of television, which Fiske and Hartley have characterized as an intersection of oral and literary language (1978, 160): but the main differences are that the linguistic code of television has rather less to do in establishing context or situation, since much of this can be done visually, and is potentially more 'literary' in the sense that it can and frequently does appear on the screen in the form of writing – as captions, tables, and so on. Yet within the overall conditions created by the medium's blindness – conditions which make themselves felt to a varying degree in different kinds of programmes – the linguistic code of radio is capable of the same variety of function as ordinary speech:

> Even by comparison with its sister medium of television, it is chaotically eclectic in the hospitality it affords to different kinds of language. The formal rhetoric of Churchill's wartime speeches would surely have sounded phoney if one had been able to watch him making them on television; radio allowed them their necessary distance and resonance. At the other end of the scale, the introduction of the phone-in programme a few years ago soon made one accustomed to hearing voices on the radio speaking as informally, often as inarticulately, as if one had heard them drifting through one's window from the street. In the course of an hour spent as an idle radio listener, twiddling between stations, one drifts from the most elaborate and carefully scripted language through every shade and tone to the most unofficial and unrehearsed grunts and squawks. On radio there is no median register, no particular way of speaking that could be said to represent the medium in neutral gear, ticking over. . . . Radio is by turns gossipy, authoritative, preachy, natural, artificial, confidential, loudly public, and not infrequently, wordless. Its languages bleed into one another. (Raban, 1981, 86–7)

We can take a more systematic look at this functional variety by using a familiar communication-model – that of Roman Jakobson (1960, 350–7). Many other models exist which could also be used (McQuail and Windahl, 1981) but Jakobson's has the merit of simplicity and flexibility. It arranges the six elements which he regards as making up the communication act (and which we have already identified in Chapter 1) in the following fashion:

	context	
sender	message	receiver

| | contact | |
| | code | |

If, as Jakobson asserts, one or other of these six elements is always dominant in a single act of communication, not only can we classify the act according to which of the elements is dominant –

	referential	
emotive	aesthetic	conative

| | phatic | |
| | metalingual | |

– but where that dominance is sustained over a series of acts of communication we can develop in radio terms an analogous theory of programme types or genres. For instance radio language whose dominant function is primarily *referential*, whose orientation is towards the context of the real world, is language which is characteristic of news and documentary programmes or of commentaries on public events. On the other hand, chat-shows or interview programmes such as *Start the Week* and *Desert Island Discs* are dominated by an *emotive* use of language in the sense that the guests are encouraged to talk about themselves, their feelings and their attitudes to life. Radio is also capable of *conative*, persuasive or rhetorical, functions – most conspicuously in commercials or 'public service' notices advising road safety, for example, but also in party political broadcasts. On the other hand, the broadcasting of plays, story-tellings and poetry-readings foregrounds the message for its own sake, for its inherent literary merits, and is therefore characterized by language in its *aesthetic* function.

Two further points should be made. First it is important not to push these classifications and the distinctions between them too far. Educational programmes might be generally recognizable by their predominantly referential language, but in making occasional use of drama or poetry-readings can also be characterized by language whose dominant function is aesthetic. And in a comic play it may be hard at times to decide whether the dominant function is conative – to make the audience laugh – or aesthetic, to foreground the 'message' for its own sake. The second point is that there is, of course, nothing exclusively 'radiogenic' about such classifications: the Jakobson model could be used to classify forms of writing or television in much the same way. I would, however, wish to suggest that there is one kind of programme classifiable in terms of this model which, if not peculiar to radio, was at least originated by it and is of unique significance therein: the phone-in. I shall be arguing in Chapter 9 that the purpose of the phone-in is to attempt the ultimately impossible feat of providing feedback for the listener and that the dominant function of the programme is therefore phatic and metalingual. In other words the phone-in enables radio broadcasters to create the illusion of a two-way medium and to verify both that they have an audience and that the audience is capable of responding to the codes they transmit. But in order to demonstrate this I have to stretch the Jakobson model somewhat, since it does not accommodate the notion of feedback: for once the receiver responds to the sender their roles – and the model – have been reversed, the receiver is now the sender. But if we were to regard the original situation as persisting and the radio phone-caller's remarks as a *response* to the broadcaster's communication rather than a part of it, the function of that response is both *phatic* – a demonstration that the audience is 'present' and can hear the radio message – and *metalingual* – that it is capable of understanding and even contributing to it. Such a concept of the phone-in does of course imply some divergence between what is actually and what is only apparently the dominant function of its language. The apparent function of a phone-in on the subject of nuclear disarmament may be to allow the listeners to become broadcasters and air their views in an emotive or conative way, like the speakers on *Any Questions*; but its actual function will simply be to demonstrate that the radio station has many listeners and that they are responsive to the publicity which it chooses to afford to such an issue.

Yet even if it is the case that phone-ins exist primarily to demonstrate the presence and understanding of an audience rather than to ascertain what any individual member of that audience may think, it might still be doubted whether they are of unique significance to radio. The other mass media are equally bereft of feedback in the real sense, and television has also made use of the phone-in to create a semblance thereof. But I would argue that in none of the other media, with their images or visible texts, are the phatic and metalingual considerations – the need for feedback to the communicator – so pressing or persistent.

In Chapters 4 to 9 I shall be looking at various kinds of radio programmes which seem to use the medium in particularly illuminating ways, and in Chapter 10 at radio audiences and the functions the medium has for them.

Suggestions for further work

Form a small group with your fellow-students – say, five or six of you – and each write a two-minute 'voicepiece' or radio talk (360 words maximum) on any subject which will suit the length and the medium. Remember that your listeners will not be able to see you or your text and will be 'absent'. Its register should therefore be colloquial, rather like that of a letter you might write to a friend, and it should be 'chatted' to the microphone – *performed* rather than merely read out. McLeish (1978) provides invaluable hints on writing for radio. When you have written your piece rehearse it *aloud* to ensure that it reads easily and effectively. The group members should record their pieces in isolation, then re-group for playback and evaluation. The less experienced and more nervous you are at the microphone, the more likely it will be that your remarks will sound 'literary', like those of an essay, your voice-tone impersonal and 'read', and your delivery hurried. But you might notice how quickly you can improve with practice (and you will have an opportunity to do another voicepiece at the end of Chapter 5). Your eventual aim might be to see if you can make your talk sound so 'warm' and natural that you can convince an uninitiated listener that it is extemporized!

PART TWO
THE WORLD OUTSIDE

4 NEWS AND CURRENT AFFAIRS

A man may see how this world goes with no eyes. Look with
thine ears.   (Shakespeare, *King Lear*, IV, vi)

Radio news has a long and venerable tradition. One can still
listen to the Second World War bulletins read by Alvar Lidell
and Frank Phillips and appreciate them both as broadcasting
models and historical documents. Indeed radio seems so natural
and successful a way of presenting the news that we tend to
underestimate the demands which the medium makes and the
restrictions it imposes, especially in comparison with the two
other main news media, newspapers and television. Its lack of a
visual dimension means that radio lacks the printed words of the
former, nor can it complement its sounds with the images of the
latter.

The limitations of radio news are most seriously exposed
when it is compared to the newspaper. The newspaper sets out
diverse material across several pages. The reader can take an
overview of the material, see several items at a glance, decide
which she will read and in what order, and re-read anything if
she needs to. Radio perforce offers much *less* news. Why?

In semiotic terms we might say that signs which exist in *time*
are rather less efficient than those which exist primarily in space;
or to put it more simply, it is quicker to read something for
oneself than to listen to somebody else reading it. The average
newsreader utters 160 to 180 words per minute. A ten-minute
radio bulletin is equivalent to a mere one-and-a-half columns of
news copy – and a newspaper may carry thirty or forty columns
of such copy (McLeish, 1978, 19–20). Thus even an hour of

radio news and current affairs cannot equal the coverage of a newspaper, and since it has to be much more selective and summary than a newspaper listeners get the impression that radio news is much more highly edited. This has led to the view that radio (and television) really offers a different *kind* of news from the press:

> Radio and television can offer instantaneous coverage of an event – an air disaster, a kidnapping, a freak storm, the falling to earth of a satellite – but the press alone can offer extensive explanation and amplification of such occurrences. Newspapers, by providing comprehensive coverage of complex issues, can thus complement the more immediate reports of radio and television. (O'Donnell and Todd, 1980, 99)

Programme planners have long been sensitive to the limitations of the medium and have attempted to give width and depth to the news through lots of ancillary current affairs and 'background' programmes – programmes which complement the questions of fact which are raised and answered by the news with attempts to explain *why* such facts occur (Paulu, 1981, 193). No less than 62 per cent of Radio 4's total output consists of news and current affairs programmes (*BBC Annual Report and Handbook 1985*, 1984, 145) such as *The World at One*, *Yesterday in Parliament*, *PM*, *The Financial World Tonight*, *Analysis*, *Today*, *File on Four*, *From Our Own Correspondent* and *International Assignment*; and one of the independent stations, LBC, is almost wholly given over to news and current affairs.

Nevertheless on a ratio of quantity to time all this is a less efficient mode of news presentation than is print; nor within any programme can the listener get so detailed an *overview* of the material as the newspaper reader. It is true that many bulletins begin with a general announcement of the items to follow, but it is seldom exhaustive – and unless the item she wishes to hear is broadcast first the selective listener cannot go straight to what she wants, as the reader can. She is presented instead with a sequence or 'thread' of items from which no deviation is possible. Hence the need for 'signposting' not just in the news but in *all* kinds of radio – 'Coming up shortly . . . ', 'Later in this bulletin . . . ' – a need which was referred to in Chapter 1.

Indeed, in contrast to the newspapers radio news programmes pose problems for the selective and non-selective listener alike – for she who wishes to hear only certain items and she who wants an overall perspective on the news. In newspapers a kind of prioritization (albeit one which is determined by the political and social bias of the individual paper) is suggested to the reader by typographical devices, photographs and overall layout. The most important item or items tend to be located under large headlines at the top of the front page, the least important occupy three lines at the foot of the inner pages. It is evident that newspapers pay as much attention to spatial composition as to the individual news items (Hartley, 1982, 31). Nevertheless the reader can, if she chooses, ignore this implied order of priorities by going straight past the 'lead' story on page 1 to read about sport or scan the weather forecast in the inner pages: but she can scarcely fail to notice that a *kind* of order exists.

On radio, order is both a more and a less rigid matter. It is more rigid in the sense that unlike the reader the listener cannot ignore it and adopt her own. She must at least half attend to the items she is not interested in so that she can catch those she is interested in – a situation which may be good for the news editor but is frustrating for the listener. One solution is that adopted by the current affairs magazine, *Today* (Radio 4), which broadcasts such 'fixed' items as the sports news and weather forecast at the same times every day, but this may still mean a wait for the impatient listener. But order in radio news is less rigid in the sense that the sequence in which the items are broadcast is not necessarily the same as the order of their importance. The non-selective listener, who wants an overall perspective on the news, is likely to assume that the most important items will come first, the less important later. But while this is generally the rule it sometimes gives way to another rule of sound broadcasting, especially in the more expansive 'news background' and current affairs programmes – that that inattentive organ, the ear, must be offered fresh stimulus through variety. The reader can introduce her own variety by turning the pages and turning back again: the listener must have her variety introduced for her, which means that the sequence and indeed the *choice* of items are partly dictated by the nature of the medium (Smith, 1976, 173).

Serious items are often interlarded with light or humorous ones which might otherwise have been thought unworthy of inclusion, but such a measure avoids monotony only to run the risk of dilettantism and lack of perspective. The news editor has no visual means of indicating that certain items are more important than others. Some may last longer than others but longer is not necessarily the same as more important, and in any case our sense of duration is less certain than our awareness of spatial length. There is therefore a risk that everything in radio news will assume an *equal* importance – or lack of it.

Let us summarize what we have asserted so far. As a result of being purveyed purely through sound, radio news suffers from a number of handicaps. In its overall range it is perforce much more *selective* than a newspaper, yet makes selection on the listener's part a much more difficult matter than for the newspaper reader; and it also affords her much less of a sense of the relative importance of the items it includes.

But radio news suffers from a further problem – the *kind* and *compass* of language in which it has to be expressed. The language of newspapers is permanent: the reader sets her own pace and can re-read what she has missed or cannot understand. This means that the press is capable of considerable linguistic variety. It can therefore divide the heterogeneous audience with which every mass medium is confronted into different intellectual levels by providing different kinds of newspapers for different kinds of reader. Their varying treatments of a single event can often be amusing. Where *The Times* might announce in a headline 'Employment Secretary Plans New Trade Union Legislation', the *Daily Mirror* might content itself with the exhortation 'Come off it, Norman!' But as we saw in the last chapter the language of radio is evanescent. The radio newsreader sets an arbitrary pace and his words dissolve into thin air. (It is possible for the listener to record and 'retrieve' news bulletins but in practice this is seldom done and is probably illegal.) This means that however complex the material – and complexity is especially likely in news, documentary and educational programmes – it must be expressed in language which is fairly simple and straightforward in style and diction. Since radio lacks the linguistic range of the newspapers we would expect it to be less capable of providing different levels of output for different kinds of listeners and to remain confronted with a largely heterogeneous audience. This certainly seems to be the case with television, whose language code is also evanescent – a point made by Fiske and Hartley (1978). They argue that the heterogeneity of the television audience dominates and even 'originates' the television message, creating a tendency towards cultural centrality. From this they develop their concept of 'bardic' television (pp. 85–6). Most of its output, they suggest, uses a 'broadcast' linguistic code – that is, language which is colloquial, contains much redundancy, is phatic rather than referential (relatively easy where pictures and images can supply much of the referential content) and assumes a background of shared experience to emphasize things its audience has in common rather than apart. Students of language will recognize a similarity, if not identity, between the notion of a broadcast code and Bernstein's restricted code (Fiske, 1982, 74–81; Bernstein, 1971, 76–92, 123–37). Hence the function of the television message is very largely one of reassurance and confirmation. Generally it avoids the use of 'narrowcast' language (analogous to Bernstein's elaborated code) which is typically literary, contains little redundancy, is highly referential and assumes a shared educational or intellectual experience to teach what is not known. Its function is to challenge or enrich audiences.

But if the television message is influenced by the heterogeneous nature of the audience I would suggest that it is even more fundamentally determined by the evanescent nature of its language – and indeed that this evanescence is the main reason *why* the audience remains heterogeneous. Moreover I would argue that such language is an even more powerful determinant in radio than in television because in the latter we can at least *see*, however briefly, what some of the words refer to and even, on occasions, the words themselves. But on the radio we can see nothing. We might sum this up in terms of the Jakobson model: in both television and radio the heterogeneous nature of the receivers imposes constraints and restraints on the referential power of the message, but the nature of the contact makes a prior, even more basic imposition for it requires that the message should be relatively simple: and it must be even simpler in the case of radio since it is unassisted by visual codes and must therefore be apprehensible through the ear alone.

Yet as I mentioned earlier, despite all these difficulties radio has an illustrious history as a news medium and in the last ten years or so has set out to emulate the press by providing its audience with both quality news (for example *The World at One* on Radio 4) and popular news (*Newsbeat* on Radio 1). How do these types of programmes set out to offer a choice of news content and mode of presentation comparable with that offered by *The Times* and the popular press such as the *Daily Mirror* or the *Sun*? Can they match the visual differences of language and layout which are immediately obvious to the reader with acoustic differences that are equally obvious to the listener? What follows is an outline of an edition of *Newsbeat* followed by an outline of *The World at One*. They were broadcast on the same day – Monday, 25 February 1985 – and within half an hour of each other. In both I have reproduced the news headlines and the first news items in full, and all the other items I have either summarized or paraphrased in order to give some idea of the sequence and shape of each programme. The points of interest and comparison in the programmes and the points of comparison between both programmes and the corresponding types of newspapers could occupy a book in themselves, but although I sometimes mention certain common features of radio news which do not occur in these particular broadcasts I have kept my findings as brief as possible.

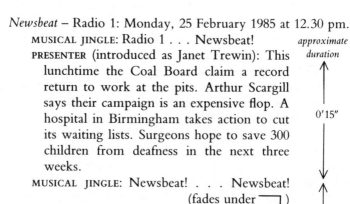

Newsbeat – Radio 1: Monday, 25 February 1985 at 12.30 pm.

MUSICAL JINGLE: Radio 1 . . . Newsbeat!   *approximate*

PRESENTER (introduced as Janet Trewin): This   *duration*
lunchtime the Coal Board claim a record return to work at the pits. Arthur Scargill says their campaign is an expensive flop. A hospital in Birmingham takes action to cut its waiting lists. Surgeons hope to save 300 children from deafness in the next three weeks.   0'15"

MUSICAL JINGLE: Newsbeat! . . . Newsbeat!
(fades under ⌐⌐)

(1) PRESENTER: As the coal industry enters the fifty-first week of its strike action furious arguments are raging over just how close the Coal Board is to a 51 per cent return to work. The NCB says 48 per cent of miners are now back but NUM President, Arthur Scargill, continues to dispute their figures and claims that 64 per cent are still out on strike. The Coal Board says more than 3500 new faces turned up for work this morning, which would be a record for a Monday, but Mr Scargill says the NCB's return-to-work compaign, costing hundreds of thousands of pounds, has been a flop.

3'19"

Male voice gives more details of return to work and introduces:

Telephone interview with a South Wales miner who has just given up the strike. He explains why he thinks the strike will shortly end.

Male voice – studio link.

Telephone interview with female NUM member, a white-collar worker who has just given up the strike in South Wales.

Male voice – studio link.

Studio interview with BBC's Labour Correspondent, Nick Jones.

(2) Presenter introduces item about surgeons at a Birmingham hospital who are attempting to clear a backlog of children requiring ear surgery.

Actuality of children's ward leading into interview with child's parent:

3'10"

Female voice – studio link.

Interview with one of the surgeons.

Female voice – studio link.

Interview with Head of Medical Staff Committee.

Female voice – studio link.

Interview with Deputy Administrator of the Hospital.
Female voice – studio link.
Interview with child about to have ear surgery. ↓

(3) Presenter introduces item about first Pakistani Elections for eight years.
Recorded interview with President of Pakistan, General Zia.
Male voice – studio link.
Interview with expert on Pakistan from the School of Oriental Studies.
MUSICAL JINGLE: Newsbeat! (fades under ⌐) ↓

2'25"

(4) Presenter reads news round-up – two sentences each on the following items:
The pound's fall against the dollar.
An underground explosion at a coal-mine in Eastern France.
The Northern Ireland Tourist Board announces a record number of visitors.
Bulletin on comedian Les Dawson after his operation.
MUSICAL JINGLE: Newsbeat! ↓

0'35"

(5) Presenter introduces item on 'Franglais' – the invasion of the French language by English words. The French have enlisted the help of an English university to resist it.
Interview with a lecturer at London University.
MUSICAL JINGLE: Newsbeat! . . . Radio 1. ↓

2'16"

(6) Presenter introduces interview with pop singer, Leonard Cohen, currently touring Britain.
Interview with Leonard Cohen – and fading in under his voice a song from his latest album. Song ends, impromptu remark from Presenter and back to the Gary Davies programme. ↓

2'45"

Total 14 min. 45 sec.

The World at One – Radio 4: Monday, 25 February 1985 at 1 pm.

PRESENTER – Brian Widlake – identifies himself and the programme, then the news headlines as follows:

NEWSREADER: The Coal Board says more than three and a half thousand mineworkers gave up their strike this morning, well above the previous record figure. Four miners have been killed and a dozen others are missing after a pit accident in Eastern France.

The pound has fallen further against the dollar, but it's risen against some European currencies.

First reports from Pakistan indicate that the Opposition boycott of today's election has been unsuccessful.

1'00"

Presenter introduces the following items in today's programme:

In the face of today's return to work a Welsh union official calls on the miners' leaders to take the men back to work.

A Coal Board spokesman says that the men going back understand pits can't stay open for ever.

Is a Spanish holidays 'price war' on the way?

A new way to eat snails – shells and all.

'The lunch-time news is read by Brian Martin.'

NEWSREADER: (i) The National Coal Board says more than 3500 miners abandoned their strike this morning – that's 1200 more than the previous record for a Monday, last November. The Energy Secretary, Mr Peter Walker, said the men now returning were helping to save their industry from further disaster and were also probably saving their

77

union. The Coal Board has said the number of miners at work is now well over 48 per cent of the total – a claim immediately challenged by the mineworkers' President, Mr Arthur Scargill. Here's our Labour Correspondent, Nicholas Jones.

Labour Correspondent reports on the return to work figures and on Mr Scargill's reaction, and introduces

Recorded remarks of the Welsh NUM's Research Officer.

He concludes with a prediction on the workforce's return.

(ii) Item on a man who has been fined for assaulting Mr Scargill.

(iii) Pit explosion in Eastern France –

Report from Paris correspondent, Philip Short.   9'15"

(iv) INLA claims it killed the former member of the UDA who was shot in Londonderry last night.

(v) The pound's continuing fall in value against the dollar.

Report from Economics Editor, Dominic Harrod.

(vi) Industrial action in support of a pay-claim by the teachers' unions.

(vii) Riots and violence in black townships in South Africa.

(viii) Voting in the General Election in Pakistan.

Report from Alex Brodie in Islamabad.

(ix) Lebanon requests UN meeting about Israeli raids on its southern villages.

(x) Man appears before magistrates on a charge connected with the anti-Apartheid demonstration against the runner, Zola Budd.

(xi) Report on recovery of comedian, Les Dawson.

(xii) Former captain of the Welsh Rugby Union team resigns from playing in international matches.

(1) Presenter introduces item about the record return to work by the miners.
  Interview with Lodge Chairman at Cynheidre Colliery by Gilbert John.
Presenter – studio link.
  Interview with Research Officer of Welsh NUM by Welsh Affairs Correspondent, Chris Powell.
Presenter – studio link.
  Interview with a Scottish miner who has just given up the strike. Interviewer: Craig Millar.
Presenter – studio link.
  Interview with Scottish Vice-President of the NUM by Nigel Robson.
Presenter – studio link.
  Telephone interview with NCB spokesman by Brian Widlake.

16'35"

(2) Presenter introduces item on the slump in Spanish holiday bookings and the possibility of a price war.
  Telephone interview with the Managing Director of Thompson Holidays by Carol West.
  C. West – studio link.
  Telephone interview with Managing Director of Thomas Cook by Carol West.

4'00"

(3) Presenter introduces item on Polish refugees in Britain, who are presently being visited by the Primate of Poland, Cardinal Glemp.
  Location interview of Polish refugee by Kevin Ruane.
  K. Ruane – studio link.
  Polish woman's account of her experiences.

4'38"

K. Ruane – studio link.

Polish man's account of his flight from Poland.

K. Ruane – studio link.

Location interview with Yorkshire-born teacher of Polish extraction by Kevin Ruane.

(4) Presenter introduces item about a food company's attempt to market edible snails complete with shells.

Location interview at a food fair with company's representative by Richard Barr.

Then actuality of interviewer sampling the snails and straight into another –

Location interview with the head of the company and more actuality of snail sampling.

3'38"

Presenter concludes Item (4) and delivers closing news headlines comprising the following topics.

   (i)   The miners' return to work.

   (ii) The pound's fall against the dollar.

   (iii) The FT share index.

   (iv) The weather.

Presenter signs off.

0'47"

Total   39 min. 53 sec.

Language and presentation

On the linguistic differences between popular and quality newspapers we might venture the following generalization: that whereas the language of the latter is relatively complex in structure, 'literary' in vocabulary and objective in tone, that of the former is relatively simple in structure, colloquial in vocabulary and emotive or sensational in tone. But one's first impression of the headlines and news copy of *The World at One* (WO) and *Newsbeat* (NB) is that they are couched in very similar language: indeed if the programmes had exchanged their copy it seems doubtful whether their respective listeners would have noticed anything much amiss. The language of WO is clearly not that of *The Times*. In order to be easily intelligible to the ear its vocabulary is familiar and its syntax uncomplicated. The newsreader does not scruple to say 'it's' for 'it is', 'that's' for 'that is', and there is an element of simplification, even personification, in 'The Coal Board says . . . ', where a quality newspaper would be likely to identify a Coal Board spokesman. The fairly elementary nature of radio news language has often been pointed out, even in quality news where one might hear such colloquialisms as 'a *row* in the House of Commons', and in analysing a script from Radio 4's *PM* programme O'Donnell and Todd (1980, 92) point out the relative simplicity of sentence structure and the occurrence of verbless sentences. Despite this simplicity radio news also acknowledges the need for 'redundancy', or reinforcement through repetition, which is a characteristic of colloquial language. WO mentions its main stories three times: in the headlines, the bulletin proper and the closing summary.

But if the language of WO does not closely resemble that of *The Times*, neither does the language of NB altogether resemble that of the popular newspapers. On 27 February 1985, I purchased copies of *The Times* and the *Sun*. Whereas *The Times* led with the collapse of the miners' strike, the *Sun* led with the conviction of a rapist known as 'the Fox'. This item, which was headlined 'PORN LUST OF THE FOX' was included in *The Times* on page 3, under the headline 'The Fox's reign of terror ends in jail for life'. It is highly unlikely that the *Sun*'s baldly sensational headline, which is fairly representative of popular press presentation, would be heard on NB: 'Porn lust of the Fox – details in a moment'. Such language would be used only as a quotation which could be ascribed to its outside source – and in this respect all radio news resembles the quality press in its concern to keep the reportage of the news as free as possible from comment and emotive judgement, a concern which is not greatly shared by the popular newspapers. In the case of the BBC the obvious reason for this is that the Corporation is forbidden to editorialize, but I would suggest that there is another reason which is to do with the nature of radio itself.

Whatever the language it conveys, print is a machine-made medium. It bears no mark of individual authorship but seems impersonally initiated, *authoritative*. This gives statements like the *Sun* headline a superficial air of objectivity, of fact or truth. But radio news is always heard in the voice of an individual and such statements would sound idiosyncratic – be attributed to the newsreader, dismissed as propaganda, or even more likely, misunderstood as drama or comedy. Hence I would argue that irrespective of any charter obligations radio news is recognizable for what it is only when couched in quasi-objective language. Furthermore the nature of the medium produces a kind of *inversion* of the relationship between news and comment which exists in the press, and in so doing establishes the editor's presence in a quite different way. In the press, comment and opinion are felt to be at the heart of the enterprise, matters of much greater editorial import than the accuracy of the news, which seems to be declared in the medium itself. We are accustomed to describe his leading articles somewhat loosely as 'editorials', as though the editor had no responsibility for other parts of the paper, and to ask first of all what a newspaper's political views are – whether it is Conservative or left-wing, for example – and only secondly how comprehensive or accurate its news reportage is. In radio it is the reportage of the news which is felt to be at the heart of the enterprise and where a strong editorial presence is often established in the person of the newsreader or news presenter, while comment, speculation and argument are dependent, peripheral matters from which the broadcasting institution is at some pains to distance itself. Alistair Cooke's *Letter from America* is in many respects similar to a *Times* leading article, but whereas the latter is understood to be the paper's editorial voice there is no corresponding suggestion that Alistair Cooke's views are those of the BBC. This means that much radio news is at an advantage over the newspapers in that on the face of it at least its editorial stance is non-partisan – a position brought about by the unavoidable presence of voices in the medium. This is not, of course, to say that radio news is never distorted or biased, only that to be recognized as news it must at least be objective in *tone*.

This objectivity is reinforced by the fact that the newsreaders of both popular and quality programmes speak in RP, whose somewhat paradoxical effects are equally useful. On the one hand RP is still commonly regarded as the badge of the well-educated, professionally successful or the socially privileged and therefore as the accent of 'those who know best, the most authoritative'. On the other hand, its universal intelligibility accords it the status of a 'non-accent': it minimizes the element of idiosyncrasy and even of 'personality' in the voice, for which reason the BBC has seldom allowed it to be replaced in the delivery of the news or official announcements by the regional accents which are widely heard elsewhere on the networks (O'Donnell and Todd, 1980, 91). I recently heard a female newsreader with a Scottish accent, which is to some extent the exception that proves the rule, although I would add that she spoke not in impenetrable Glaswegian but in what would be generally accepted as *modified* RP. So successful were the pre-war news bulletins in minimizing personality that many listeners believed there was only one newsreader (Black, 1972, 69). If this was so, why are the readers now identified by name when previously they were anonymous? Naming began in 1940 to prevent the Germans from trying to counterfeit the news bulletins and was immediately popular, 'a recognition that the source was more important than the medium or the message' (A. Briggs, 1970, 202). By this is meant that the personality of the newsreader became a guarantee of the 'impersonality', or objectivity, of the broadcasting institution – the 'source', strictly speaking, being the organization which compiles the news not the person who reads it. It is an indexical function which the newsreaders have performed ever since.

But all this is only to declare the *similarity* between popular and quality news on the radio and the *difference* between such news and all newspapers of whatever kind, for I have been suggesting that the nature of the medium compresses its range of language and style of presentation and allows it to resemble neither *The Times* nor the *Sun* nor the *Daily Mirror*. Nevertheless I would argue that there remain certain differences between NB and WO which do evoke the difference between the popular and quality press. Whereas the news presentation of Brian Martin on WO is slow and sedate and characterized by standard RP, Janet

Trewin's is brisk and more urgent and her RP modified by a very slight regional accent. Moreover there are subtle but important differences in language, one of which – in the names of the programmes – is not present in the titles of the newspapers. Since many of them have long histories during which they have frequently been forced to seek new types of readers, newspapers do not generally reflect their differences of appeal in their titles. The name *Daily Mirror* has different connotations for us from *The Times* because we have long been aware of their different formats and different readerships, but there seems to be nothing intrinsically more populist about one title than the other. With much shorter histories, WO and NB do seem concerned to establish differing connotations through their titles. That of WO is an alliterative pun meaning 'How the world looks at one o'clock' and having the larger, more objective sense of 'The world as a unity, taken in at a single view'. 'Newsbeat' is also a pun, a compound formed by analogy with 'heartbeat' and therefore suggesting a programme with its finger on the pulse, one which keeps abreast of the latest news. 'Beat' also carries the suggestion of a patrol or assignment, but for a programme set into a pop music network its primary association is with rhythm and music. Generally, then, the title has connotations of pace, 'up-to-dateness' and vitality – very different from the judicious detachment implied by 'The World at One'.

But there are also important linguistic differences in the headlines and news copy of the two programmes. NB foregrounds the dispute over the numbers of returning miners and uses slightly more emotive language ('furious arguments are raging'), quoting Mr Scargill's colloquial verdict, 'a flop', in the headlines. Indeed the opening news item is presented in simple adversarial terms – the repetition and balance of *says* ('The NCB says . . . The Coal Board says . . . but Mr Scargill says') resembling the report of an informal argument. The issues are reduced to straightforward personal confrontation. Nor is the grammar always consistent, the Coal Board being treated first as a collective singular and then as a plural, 'Arthur Scargill [disputes] *their* figures'. The diction is simple and fairly informal – the 'new faces [Coal Board jargon] . . . *turned up* for work', rather than 'arrived'; Mr Scargill's colloquialism 'a flop' makes an effective end to the piece; and later on the Labour Correspondent, who is Nicholas Jones on Radio 4, is introduced as 'Nick Jones'. In contrast, the language of WO is rather more formal. It is more scrupulous about assigning the title 'Mr' to those involved in the dispute, nor is it simply 'the Coal Board' but 'the National Coal Board'. Moreover WO concentrates not on the dispute over the numbers who are returning but on the mere *fact* of the return. It includes a government view of the situation and does not refer until well into the item to Mr Scargill's disbelief in the numbers alleged to have returned. His term 'flop' is not included in the bulletin itself but in the correspondent's report, while his action – 'immediately challenged' – sounds slightly more literary than we might expect from NB, as does the mention of miners who have 'abandoned their strike' rather than merely 'gone back to work'.

Content and format

As with language and presentation it is useful to begin by making one or two generalizations about the differences in content and format between quality and popular newspapers. The former devote a large proportion of their space to serious, 'hard' news – that is, to occurrences of major importance in the spheres of politics, economics, technology, the arts, and so on, as well as to isolated events such as accidents, crimes and court cases. They also attempt to set the news in some form of perspective by grouping it into themes and subjects – headline news, further news, 'Home', 'Foreign', 'Financial', 'Arts' pages; by using layout to distinguish the important from the less important items; and by locating features or 'background' articles on separate pages from those which contain the hard news items. With respect to format, their pages are large, the headlines relatively small (with the frequent inclusion of lower-case lettering), they are characterized by little typographical variety; and they contain a considerable amount of text, much of it divided into items of substantial length, and relatively few photographs and illustrations.

In contrast the popular newspapers seem less concerned to set the news in perspective than to demonstrate its interest to their readers or its relevance to their ordinary preoccupations. They devote a large amount of space to lighter, 'human interest' items and make no obvious distinction between these and the more serious items they include. They focus upon such subjects as accidents or crimes, dramatic court cases, news about pop stars, actors and other celebrities, and unusual stories involving people or animals. They also devote considerable space to sport, which like television and 'leisure' news, is slightly atypical in having a section to itself. Their pages are of a smaller size ('tabloid') and rather fewer in number than those of the quality newspapers and their format is spectacularly different. Their headlines are huge (there may be room for little other than headlines and a photograph on the front page) and mostly consist of block capitals; there is a large proportion of photographs and illustrations to text, and the latter is broken up into articles which are mostly short. These papers are also characterized by considerable typographical variety, for there are differences in print not only between articles but *within* them. There is heavy print and lighter print, white letters on a black ground, black on white, white on grey, black on grey. Block capitals may occur within the text, and the items and photographs are framed by dots, borders, asterisks and similar devices.

What is the purpose of this typographical variety? Print is a formidable medium for people for whom reading is not a frequent or congenial activity, and so its intrinsically authoritative nature will count for nothing if it remains unread. The typography therefore has two related functions. First it enables the text to advertise itself and make the business of reading more attractive. Articles begin in bold type and wide spacing to lure the reader into them and continue in closer, lighter print. The general effect of the changes is to break up the text into small and distinctive units. A whole article may be printed in bold to catch the eye amongst others in light, and vice versa. The second function, especially common in the popular newspapers, is to make the business of reading, once undertaken, much easier by reinforcing – one might almost say, exaggerating – conventional punctuation. Key words are printed in block capitals or underlined, quotation marks enlarged and set in bold type, and so on. Since it remains impersonal the printed text retains an air of authority; but to the extent that it is no longer of uniform appearance but organized into shapes and shades which clarify, although they do not appreciably add to, its meaning it acquires an almost pictorial quality. The purpose of this typographical variety is, then, to make reading as inviting and easy as looking at pictures.

How can radio set about imitating these differences in content and format? The short answer is that it can match the visual resources of newspapers with its own acoustic resources. It can match the differences of size with differences of duration; words in different kinds of print with words in different tones or voices; dots, borders and asterisks with pips or musical jingles; and the photographs or icons of people and things with indexes – the sounds made by people and things. But the correspondences are not quite that straightforward, for the sound of words on the radio and the image of words in print are not strictly analogous. Indeed, as was suggested in Chapter 3, print is a technological development of speech, which is the only 'natural' form of language, and the punctuation system of print is an attempt to fix meaning, which inheres not only in the words but also in the inflections of the human voice. The typographical exaggerations of punctuation which occur in some newspapers are simply attempts to convey that meaning more clearly, they are not attempts to enhance or heighten it. So for the radio newsreader to try to reproduce them would be to reverse cause and effect, to imitate through speech something which is *itself* an imitation of speech. In one sense, then, to imitate these typographical devices would be an absurdity; but in another sense we could say that they already exist in the naturally expressive tone of the newsreader, for expression is determined by meaning not by punctuation, which is a purely visual *guide* to meaning. But there are, as we have seen, other typographical devices which are to a great extent independent of the meaning. They are simply there to catch the eye, to relieve the impersonality of print without impairing its authority, and there may be as many as four different kinds of typefaces in a single article. These could be – and are – matched by changes of voice among the news presenters, but to nothing like the same extent since the voice is a live, personal medium and does not require the same measure of relief. Indeed to match the number of changes in the typeface with the same number of changes of voice would make us conscious of the news presenters to an extent which would compromise radio news's necessary attempt at an 'impersonal' style of presentation. The amount of human 'presence' must be enough to make the reading of the news expressive and interesting, but not so great as to make us more conscious of the reader than of what is being read. Hence when a change of voice occurs in radio news it must be dictated by the logic of the news itself – by a change from one item to another or a switch from the actual text of the bulletin to a correspondent's report. But not only must the acoustic resources of radio be more sparingly deployed than the visual resources of the newspapers, but they are inherently more *limited*, for while most things in the physical world are visible many are soundless, at least for some of the time. Among these things are people, and the only noises which they make which are adequately meaningful are words. Yet people make up the subject of the vast majority of newspaper photographs. Of the fifty-nine which I counted in the *Sun* for 25 February, all but three were of people, as were all but six of the fifty-seven in the same day's issue of *The Times*. This means that in radio news both bulletins and actuality consist mostly of words, or to put it another way, that speech must be regarded as both typographic and photographic, as the equivalent not only of the newspaper text but in many cases of its photographs.

With different exigencies to meet, then, in what way and with what success do WO and NB imitate the quality and popular newspapers? Superficially WO seems to fall well short of what quality newspapers provide. The ratio of quantity to time makes the provision of news in breadth or in depth seem impossible. Since the number of items to the duration of the news bulletin can allow for an average of only about 130 words per item the news coverage may be more reminiscent of the popular than of the quality press. Furthermore there is insufficient time for the grouping of the news into the 'Home', 'Foreign', and other sections which characterize the quality newspapers and so such specialized forms of news must be allocated to separate programmes. Nevertheless by being sedately paced over forty minutes and by 'packing' its news coverage on the one hand and extending its features presentation on the other, WO does succeed in conveying what is in radio terms a strong suggestion of news in breadth and in depth. With no apparent air of haste it compresses twelve items of news, some of them containing recorded inserts, into a nine-minute bulletin and devotes its remaining half an hour or so to just four features, one of which – on the miners' return to work – lasts over a quarter of an hour.

It is worth taking a closer look at the format of WO. The sedateness of its approach is partly established by the extended headlining at the beginning, which incidentally points to the risk of drawing false analogies between radio and press news. From the fact that the newsreader and presenter spend a full minute in previewing the news and features to follow we might be tempted to see an analogy with the huge headlines of the popular papers, but a truer analogy would be with the table of contents which somewhat inconspicuously runs down the side of the front page of the quality newspapers. They can be so situated because in a spatial medium they can be perused at a glance, as can the contents themselves; but on the radio they must be heard first and in some detail since the listener cannot otherwise know what is 'coming up'. Hence radio headlines are not closely analogous to newspaper headlines and their length implies not sensationalism but quantity and depth – a perspective on the news and on current affairs.

This sense of amplitude and depth is created by two other aspects of the format of WO. The first is the strong presence of what I will refer to by the generic term 'newsgatherers' – correspondents, specialist editors, interviewers, reporters – all of whom are named and heard. They are equally apparent in the newspapers, but we must again beware of simple analogies. The impersonal, authoritative nature of print seems to allow the newsgatherer to take entire responsibility for the article he writes, for more often than not the whole of it is written in his name. In those radio news broadcasts where the presence of newsgatherers is not apparent it is therefore the newsreader himself who is the counterpart of the press newsgatherers, for he too seems solely responsible for the items he presents. In both cases an editorial presence is merely implicit. We are, of course, aware that both radio news items and newspaper articles are subject to editorial mediation, but there is nothing in either to *indicate* this mediation. However, when the voices of news-gatherers are included in radio news the reader seems to acquire a higher, editorial status, indicating by the way in which he contextualizes the gatherers' reports what credence the listener should give them. He may make it clear that he is entirely dependent on a particular correspondent for the information and that he endorses it entirely. He summarizes the item and the correspondent then provides the full details. On the other hand the newsreader may imply that his endorsement of the correspondent's report is only partial, that it should be treated as no more than a fragment of the total picture which has been, or will be, balanced with others. There is therefore a sense in which the role of each transcends that of the other, but we are never in doubt of the editorial authority vested in the reader: his words may imply that he trusts his correspondent's report entirely but that in itself is an editorial judgement, a taking of full responsibility for what the correspondent says. The nature of this relationship between newsreader and newsgatherers is signalled in various ways in the broadcast itself. Though the reader delivers his words in an expressive, 'speech' tone we know from what we are told and/or from the fluency of pace and occasional 'literariness' of the language that it is not being extemporized. The newsgatherers normally deliver their reports in much the same way, but when events are of a dramatic or emotive nature and/or are still occurring their reports may be extemporized: but they are then 'legitimized' as news, set in perspective, by the voice of the reader or presenter, who in certain circumstances may interview the gatherer and thus treat him as a 'witness' of the news rather than as the initial 'judge' of it. Because of this subordinate status the newsgatherer may even have a strong regional accent (the Northern Irish brogue of the BBC's Political Editor, John Cole, is a frequent object of parody) and whereas his reports may often be broadcast from the scene of the news itself, the reader will always present the news from a studio. A central paradox of radio (and television) news is that if there is one thing more vital to it than a sense of

90

authenticity, of proximity to the events themselves, it is a sense of clear-sighted detachment from them – of this authenticity being mediated through the remote, sterile atmosphere of the studio. The final proof of this is the fact that whereas the former quality is dispensable, the latter is not. In news *summaries* we seldom hear newsgatherers or news actuality, merely the reader in what is always a studio acoustic.

If the newsgatherers do not *need* to be heard what, then, is the point of their strong presence in WO? There is a sense in which the impersonality of print is a limitation. It gives no hint of the eclectic nature of the information which goes into many of the articles. But the variety of voices and acoustics on radio news suggests the gleaning of its information from a multitude of sources and allows WO to show that whatever the quantitative limitations of its output its newsgathering operation is as extensive as that of. the quality newspapers. But even more important, the sound of newsgatherers on the medium seems to introduce an extra *level* into the production of the news and, indeed, exposes the mechanism of that production by making overt the processes of news collection and editorial mediation which are merely implicit in the news sections of the quality press. Thus in its own way the programme achieves that sense of depth, balance and perspective which the quality press can achieve through the sheer quantity of its news coverage and its freedom to editorialize on other pages. Even a short piece such as item (viii), on the Pakistani election, conveys this sense merely by its change of acoustic from the newsreader in the studio to the reporter on the telephone from Islamabad. Moreover since despite the acoustic variety they help to provide, the newsgatherers are, along with the newsreader, the *purveyors* of the news rather than a part of it, they help to form a substantial ratio of reportage to actuality which mirrors the ratio of text to photographs in the quality newspapers. In a recent book about television news it was suggested that the framework which this reportage provides for the 'voices in the news' is somewhat analogous to the narrative framework provided by the author of a novel, within which we are 'privileged' to hear the actual remarks of his characters: 'Even though the dialogue "belongs" to the characters who speak it, it is *produced* by the author' (Hartley, 1982, 109). But the author in this context should be seen not as a fabricator but an *authority*, the guarantor of the reality he is purveying.

The second aspect of the format of WO which helps to create a sense of breadth and depth is the division of the programme into hard news and what I shall call with convenient vagueness 'features'. Though they are also in a position to arrange their news under subject headings such as 'Home' and 'Foreign', something of this same division is apparent in the quality papers. On WO it is faintly suggested by the opening announcement 'forty minutes of news and comment' and necessitates not only a newsreader (Brian Martin) but also a programme presenter of similar editorial status (Brian Widlake). Moreover it mirrors in a structural way the presentational distinction we have made between the newsreader's text and the newsgatherers' reports, since the Features section is to some extent an illustration or expansion of the News section. In the News section we are apprised of the latest events in the 'serious' world of politics, economics, military affairs and general human concerns. The WO Features section, as our outline shows, may function partly as a background to those events (cf. the item on the miners), providing material which explains or amplifies them or gives people's reactions to them where those reactions do not in themselves amount to 'an event'. It may also provide 'current affairs' – that is, cover issues which are a part of contemporary life even though they may presently lack 'hard news' content. The item on Spanish holidays would fall into this category, since the suggestion that a price war *may* be about to start is scarcely hard news: likewise the item on Polish refugees, though loosely related to Cardinal Glemp's visit, really focuses on an abiding feature of contemporary life. Finally the Features section may complement serious news with news of a lighter, more frivolous nature as is aptly illustrated by the final and brief item on snails. Hence in structure as in presentation WO is able to evoke something of the substance and perspective of the quality press.

In format and content NB differs radically from WO. It lasts a mere fifteen minutes, less than half WO's length, yet contains five 'illustrated' features to WO's four – a fair imitation of the bright, 'urgent' format of the popular papers. Such a feat of compression allows the minimum time for headlining (a mere fifteen seconds) and reminds us yet again that analogies between time and spatial quantity are not entirely straightforward. Although the compactness of the popular newspapers is well matched by the brevity of the programme, it does not follow that their large headlines would be matched by lengthy previewing. Such headlines are, in fact, more quickly scanned than small ones, and NB gets much nearer to the spirit of its counterparts by moving as swiftly as possible into the first item. It is also characterized by musical jingles, a feature wholly absent from WO. What are they and what are their functions? There are five jingles in NB, all very similar but not identical. Since they are staccato and repetitive in style they seem to be an iconic index suggestive of various forms of information technology – a typewriter, Morse telegraph, computer or teleprinter – and thus identify the genre of programme, tell us that what we are hearing is the news as distinct from records, for instance. The programme's title is proclaimed in all of them and the network, Radio 1, in the first and final ones. Furthermore, the *musical* quality of the jingles helps to indicate that its news appeal is popular. Since news presentation and reception entail an exercise of balance and judgement, are in a word dispassionate activities, and since music is commonly regarded as producing emotional effects, we might take its mere inclusion in NB as a sign that we are hearing popular rather than quality news. Nevertheless the theme-tune of Radio 4's *PM* programme reminds us that music may characterize quality news, too. Yet quite aside from the implications of the title there is a bounce and exuberance about the NB jingles which suggest that its news appeal *is* a popular one.

But as well as conveying information in their own right the jingles have specific functions in respect of the programme's format and sequence. The first precedes, and the second follows, the headlines and in so doing they invest them with an emotive import, a combined lightness and urgency of tone which makes them in spite of their brevity equivalent to the sensationalist block capitals of the popular papers. This function is, then, an extension of their primary role in establishing the 'feel' or flavour of the programme as a whole. The third follows the item on Pakistan and with the fourth frames the news round-up in the middle of the programme. Following the item on Franglais and preceding the Leonard Cohen interview the fifth signifies a change of mood which might be expressed as 'Enough of the news, back to music!' and eases the transition back to the Gary Davies show. These jingles, then, are also used as frames, they revive the listener's attention and thus increase the appeal or intelligibility of certain items by isolating them from others. We can therefore regard them as a form of radio typography since they are 'redundant' sounds in the way that the dots, borders and rows of asterisks are redundant images in the papers, there to adorn the text without appreciably adding to its meaning: and a measure of their general effect can be taken from the fact that in WO their various functions are performed entirely by the sober tones of Brian Widlake.

But not only is there a sense of contrast and variety which the jingles help to create in the *sequence* of items, there is a considerable acoustic variety *within* each item. Reportage alternates with actuality, both of them involving several voices and the latter occurring in a range of acoustics – studio, locational and telephonic. And since the alternations are frequent and no item lasts longer than a few minutes we never hear more than snatches or snippets of each. In the item on the miners, which runs for just over three and a quarter minutes, there are *seven* changes of acoustic, involving the voices of Janet Trewin and an unnamed male newsgatherer, the BBC Labour Correspondent, and two Welsh people heard over the telephone. But in the item on the Birmingham hospital even more is condensed into less. There are ten tightly edited changes of acoustic – Janet Trewin's introduction and the alternations between four studio links delivered by an unnamed female newsgatherer and five different voices heard against a background of hospital noises, the whole item packed into three minutes and ten seconds. There is a similar acoustic variety in the WO feature on the coal strike, but it does not convey the same tautness, pace and variation since it is longer than the entire NB programme. Indeed in terms of the production and editing techniques which must be used to meet its requirements NB is much more impressive than WO, just as, no doubt, the typographical demands of the *Sun* display the skills of layout staff much more than do those of *The Times*. In popular news, whether on the radio or in print, one gains a strong sense of the medium itself, of technology flexing its muscles. To sum up, then, we can say that just as the popular papers are characterized by short articles in different kinds of typefaces, numerous photographs and illustrations, a number of typographical devices which enhance visual appeal, and by an overall compactness, so NB is characterized by brief spells of reportage delivered in different voices, lots of sound actuality or illustration, a number of jingles which enhance auditory appeal, and by an overall brevity – what we might describe as 'tabloid length'.

Two further aspects of NB's format must be noted – aspects which also distinguish it from WO and reinforce its similarity to the popular press. The first is that whereas in WO the newsgatherers maintain what might be termed a high profile, they are virtually absent from NB. Though their contribution is discernible few of them are heard and only one is named. The presenter, Janet Trewin, is of course named, but she introduces the recorded interviews made by the newsgatherers with some such formula as 'X told us . . . ', 'Y spoke to the BBC recently . . . ', 'We were at the hospital . . . '. The interviewer's question is then edited out, so that the first words we hear in the recording are the interviewee's. Even if the interviewer is heard asking a subsequent question she remains unidentified, as do those newsgatherers who are heard introducing certain items – for example the male newsgatherer who introduces and links the elements in the second half of the item on the miners, the female newsgatherer who links the elements of the item on the children in hospital. The only newsgatherer who is named is the Labour Correspondent, Nick Jones, but he is used not as an interviewer but an interviewee and thus treated as a *part* of the news rather than as a gatherer of it. Hence those newsgatherers who are heard are not so much used as an intermediate presence between the presenter on the one hand and actuality on the other, as is the case in WO: they are treated either as unnamed, temporary presenters alongside Janet Trewin or as 'voices in the news' together with the returning miners, experts on Franglais, and so on. In other words they are closely identified either with presentation or with news actuality. This virtual omission of newsgatherers gives us much less sense of a perspective on the news than in WO, yet seems to bind presentation and actuality more closely together. It means that most of the reportage is left to the presenter and that she acts rather more like a newsgatherer herself and rather less as the editor of news which has been gathered by others. Hence whereas WO uses its newsgatherers to show how the news is produced, NB seems instead to *conceal* its production processes. But it is not simply that we sense a closer connection between presentation and actuality; we are much more *aware* of the actuality than we are in WO. We are told Janet Trewin's name, but only at the beginning of the programme. Thereafter none of the presenting voices is identified, whereas all the 'voices in the news' *are*. Hence just as in many pages of the popular newspapers the text seems little more than ancillary to the numerous and often large photographs, so in NB the role of Janet Trewin and her anonymous co-presenters seems to be little more than to cue its many slices of actuality. It might be useful at this point to recapitulate my argument. I began by suggesting that an authoritative presentation of the news can be achieved on radio by nothing more than a reader with an RP accent, as is attested by the many summaries which consist of nothing else. But in WO this authoritative air is confirmed by creating a sense of depth and perspective – by demonstrating through the strong presence of correspondents, reporters and others its newsgathering and editorial processes. In the interests of brevity and vivacity, however, NB suppresses its newsgatherers and instead conveys its air of authority through authenticity – by a mode of presentation which is closely linked to actuality. And these differences of format seem to illuminate the basic differences which underlie quality and popular news in any medium: for whereas the former broadly depends for its authority upon its 'literary' resources, upon the number and accuracy of its reports and the way in which they are set in context by editorial judgement, the latter draws its authority from its nearness to reality, from its pictures or sounds of the people in the news. To make a crude generalization – quality news relies on the strength of its reportage, on an approach to the world which is essentially verbal, that is symbolic; popular news relies on its pictorial strength, on an approach to the world which is in the broadest sense iconic.

One other aspect of NB's format distinguishes it from WO and identifies it with the popular press: its integration of news and features, which reflects in a structural way the integration of presenter and actuality that occurs within each item. In WO we noticed the maintenance of a clear distinction between hard news and features, but in NB each of the main items is neither pure news nor a pure feature but something in between. Much more, for instance, is packed into the NB item on the miners than is contained in WO's *news* item thereon, but much less than in the latter's *features* item. NB's items are, then, shorter than conventional features but less abstract and summary than conventional news items and might best be termed 'illustrated news items'; moreover they only require the services of a single presenter, Janet Trewin, rather than a newsreader and a features presenter as in WO.

What is the reason for this foreshortened perspective, for this conflation of the news itself with its background of illustration and reaction? It reflects an underlying assumption shared with the popular papers that the news consists not merely of 'events' to be perceived in a detached and clinical way, but of matters which must as far as possible be assimilated to the ordinary moods and concerns of the audience – its preoccupation with employment, money, sexuality, crime, and so on. This explains the tendency in popular news towards an emotive or sensational treatment of serious events, but it also explains a greater predilection than in quality news for 'human interest' items – those which touch the heart, 'funny-bone' and sometimes the lower regions of the anatomy – and this predilection is apparent in NB. Its choice of items makes a fascinating comparison with that of WO. Of the nine items of news which it contains, only five occur in WO, including the lead story on the miners' drift back to work. NB gives extended coverage to five of its nine stories, treats them as what I have described as illustrated news items, and a large proportion of this coverage – amounting to just over half the programme, about eight of its fifteen minutes – is devoted to lighter fare, 'human' or leisure interests which closely affect our lives or will have an immediate effect on our moods: children's welfare, Franglais and pop music. Though headline news in NB, the item about children is not even mentioned in WO: had it been included it would almost certainly have been as a feature and not as hard news. It is true that two of the four features in WO are ostensibly light – namely, holidays and snails. But the former is given 'hard news' treatment while the latter is clearly differentiated from the main concerns of the programme in being treated as a short tail-piece, and together they comprise only one-fifth of the whole programme and run for less than half the time of the main feature on the miners. It is not, of course, the case that lighter stories are ignored in quality news, merely that they are more sharply distinguished from serious items. In contrast, the serious news round-up in NB is tucked between two of its illustrated items and occupies only about thirty seconds of the whole programme – a format which is also reminiscent of the popular papers where a similar round-up is often provided on one of the inside pages. Thus popular news is less concerned with perspective not only *within* its items, but also *between* them: in NB as in the papers serious and light stories are fairly freely intermingled. But perhaps what is most remarkable in NB is the concern not only to give its news-content a maximum appeal to its listeners, but to assimilate the programme as a whole to its broadcasting context, to emphasize to an audience not primarily interested in the news its relationship to the world of popular music and popular culture. We have already seen that this relationship is implied in the pun of its title 'Newsbeat' and in its jingles, which remind us in both music and words that what we are listening to is basically a continuous pop network, Radio 1. Again, the contrast with WO, a discrete, self-contained programme ('forty minutes of news and comment'), is extreme; for NB is not broadcast *between* programmes – it is an enclave *within* the Gary Davies show. Another effect of its integration of news and features which we might have mentioned is that it makes it seem more like an extended news summary than a programme in its own right, and NB further minimizes its difference from the rest of the network's output by frequently ending with an item on pop music, making the point not only that 'the news' affects us as closely as pop music does but conversely – and as the popular papers do, too – that pop music is itself *part* of the news. Hence NB concludes with the interview of Leonard Cohen, followed by a snatch of his music. There are no closing headlines, indeed the programme has no formal ending, a facetious exchange between Janet Trewin and Gary Davies easing the transition back to the latter's show.

To sum up, then. For all the linguistic compression which the medium imposes, its inability to editorialize and its need to use voices not only for reportage but also as actuality, radio news does succeed to a remarkable extent in paralleling and evoking the differences between the popular and quality newspapers. But we must now face a further question: what *advantages*, if any, does radio news possess over press news of all kinds?

Its advantages may to some extent be discernible in the comparisons we have been making. One of them is the presence of an authoritative 'news voice', the fact that radio news is a matter of speech. The potential *dis*advantage of this we have already noted: the very presence of a newsreader diminishes the required air of objectivity. Devoid of personal signs, print seems to be 'the truth' even when its language is value-loaded (something which quality as well as popular newspapers have frequently exploited in order to tickle the prejudices of their readers). But given that *all* language is a personal product – the very choice of words declares the presence of an author – the radio voice can actually make the news more vivid and effective not in any crude, sensationalist sense but in the sense of giving news language its full measure of expression – of disambiguating not only through stress but also through voice-tune such a statement as 'And the news from Fenner's is that Combined Universities won't be on the winning side yet again'; which on paper could mean either that Combined Universities have been losers many times in the past and are losers yet again or that they have been winners many times in the past but will be the losers *this* time. Though an advantage to radio in general this clarifying function of the voice is of particular importance in news, where accuracy is an absolute requirement, and in the frequent comparisons which are made between evanescent speech and permanent print it is insufficiently considered. A simpler example of its power is provided by the title of Beckett's radio play *All That Fall*, whose visual ambiguity (noun–relative pronoun–verb: 'Everybody who falls'; or adjective–demonstrative pronoun–noun: 'The whole of that collapse'?) is instantly resolved when we hear it spoken; for the unstressed second word would leave us in no doubt that the first meaning is intended. Oral presentation can of course be used to belie or distort news-content, but this is not to deny that it can, and should, enhance content when all allowances have been made for the fact that the news is always in some sense arbitrarily selected and partially treated. On the radio *due* stress and expression can be given to words which in the cold medium of print might be opaque, ambiguous – inadequate.

But the presence of sound is important with respect not only to the way in which the news is delivered but to news actuality, the people and events in the news; for it enables radio to have, in common with all the news media, its own special grasp on reality. Newspapers contain photographs of the world: we can *see* in the newspaper what radio can only *describe*. But radio has the *sounds* of the world. In contrast to the mere iconism of newspaper photographs, which are only *copies* of people and events, radio gives us an indexical sense of the news, the noises which those people and events actually make. This indexical relationship therefore declares a *direct* connection, we are not presented with an illustration which is at one remove from reality. Hence the technical term for these sounds or noises, 'actuality', is well conceived. On the radio we hear the noises of the news, or at least the informed view or the eyewitness account 'straight from the horse's mouth' and often on location – outdoors, over the telephone – that newspapers can only *report* in the bland medium of print, a medium bereft of the inflections, hesitations and emphases of the living voice which contribute so largely to meaning, and also less able to evoke the location in which the account was given. We might observe in passing that within the fifteen-minute NB programme outlined above, items on the miners, Pakistan, Franglais and pop music were 'authenticated' by Welsh, Pakistani and Canadian accents in various acoustics; while WO's items contained the voices of Welsh and Scottish miners and Polish refugees. Indeed an event can be particularly 'newsworthy' on the radio and gain much more public attention than it could through the press simply by being primarily a matter of sound. However extensive and eloquent it may be, the press coverage of a concert tour by Leonard Cohen could in one respect never equal NB's coverage since the latter includes the actual *sound* of his music. A more frivolous example which springs to my mind is a 'silly season' item which BBC Radio Newcastle once ran about a Japanese professor who during a brief visit to the city learned to play the Northumbrian bagpipes. Essentially an 'acoustic' item, it would lose much in the newspapers and was most likely ignored by them – another reminder that the very *choice* of news item is determined not simply by its inherent importance but by how effectively the medium can convey it. A more serious example of the use of sound as a news resource is *Yesterday in Parliament* (Radio 4), which comprises not only the presenter's links and the voices of the main speakers but the equally expressive background noises and reactions of the whole House.

But it could be argued that in stressing the difference between radio and newspapers and proclaiming the advantages of the former over the latter, I have merely demonstrated its similarity to television, except that television has the advantage over radio that it is endowed with pictures as well as sound. Our remaining task is therefore to see how radio fares as a news medium in comparison with television. There is by no means universal agreement that television's pictures are a straightforward asset, for it could be said that they do not materially add to the news so much as illustrate it and slow down presentation:

> there are critics who argue that it is a bad medium for handling news . . . pictures take a long time to convey simple information and are often what is called professionally 'moving wallpaper'. Radio, these critics argue with force and considerable justification, is able to convey news in more detail without the distraction of pictures and – if speed is a valid consideration – more speedily than television.
>
> (Hood, 1975, 35)

The question 'What is news?' is as knotty as any philosophical problem and to try to answer it would push us into deep waters I am keen to avoid. But it is at least arguable that news is primarily verbal, that however concrete the subjects with which it deals it is mostly concerned with the abstract relationships which exist within and between them and which can only be expressed in language. This was brought home to me recently by a television news-flash which announced that mortar bombs had landed on a police station in Newry and that pictures would follow later. These consisted of shots of a damaged building and a fire-engine departing from it and struck me as entirely dispensable. The cause of the damage and the reason for the fire-engine were not self-evident. To make sense they required *words*, all of which had been provided in the earlier news-flash; those words had not required the pictures. For a strictly intellectual understanding of the news words are entirely adequate. Indeed language is bound up with our very efforts to make sense of the world and images are seldom as explicit: even in newspapers, where the images are surrounded by text, they invariably need separate captions to explain their relevance. One may go even further and argue that in certain cases the pictorial redundancy of television can *mislead* us as to the true state of affairs, or at least encourage us to draw false conclusions. One of the arguments against televising debates in the House of Commons, for instance, could not have been brought against radio: 'if the cameras showed only a few members in attendance during a debate, the public might think its representatives were neglecting their work, whereas in fact they might be attending meetings or talking to their constituents' (Paulu, 1981, 234).

Something of this redundancy can be felt at the *production* end of television, for its studios and cameras invite the broadcaster to make a 'spectacle' of himself, with the tendency towards irrelevance and artificiality which that implies. The somewhat 'spare' nature of radio technology, on the other hand, is less likely to dilute and distort the truth: the solitary microphone is more conducive to honesty. This point was facetiously made in a critical review of the highly successful Radio 4 series, *In the Psychiatrist's Chair*:

> Down at Portland Place, with a green baize table, a waxy beaker of water, a stacker chair, a gang of technicians behind a glass partition . . . the parallel between an interview and a

private confessional conversation may be plausibly drawn. On television, with heat, lights, make-up and visible cameramen laocöonically wrapped in cable, the guest finds himself subliminally invited by the medium to entertain. To be interviewed on radio is like being asked to pause and tell them the truth; to be interviewed on television is like being asked to lie quickly in case people start switching off.

(Barnes, 1983, 32)

If it is true that radio is a 'purer', more concentrated news medium than television, then in terms of production it has another advantage over both television and newspapers, which is that the link it provides from the occurrence of the news to the audience is shorter and cheaper than that provided by the others, especially the press with its lengthy processes of reportage, editorial mediation, composition, printing and distribution. This means that it can provide 'newer' news than the press, including updates on events which have been continuing over a span of time such as wars or test-matches. As we saw in Chapter 2 the newspaper proprietors recognized this advantage very early in radio's history and took steps to prevent it, so that it was some years before it was fully exploited. One significant effect of this advantage which has emerged only gradually, and largely as a consequence of local radio, is that the medium has developed a whole new *stratum* of news, in that it can cover events which are not only very new but *ephemeral* – that is, events which would have ended in the time it takes to go to press and which the newspapers must generally ignore. One such event might be the blockage of a motorway by an accident or the presence of fog at a local airport. But it is also true that radio is quicker and cheaper than full television coverage: 'It is complicated and expensive to set up a live television outside broadcast for a news item. All that radio needs is a man and a telephone' (Herbert, 1976, 26). This is all that television needs, too: we may, and sometimes do, hear an on-the-spot report while our screens are filled with nothing more than a photograph and a caption. But here television is a victim of its own visuality: however redundant this or any other image would be, the medium leads us to expect something more. What we have is

103

something quite adequate, it is televised radio; yet it is not felt adequate as *television*. I often think that the medium reaches its nadir with the Saturday afternoon soccer reports which are accompanied by pictures of the goalscorers' faces – not, it would seem, of the greatest relevance to their feats! This means that in certain cases radio can cover events that not only would the press have to overlook on account of their ephemerality, but which television would have to overlook on the grounds that for all their news-value they are not worth sending a camera crew out for, yet could not be broadcast without some visual accompaniment. It reinforces one's conviction that for all the glamour of television, news is quintessentially a *verbal* genre, and this verbal quintessence explains why, even in this visual age of television and teletext, news is part of radio's 'rump'. It is for 'newsic' – news and music above all – that people continue to listen in.

But the last and greatest advantage of radio news over television and press news is already familiar to us: that it is quick not only because the medium can forge a link between events and audiences more rapidly than any other can, but also because there are many more circumstances in which its audience is able to attend to it at the *moment* of transmission. At the moment the newspapers arrive on the streets the aspiring reader may not be in a position to read a copy even if she is able to buy one; and when the news is broadcast on television the viewer may be nowhere near a set or in no position to watch it if she is. But radios are portable (or mobile) and cheap. They can be – and are – taken anywhere and attended to while the listener performs other activities. Thus, given that the production of the news is *always* a selective matter – a matter which depends on such factors as the editor's political views and his general sense of what is important, the relatively condensed and synoptic way in which it has to be presented on the radio is in this respect a positive advantage, affording convenient and rapid assimilation. An early slogan of LBC News Radio was 'Read the newspaper with your eyes closed' (Baron, 1975, 92). The first three words might equally have been 'Watch the television', for in certain vital respects radio news surpasses both.

Suggestions for further work

Newsbeat and *World at One* are by no means at opposite poles of the world of radio news. You might make a comparison similar to the one above (focusing on language, presentation, content and format) between a news summary on ILR and one on Radio 3. And you might even be surprised by certain resemblances between the two! Here are two other possible comparisons. (1) Examine a single news story as it appears in each of the news media, noting particularly how radio's presentation differs from that of television and the newspapers. (2) Compare a morning bulletin on any of the radio networks with the news coverage of the morning papers. Is there any evidence that the choice of news is determined by the medium in which it will be presented, that is does radio incline to certain stories because they lend themselves better to radio treatment than other stories do? In a more practical vein, listen carefully to the length and register of the items in a Radio 4 news bulletin. Then take a newspaper story and rewrite it as a radio news item. In dealing with the often complex and profuse data of the news you may find it a formidable challenge to satisfy the conflicting requirements of brevity, accuracy and clarity! Finally, listen to one or two of the 'news background' programmes on Radio 4 – *Analysis*, *From Our Own Correspondent*, or even a more specialist programme like *Medicine Now*. How far do they make good the deficiencies of the main news broadcasts? And is this *all* they can do, or do you consider that they can offer something more than is offered by the background articles in the newspapers?

5 DOCUMENTARY AND EDUCATION PROGRAMMES

> To think of the educational powers and possibilities of
> broadcasting in terms of ordinary classroom practice is
> to ignore both the wealth of resources and the obvious
> limitations of the media.
>
> (J. Scupham, *Broadcasting and the Community*)

The first task in discussing documentary and educational
broadcasting is to decide what programmes, if any, fall *outside*
this category. The BBC, for instance, which is obliged by its
Charter to educate, claims that in the first instance it fulfils this
obligation 'through its programmes as a whole, that all serious
broadcasting as well as many programmes conceived primarily
as entertainment serve educational purposes' (*An Introduction to
School Broadcasts*, 1978, 4). Nevertheless it is possible to feel
sceptical about the claim that 'good broadcasting is good
education' on the ground that people seem rapidly to forget
what they have just seen or heard (Bates, 1984, 119–20). We
might therefore distinguish programmes with a specifically
documentary or educational purpose as containing information
which is to be *retained* – which is worthy of sustained attention
and / or capable of a constructive application. Furthermore this
notion allows us to make a tenuous but tenable distinction
between these programmes and news and current affairs output,
which is also informational but whose concerns are somewhat
more topical and ephemeral. Nevertheless documentary and
educational broadcasting remains a broad category within which
we need to make further rough distinctions.

Traditionally the BBC has drawn a line between *educative* programmes, which are directed at the widest possible audience and impose no 'discipline of response' but whose contents are retained as a general impression rather than a body of knowledge or expertise; and the more truly *educational* output, which contributes systematically to the growth of knowledge and does elicit a disciplined response (Scupham, 1967, 129–208; *BBC Handbook 1978*, 1977, 283; Paulu, 1981, 250). Educational output imparts specific ideas or information or techniques and may range from an Open University radio lecture on philosophy to a 'do-it-yourself' television programme on plumbing. But the distinction between these two categories is often difficult to maintain and depends quite as much on the way in which the student uses the programmes as on their intentions or inherent content. It is possible, after all, to regard *any* kind of programme as educational in that the student might respond to it in a disciplined way, listen carefully to it, make notes from it and treat it as a systematic extension to the body of knowledge she already possesses. On the other hand, while we would expect a radio production of Shakespeare to be a merely educative experience for the casual listener, it may well be no more even for the student doing an A-level in English. She may listen harder but not 'retain' it in any systematic or disciplined way. It would thus be more of a new experience than an extension of her literary knowledge and usefully illustrates that we must not regard programmes which are associated with highly structured, educational courses as necessarily 'educational' themselves. The difficulty of separating educational and educative programmes is stressed by Bates (1984, 7–8), who prefers a more gradual classification from 'enrichment' (at the educative end of the spectrum) through 'learning resource' and 'meeting special needs' to 'direct teaching' (at the educational end) (ibid., 18–24): but it seems to me that this increases rather than resolves the difficulties of distinction and I propose to retain the traditional dichotomy despite its inadequacies. Given that programmes can be used in varying ways, it is still apparent from their formats that some intend to elicit a more, others a less, disciplined response from their listeners. We have yet to decide, however, where documentaries stand in relation to educational and educative programmes. I would suggest that they are broadly similar to the latter, though perhaps with slightly more serious, less dilettante connotations. It might therefore be possible to place news and education programmes along a spectrum thus: News – Current Affairs – Documentary and Educative Programmes – Educational Programmes. But at this point a formidable question arises: if the contents of documentary and education programmes are likely to be even more complex and needful of retention than news and current affairs output, and in some instances to be construed as capable of a constructive application, how effectively can they be conveyed through a blind medium whose codes dissolve into thin air? The question is especially pertinent to educational output, to programmes whose purpose is not simply to provide impressions or experiences but to extend knowledge and to which a significant number of students will respond in a disciplined way. Broadly speaking, they adopt one of two formats. The first consists of direct instructions to the student to perform specific actions – a scientific experiment, perhaps, or a sequence of cookery. An even more familiar example is the music-and-movement programme for young children, in which they are instructed to toss a ball into the air, pretend to fly like a bird, and so on. The second format which may be adopted by educational programmes, but which is often merely educative too, is the lecture or talk. Its concerns are frequently abstract or conceptual, though they may sometimes be concrete or material – how to keep bees or build a rockery.

We ought to begin by acknowledging that the educational limitations of radio can be over-estimated. Its oral mode is, after all, the same as that of the classroom lesson and of that other enduring (yet much criticized) teaching tool, the lecture – and like lessons and lectures it allows the student to carry out actions or to take notes. Moreover when it consists of direct instruction it differs from books and television in leaving her with the free use of her eyes and hands (a particular advantage when learning such skills as dancing or computer-programming); and even in the case of the straight lecture or talk the freedom from such visual distractions as the cut of the teacher's suit may be a salutary one. Furthermore, since in educational broadcasting the listeners are likely to be better informed and more highly motivated than in educative broadcasting, problems of presentation and language are less insistent. In Open University programmes, for instance, there is less need to vary or lighten the material and the linguistic code is more narrowcast than that of educative and documentary programmes, a fact which is evident even in some of their titles. In flicking through the *Open University Broadcast and Assignment Calender 1983*, for instance, I found a radio programme entitled 'The Moving Coil Meter and the Pneumatic Transducer' (1982, 204) and another even more esoteric – 'Measuring $\triangle$H by Calorimetry' (ibid., 184). (While on this subject I would briefly mention a recent BBC series entitled *The Chip Shop* (Radio 4) which was something of a broadcasting innovation. Produced by the Continuing Education Department it was not simply a radio magazine about developments in the world of computer technology but included a forty-second computer-programme, a sound-strip of bleeps which listeners could key into their own machines. This could be regarded as the effective transmission of an instruction in a code which was much more narrowcast than words could ever be, except that it was addressed to the listeners' *computers* rather than to the listeners themselves, who would in any case be well versed in the art of programming.) But the intelligibility of narrowcast language can be enhanced by one element in radio which is always missing from the print media: the speaker's voice. What, asks David Wade, is the point of listening to a Reith Lecturer 'when I could read what he has to say in half the time with twice the comprehension?' (1984b, 7). The answer, he suggests, lies in the lecturer's manner of delivery, 'the contrast of pace and tone, emotional stimuli of various kinds' (ibid.), but the effect of this must surely be to *enhance* comprehension, albeit at a slow rate. And one other advantage of radio as an educational medium – an advantage it shares with television and the print media – is that it can span long distances and reach much larger numbers of students than could ever assemble in a classroom or lecture theatre.

Its limitations are, nevertheless, real. The most intractable one, especially in comparison with books, is the temporal, and indeed temporary, nature of its codes: the student is likely to find it much harder to understand messages and/or carry out instructions which do not allow her to pause or refer back. Her use of books, on the other hand, is not confined to broadcasting hours; she can ponder over parts of them and re-read them with ease. Like radio programmes lessons and lectures can exist only in time and we have already noted that their visual dimension can actually be a hindrance; but in general it must be more of a help. The students can see not only the blackboard and other teaching aids but the teacher herself – her posture, facial expression and gestures. They can interrupt her, ask questions, make points of their own. And the teacher can see them, gauge their reactions and if necessary make ad hoc adjustments to her material. None of this two-way communication is possible on radio, or on television for that matter. Learning-pace must be teacher- rather than student-centred, but on television the student at least has the advantage of a visual dimension. All this means that radio remains a somewhat crude medium for conveying esoteric or abstract concepts even to highly motivated students, for the complex syntax, specialist terminology and long sentences which such concepts normally involve are hard to assimilate over the air: the methodologies and principles of such disciplines as philosophy, music, linguistics, mathematics, science and technology are more effectively dealt with by other media. An 'ideas' talk *is* feasible on the radio (the annual Reith Lectures are only one example) and has been found to be most effective if it makes a limited number of main points, reinforces them through repetition, and provides concrete illustrations of abstract principles (Silvey, 1978, 281, 284–5): but its inherent limitations are suggested by the regularity with which such talks are reprinted in *The Listener*, presumably in order to give the audience a fuller opportunity to digest them, and by the fact that when we see them in print, we are aware that their style is rather more terse and rudimentary than conventional 'literary' language.

Yet not only is radio ill at ease with abstractions, it is not always very effective in dealing with concrete, material phenomena – at teaching students about simple physical skills. Both kinds of limitation have been neatly summarized by an experienced programme producer: 'there are some subjects which defy radio treatment, subjects for which spoken words are just not enough – advanced chemistry, for instance, with its diagrams and equations, or, on a homelier level, how to tie knots' (Evans, 1977, 17). There is a common factor in these contrasting limitations and that is, inevitably, the absence of vision. In the concrete world of knot-tying images speak louder than words, and in the abstract world of philosophy or linguistics which is in itself devoid of images we are heavily dependent upon images of *words* – upon a stable, visible text which we can study at leisure.. This means that even television, whose codes also exist in time, is better than radio at conveying not only knot-tying but also abstract ideas, for its images of words and things provide a broader, more stable base from which the student can conceptualize.

Many of radio's limitations can, however, be alleviated by the use of audio-cassettes and tapes, whose value may be summed up in a single word – retention. By storing radio programmes they allow the student to make use of them at any time, just as she may use books, and, like books also, they make for a fuller understanding of the material by giving her a chance to pause and/or refer back. This facility is particularly useful in the case of talks and lectures, but it can also enhance direct-instruction programmes by enabling students to master techniques through repetition. Two obvious examples are exercises for physical fitness and the pronunciation of phrases in a foreign language. Furthermore cassettes can provide a pause in the instruction while the student carries out the activities before returning to the tape for the correct answer, comment and the next stage of instruction. This facility is of particular use in instructing students how to key into a computer and commenting on what appears on the screen. Unlike conventional radio, then, cassettes allow learning-pace to be adjusted to the needs of the individual: they are student- not teacher-centred, and it is not surprising that they are superseding live broadcasts at all levels of education. Many schools programmes are now transmitted at night for the purposes of cassetting, and in 1983 over 90 per cent of all the schools which took the BBC's education programmes used them on a time-shift basis (*BBC Annual Report and Handbook 1984*, 1983, 26). Since 1980 the Open University has made a similar switch from live broadcasts to cassettes. In 1983

111

radio transmissions dropped to less than thirteen hours a week, while over half a million cassettes were mailed to students. Moreover more than one-third of the students who listened to the radio transmissions did so on recordings (Bates, 1984, 204).

The use of audio-cassettes in education gives rise to two speculations which are of relevance to our concern with radio in general. First they are a reminder that radio is not the only pure sound medium: as well as cassettes, records and tapes have been in existence for many years and all have pedagogical advantages over radio in that they can be started and stopped at any time and also permit the selection and review of the material they contain. The question is whether we regard them merely as varieties of 'time-shift' radio or whether their differences are significant enough for us to regard them as separate media. If we were simply to consider commercially pre-recorded cassettes other than those which consist only of music we would find that many, probably most, consist of material (for example story-readings or keep-fit-through-dance routines) which did *not* originate as radio programmes. Nor are the differences in these 'canned' media entirely to their advantage, for they do not of themselves generate new material as radio does; and since radio's output can be instantly recorded it can easily acquire their advantages. The second speculation is prompted by Bates's point that 'there is a big difference, both in production style and educational effectiveness, between programmes made originally as radio programmes, and programmes created from the beginning for use specifically in a cassette format' (1984, 204–5); and it is one which extends beyond education to sound broadcasting in general. Despite the ubiquity of radiocassette players, the off-air recording of radio programmes is more often than not illegal, but if at some stage the legal difficulties were removed so that the cassetting of much radio output became almost a matter of routine, this could have revolutionary effects on production styles and programme techniques. Radio producers might become less concerned with what 'communicates at first hearing', less frightened of pauses and silences and more conscious of the fact that their programmes were being pondered over and replayed. At the very least the language of certain kinds of programmes might become more 'literary' and listeners respond to them as to the less ephemeral medium of print. It is an interesting thought.

But to return to education. We can sum up by saying that in terms of educational output radio itself seems to be virtually obsolescent and that the future lies with cassettes, over which the student has full control. Nevertheless it must be added that for all their advantages cassettes are generally a less efficient means of storage and retrieval than are books. We have already seen that telling something to a listener takes longer than if she read it for herself, which means that cassettes are able to store much *less* material than books can. Furthermore the retrieval of information from cassettes is a less easy matter than from books, where turning back the pages allows the continuous monitoring of intervening material and permits scannings and overviews of the text. And even when the required information is located on cassette it still exists 'in time' rather than in space, still addresses what is even for committed students that slow learner, the ear, since it lacks the 'simultaneity' of spatial information. The advantages of cassettes over books are that they leave the student with the free use of her eyes and hands and they provide her with sound, which can enhance a teacher's meaning and is a valuable resource in acquiring such skills as foreign language pronunciation; yet books can offer a *stable* text of words, images and phonetic script which all but neutralizes these advantages. It is of course true that no single medium is equal to all pedagogical needs and that the most elementary teaching is likely to be 'mixed media' even if it consists only of the teacher and a blackboard. But the permanence of print would seem to make it more nearly equal to these needs than any other single medium and certainly more so than any other 'distance' medium. The next most effective of the latter is television since its codes are partly visual even if they are temporal: but radio, as we observed at the very beginning of this book, is characterized by codes which are neither stable nor visual and this explains why even those educational programmes which are effective on radio, whether as live broadcasts or on cassette, invariably require ancillary material. This may take the form of visual codes which are also temporal (BBC Schools Radio has for some years offered with many of its programmes a

35 mm film-strip known as radiovision); or more frequently by visual codes which are spatial – print and/or pictures; or sometimes by both. By using such material radio is virtually unlimited in what it can teach – even knot-tying and mathematics would be within its powers. But the question then arises whether radio is not simply insufficient as an educational medium but altogether redundant. In its use with radiovision it is effectively little more than a half-medium since it performs no function which could not equally be performed by a film or television soundtrack; and even in its use with books it seems to add little of significance. At the level of Continuing Education, for instance, we are told that series are *always* accompanied by 'support notes' (*BBC Annual Report and Handbook 1984*, 1983, 28) and that many publications of this nature 'have a "life" of their own independent of series and continue to sell after the broadcasts have long since ceased' (*An Introduction to Further Education Broadcasts*, 1977, 8); which rather suggests that the one dispensable element in this form of educational broadcasting is the broadcasting. And even when these publications would not of themselves make sense without the broadcasts, they often give the impression that they are being used in an unnecessarily restrictive way in order to allocate some distinctive role to radio. There is other evidence which hints at its redundancy as an educational medium. On courses where there exist alternative ways of learning the same material, such as many of those run by the Open University, radio (and television) is likely to be used fairly little. Paulu has pointed out that students of the Open University are expected to spend 65 per cent of their time reading and only 10 per cent of their time listening or viewing (1981, 270); and more recently Bates has conceded that broadcasting is a relatively minor component of its teaching system (1984, 139). Moreover its seems to be the case that even radio programmes which contain direct instructions are often used merely for revision or reinforcement since the skills which they impart have already been acquired through other teaching media, notably books; and in the case of talks and lectures which do not contain direct instructions many are used merely to gain a general impression of their subject even when their intention is to impart specific knowledge. In other words, even though

many of these talks are conceived as *educational* there is some tendency for students to treat them as *educative*; and this tendency is strengthened by their ingrained habit of regarding radio and television as 'leisure media' to a much greater extent than they regard books and newspapers: for since students do not respond to them in a critical or analytical way while at leisure, but indeed tend to regard them as an aid to relaxation, they are also likely to allow education programmes to 'wash over' them. This was found to be a particular problem at Open University level and is the so-called 'Warm Bath' theory of educational media consumption (Bates, 1984, 176). The various difficulties which broadcasting must contend with has led Bates to take a very sombre view of its educational potential: 'The basic problem is that broadcasting is a weak instructional medium. It is difficult for students to master skills or acquire deep understanding through broadcasting alone, and difficult for teachers to integrate broadcasting with other learning activities' (ibid., 234).

But if radio's educational potential is limited, it can offer a third kind of format – one which is educative in intention as well as in effect and which transcends the possibilities of its other two formats and of the print media. Like books, programmes consisting of talks or instructions describe the world to the student or tell her to do various things within it; but radio can also offer a direct impression of that world. In other words, within its natural domain, which as we have seen lies between abstract concepts on the one hand and what is visually or physically intricate on the other, it can provide *experiences* which would otherwise be inaccessible to the student (Palmer, 1947, 18–22; Bates, 1984, 20). Since this kind of broadcasting is not overtly conative it is distinguishable from educational formats by its absence of direct address: material is presented before a listener rather than aimed at a respondent and may take the form of foreign languages spoken in context by native speakers, not as a model for direct imitation but simply as an authentic impression; music recitals; dramatic productions of major literary works such as Shakespeare; and actuality (real or simulated) of manufacturing processes or historical events. Under the last heading we might also include eyewitnesses' accounts of those events, for even though they are at one remove from them and to that extent much the same as an account delivered by a history lecturer, they might strike the listener as a part of the original experience because she knows that the speakers participated in, or were at least present at, the events. Yet even if we argue that radio can enlarge the student's experience of the world in a way that books, talks or a teacher cannot we would have to concede that it cannot do so to the extent that the visual media – film and television – can. In certain circumstances this is, of course, to radio's advantage. Language learners can hear what Finnish sounds like, music students can hear what a clavichord sounds like, instead of just reading about it in a book or being told about it in a talk: but they can also do so without being distracted by an irrelevant image of the speaker or the musician. However it is true that these experiences are usually more than a matter of mere sound, in which case the listener (unlike the viewer) must compensate for the deficiencies of the medium by using her imagination. Nevertheless, what is in one respect a deficiency is in another an advantage: not only the provision of experience but also the disciplined use of the imagination is held to be of value in education. Thus radio's major contribution to education is its unique combination of two processes which are both regarded as important yet which the other media can provide only separately: it is the only medium in which reality is in some sense directly presented yet must *at the same time* be imagined. Not the least reason why both these processes are prized in education is that they can increase learning motivation – and radio is capable of doing this even with respect to those disciplines in which it can offer little by way of direct instruction. We have already seen that it is inherently unsuited to the teaching of scientific and mathematical principles: nevertheless a radio dramatization of Darwin's voyage to South America on HMS *Beagle* may stimulate a scientific interest in theories of evolution. This inability to convey methodologies combined with an ability to arouse interest therein has often been noted by experts in educational broadcasting (Palmer, 1947, 101; Bailey, 1957, 55).

We might conclude our discussion of the use of radio in

116

education with a summary and a general observation. We can sum up by saying that radio's relative inefficiency as an educational medium, even when its output is recorded on cassette, creates a tendency among students to use direct-instruction programmes in a marginal way – not as the main teaching medium but as a reinforcement of knowledge first acquired through other media – and to treat radio talks and lectures, however educational their intentions, as merely educative, as a way of gaining an impression of the subject rather than specific knowledge of it. On the other hand, radio's ability to present experiences and to stimulate the student's imagination means that its importance is felt to be predominantly, though not exclusively, educative and documentary. Generally speaking teachers prefer to use broadcasts as enrichment rather than as a means of direct teaching (Bates, 1984, 42–3). Furthermore, since their content tends to be retained in an impressionistic and indeterminate rather than a precise or detailed way, the cassetting of such broadcasts is perhaps less imperative than the cassetting of educational broadcasts. This really returns us to the initial question of how far certain kinds of education programmes are distinguishable from general output; to which our answer might be that there is often little *intrinsic* difference but that the content of the former is more likely to be retained simply because they are located in an education context – heard, perhaps, as part of an Open University course which in general demands a considerable 'discipline of response'.

Our final observation arises from having noted that radio's ability to extend the student's experience rests largely on its power to stimulate her imagination. It is often, though not always, of a factual nature – experience of the 'real' world. But we may recall from Chapter 1 that the listener's imagination is an instrument of fiction: it *constructs* a reality inside the mind or reconstructs one which is in many respects *different* from the original. Thus radio has a close yet strangely ambivalent relationship with the world outside, as is aptly illustrated by outide broadcasts – the occasions when it leaves the hermetic environs of the studio to describe the world directly through commentary.

117

Suggestions for further work

1 Write and record a four- or five-minute radio talk (700–900 words) whose purpose is broadly informative and instructive. Again bear in mind the limitations of the medium – Silvey (1978) gives a good account of what should be aimed for and avoided in talks of this kind, but the general rule is: Keep it simple. Get your fellow students to listen to the recording of your talk *without* taking notes and then, either orally or in writing, ask follow-up questions to see how much they have understood and retained.

2 Imagine that you are going to make a radio programme to help the young unemployed to improve their skills when attending interviews for jobs. Write a detailed scenario of what the programme would include, bearing in mind that it must win and hold the listener's attention before it can inform and teach, and that the broadcasting techniques available to you range from interviews and actuality through voicepieces, dramatic dialogue, comedy sketches and pop songs.

6 OUTSIDE BROADCASTS: COMMENTARY ON PUBLIC EVENTS

> Before I joined the B.B.C. . . . I rarely listened to
> anything except concerts and running commentaries on
> sports events. These latter, which gave me a pleasure
> distinct from that which lies in *seeing* a game or race,
> should have provided a hint of radio's possibilities.
>
> (Louis MacNeice, Introduction to *The Dark Tower*)

Outside broadcasts (OBs) consist of live coverage of an event
which takes place outside the studio. Their various forms were
categorized as long ago as 1929 (S. Briggs, 1981a, 165) and in
both radio and television they are extremely popular with
broadcasters and audiences alike. Why?

They are a necessary, or at least desirable, proof that media
messages can be originated in places other than the womb of the
studio, an acknowledgement that radio and television not only
serve the community but draw their raw material from it.
One might expect that radio would have ceded outside
broadcasting to television, which is in an obvious respect better
qualified to do it. But precisely because its codes are limited
radio has found it even more important than television to
demonstrate its links with the 'real' world and has over the years
more than maintained its OB output. The most effective means
of doing this is *commentary*, the improvised description or word-
picture of an event. Thus commentary is even more referential
or 'realistic' than News because it is immediate and spontaneous
– unscripted by a news editor – and occurs entirely *in situ*: it is
not transmitted from a studio or newsroom. Commentary exists

and is important in television as well as radio, but the differences in the media mean that radio commentary is usually different in nature and always in effect from that of television. It is not simply the special abilities of a John Snagge or Richard Dimbleby which make them more memorable than television commentators but the difference in their *function*.

In television the outside world exists as an icon or picture. It can be watched on a screen, where it engrosses most of the audience's attention. The commentator exists, as it were, off-stage: his role is largely secondary since his words are an elaboration of what we can already see. In radio the outside world exists as an index, if it exists at all. 'Effects' microphones are invariably installed to gather the sound of the action and/or crowd reaction, but as often as not it is inaudible or at best exists as a collection of distant and isolated noises – applause, shouts, the click of ball on bat. Beyond these the commentator must create the picture for us, so that his role is central. He acts as our eyes and to a large extent our ears. This means that while all good radio commentators know the eloquence of a pause their commentary must be more nearly continuous than that of television. Its speed and style reflect the mood of the event and its language tends to be more explicit, creates its own context much more, than television commentary. It includes not simply a concrete description of the event but what has been described as 'associative material' (Evans, 1977, 159) – other sense-impressions such as the smell of new-mown grass, the weather and the human 'atmosphere', and also the historical background, those facts and causes beyond the event which remind the listener that there is more to it than meets the eye.

Primarily as a result of radio commentary a necessary new verb 'to commentate' has appeared alongside the traditional 'to comment'; for whereas 'comment' implies subjectivity – 'to express an opinion on something' – 'commentate' implies the more objective process of describing something as it happens. These functions are often quite sharply distinguished in live sports coverage, a commentator breaking off his *commentary* at intervals to invite *comments* from an expert sitting beside him. A somewhat similar arrangement occurs on television, except that since the action is largely self-evident the functions are less sharply distinguished: the commentator will not infrequently 'comment' as well as commentate. But within the total impression of the event which both media seek to convey the radio commentator must first create the picture or image of it which his television counterpart can take for granted – and however 'vivid' that picture may be it can never be iconic but merely *symbolic*, created in the opaque material of words.

Despite this apparent handicap radio commentary has always enjoyed a huge popularity, creating an impression in the minds of its devotees which is often more vivid than that made by the events themselves upon those who are watching them. It is not altogether surprising, then, that such commentary has maintained its popularity even in the age of television (Trethowan, 1970, 8). The two great BBC commentators were Richard Dimbleby on state occasions and John Arlott on cricket, and many people have preferred to have test matches mediated through the commentary of the latter than through the television cameras. One likely reason for this is that unlike television or watching from the terraces, it left them free to do other things at the same time. Yet it is still listened to even by those who have time to view – the reason for which can only be that such people prefer words to images, signs which do not resemble the things they stand for to those which do. In brief, they prefer to *imagine* the cricket match than to *see* it. Nevertheless, as the following extract illustrates, radio commentary attempts to be as exhaustive and accurate as possible:

England vs. West Indies – Second Test Match
Transmission: 25 June 1963. Commentator: John Arlott.
England want 43 to win in 55 minutes . . . and Hall . . .
that little shower apparently wetted the outfield and for
the first time today a bowler has recourse to the sawdust
heap, Hall comes down . . . dries it . . . turns at the pavilion
5 end, comes up . . . great tigerish run, the leap . . . he bowls
to Titmus . . . Titmus covers up . . . its goes off the edge of
the bat and he takes a single to gully. (Applause)
A single to gully there, the ball didn't travel a third as
far as the batsmen ran. A very quickly taken single makes
10 England 192 for 5. And this is where one's almost afraid

to breathe for fear of rocking the boat: and these two
batsmen now faced with a tactical decision on almost
every ball. Two slips, leg slip, silly mid-on for Close,
Hall comes in, bowls to him and he plays that straight
15 up to silly mid-on, Worrell. Hall turns and walks back,
Close again goes out and prods the pitch. The trees
away in the distance heaving under this strong wind which,
in fact, would help Hall to swing the ball in to Close.
The wind is coming in from about cover point – say extra
20 cover. The trees heaving and bending under it, the light
murky: and Hall comes up again, past Umpire Phillips and
bowls to Close, Close a hook, he's beaten long leg, it's
through, it's four runs. (Applause)
Close is 50 and the people here are only sorry they couldn't
25 make ten times as much noise. An innings of remarkable
shrewdness, good judgement, courage and very sound techniqu
50 in 3 hours fifteen minutes with five fours, his
first 50 in a Test: his previous best, 42 against the
West Indies at Birmingham in 1957: and now it's Hall
30 again from the pavilion end; in, bowls to Close and Close . . .
oh! tried to cut outside the off stump, through to the
wicket keeper and about six rows of members down here
fidget as if their ants were full of pants . . . pants were
full of ants . . . absolutely unable to stay still there. This
35 awful moment when you see a batsman play outside the
off stump at pace and it goes through.
196 for 5. 196 for 5. Hall comes in again, bowls to Close,
Close tries to turn that on the on side, takes it on the
thigh again as he turns, walks away with a little hobble,
40 still disdaining to rub . . . a very hard man this. He's
been hit, I would think, a couple of dozen times on
the thigh, he's resolutely refused to rub; he was cracked
once on the forearm . . . and I would think that that was
the first time in this innings that Brian Close has flashed
45 outside the off stump. And the reaction amongst the crowd
was almost terrifying, 196 for 5, then.
38 wanted and Hall comes in, bowls to Close, Close hooks and
again he's beaten long leg . . . leg slip but not long leg,
beautifully fielded by Butcher, they take a single

50 (Applause) – a Constantine-style spring, pick-up and
   return, it's 197 for 5. Titmus 11, Close 52. England,
   197 for 5, want 37 to win and there are 52 minutes left.
   Well, still anybody's game but Close, I think, realizes the
   position, he's hitting at everything on the leg side and
55 really, for the first time in this innings, since tea he's
   been connecting with the ball on the leg side. He had one
   or two swings before tea and never got a run from it; but this
   time he's got two fours and two singles down to fine leg.
   And Gibbs comes in, bowls to Close who goes down the
60 pitch, but checks the stroke, Worrell fields, and you
   can hear the sighs come out of the spectators like
   punctured bicycle tyres. Every time a risk is taken, everybody
   walking the tightrope.
   Gibbs to Close, tries to swing it, an appeal for LBW, not
65 out; taken by Close at slip and he appeals for it, Sobers
   at slip, and he appeals for a catch. A few brows being
   mopped though it's not a warm afternoon; and Gibbs comes
   again and bowls to Close – a little short but Close, using
   his reach, goes forward, smothers any turn and plays it
70 out on the off side. 197 for 5 and still with this very
   economic field: eight men saving the one. Gibbs comes in,
   bowls to Close, Close swings it on the leg side. (Roar of
   crowd) Four again. (Applause) 200's up. It's been a long,
   long road to home, this, and now England want 33. Gibbs
75 bowls to Close and Close plays out on the off side, 201
   for 5. Close 56, Titmus 11, and that grotesque tower away
   in the distance suddenly catching the sun like a beacon,
   the ground in bloom as Gibbs comes in, bowls, and Close
   steers him to short third man and takes a quick single,
80 as Nurse closes in to field. 202 for 5, Close 57, every
   Englishman in the ground with him. Every West Indian in
   the ground after his blood.

Radio commentary entails a relationship between commentator
and listener which is complex and appears to operate at several
levels. At the first level there is the 'real' John Arlott and the
'real' listener, who cannot know each other to the extent that
they might in circumstances of ordinary personal interaction.

123

They are mutually invisible and physically remote from each other. Yet these 'real' individuals are, of course, the precondition of interaction at any other level. At the second level the commentator and listener assume the minimal roles of 'mouthpiece' and 'hearer' respectively. The commentator is the mere purveyor of actuality. He is as self-effacing as possible, his primary duty is to events rather than to the listener, he is interested only in what is happening 'out there'. He is not present 'in propria persona', nor is he expected to be, but in a sense pretends not to be present at all. Like the newsreader he submerges himself in the reality he reports. John Arlott's language in this passage is very largely referential, concerned with the objective world of deeds and facts – 'Hall comes in again, bowls to Close' (l. 37), and so on. In sum the passage consists of a description of every ball bowled, the number of runs England require to win, the physical and psychological duel between Hall and Close, the air of tension and excitement in the ground, the weather conditions. What confirm the existence of that objective world are the intermittent sounds of applause and Arlott's occasional unfinished remarks (l. 1), ungrammatical sentences (ll. 34–6) and errors of fact (ll. 65–6), which suggest that the events are putting him under pressure. In the sense that the commentator has no rhetorical design upon the listener but is presenting the facts on a take-it-or-leave-it basis, the listener 'pretends' not to be present, too. He merely eavesdrops on John Arlott's words as symbols of the action.

Nevertheless as we saw in Chapter 1, the lack of resemblance between words and the things they represent means that however factual the events which the commentary describes they must be 'created' in the listener's mind, very probably in a form which is in many respects different from the reality itself, and are in that sense a 'fiction'. One broadcasting historian recalls that after hearing a particular OB 'I was taken to Rushmoor Arena to watch the Aldershot Tattoo, and was disappointed to find how small the spectacle seemed compared to the stupendous thing my mind's eye had seen' (Black, 1972, 68). This is a disturbing reminder of the old philosophical dilemma that ultimately only words can explain the world yet do so by 'falsifying' it. Thus however accurate John Arlott's account, the test match which the listener experiences is in the strict sense of the world *imaginary* and when he prefers this account to television coverage we must conclude that he is more interested in a fiction than in the 'truth'. We glibly refer to television as the truth since its photographic images seem to represent things 'as they really are': we are hardly conscious of the human agency (choice of camera locations, sequence of pictures, and so on) which is always involved. But in radio commentary the very fact that things are not 'apparent' in the words which represent them gives us scope to be much more conscious of the person who provides those words, and I would suggest that for all the commentator's objectivity there is a sense in which we become almost as conscious of him as of the events themselves.

In what way, then, do John Arlott's words proclaim his personality almost as much as they proclaim the events they describe? At the beginning of the extract he describes Hall's run as 'tigerish' (l. 5), a word which conveys to us something more than the objective nature of the bowler's action, for it is a metaphor which briefly superimposes upon that action the image of a wild animal and thus invests it not only with speed but with a primitive aggression, a suggestion of hunger and predacity. But at the heart of this as of all metaphors lies an incongruity. We would not notice the image if in most respects Hall were not quite unlike a tiger, and the incongruity thus declares the inventiveness of the commentator, his ability to sharpen our awareness of the familiar by discovering between objects connections which are unfamiliar. We see this same inventiveness in ll. 17 and 20 when Arlott describes the trees in the distance as 'heaving . . . heaving and bending', which is a buried metaphor and much more than such effete verbs as 'shaking' or 'waving' invests the trees with a kind of arduous, sentient life and suggests by implication the force of the wind which in helping Hall to 'swing the ball in to Close' (l. 18) may have a decisive effect on the match. In l. 63 Arlott describes cricketers and spectators alike as 'walking the tightrope', a momentary superimposition of images which the 'impersonal' iconic media would find hard to emulate! And when, facing Gibbs, Close changes his stroke at the last moment and Arlott avers that 'you can hear the sighs come out of the spectators like punctured bicycle tyres' (ll. 60–2) the comparison evokes the tension in the ground, but its bathos declares him, too, for he is momentarily detached enough from the proceedings to glimpse them in a comical light. One or two other expressions highlight the commentator's sensibilities and his gift of words quite as much as the atmosphere of the match itself. He notices a 'grotesque tower away in the distance' (ll. 76–7), an observation and a description which are so idiosyncratic that we picture not only the object itself but also Arlott observing it. Yet with an author's instinct he provides the tower with an aesthetic relevance to the events on the pitch. It suddenly catches the sun 'like a beacon' (l. 77) and this, together with 'the ground in bloom' (l. 78), which suggests not only the beauty of the summer but also the colourfulness of the spectators, creates a sense of incipient celebration, is perhaps a portent that England will achieve a great victory. Arlott concludes this phase of the action with a summary of Close's situation – 'every Englishman in the ground with him. Every West Indian in the ground after his blood' (ll. 80–2) – and like his previous expressions it is elegant enough to call attention to its creator as well as to its subject. The antithesis could hardly have been bettered had Arlott had the opportunity for a writer's premeditation.

But not only is Arlott's personality revealed in his choice of words – his distinctive epithets and his ability to find linguistic connections between the happenings in the test match and other, quite different, areas of experience; it emerges in his ability to find simultaneous and causal connections which exist within the match itself but which are by no means obvious to everyone who is watching it. For instance even those viewers who saw Titmus's quick single on television may have failed to notice that 'the ball didn't travel a third as far as the batsmen ran' (ll. 8–9), an arithmetical comparison which precisely conveys the pressures on the England batsmen to take risks. Not only, then, do we have signs which do not resemble what they describe and are therefore just as likely to proclaim their author, they describe connections which may be partly visible within the photographic images of television but are by no means self-evident. They do not simply exist 'out there' but are made explicit by the commentator and therefore declare his presence and percipience to an even greater degree than his use of metaphors and epithets. Likewise, his subsequent observations that 'one's almost afraid to breathe' (ll. 10–11) and that 'A few brows [are] being mopped though it's not a warm afternoon' (ll. 66–7) confirm the existence of a tension within the ground whose cause is not at the moment wholly visible, as the last clause concedes. Ll. 38–40 describe Close being struck on the thigh and hobbling away but disdaining to rub it. A spectator relying solely upon his own eyes might simply assume from this that Close was hit hard, but not very hard. He might have 'failed' to notice what Arlott perceives as a significant 'non-event', the refusal to rub, a perception which in its very utterance draws the listener's attention to the psychological as well as physical battle between Close and the West Indian fast bowler, Hall. Finally, in ll. 54–5, Arlott observes a change in Close's batting behaviour, 'he's hitting at everything on the leg side . . . really, for the first time in this innings since tea' and spells out the tactical significance: 'still anybody's game but Close, I think, realizes the position' – an observation which is at least partly based on visual data, but data which have been abstracted from a welter of other physical detail and over a period of time. What Arlott is doing here, then, is conveying more than is conveyed by photographic images, he is 'reading the game'. His ability to describe a reality which is only partly visual and to make connections between superficially disparate phenomena or between aspects of the past and those of the present is essentially a human, an intellectual faculty. In all these remarks, no matter how objective they may seem, the mediating intelligence of the commentator is strongly declared. I do not, of course, mean to suggest that this cannot be done by television commentators, indeed they do very little else, merely that this reality is not established through images alone. But whereas on television it is done as an accompaniment to the events that the viewer can see for himself, it is done for the listener by the same person who has described those events to him and very often in words which are an inseparable *part* of that description, and it thus makes the commentator a much more pervasive presence on the radio medium.

But in concentrating on the commentator's stock-in-trade of

127

words we have so far ignored an obvious sense in which radio commentary is more personal than other accounts of the world: it is *voiced*. Newspaper accounts are also personal in the sense of being written by individuals, but as we saw in Chapter 4 the medium of print lends them an air of impersonality. By different means the radio presentation of the news also acquires an impersonal air, for we know that it is being *read* – a fact which suggests that it has originated elsewhere, been observed and set down by someone other than the speaker, and this deflects our attention from him. But commentary is improvised under pressure of events, as is clear from the variations of volume and pace in the commentator's voice – his alternating murmurs and shouts as the significance of the events changes, his fluency then hesitancy as he strives to keep abreast of them. The effect of this is, as we have seen, to convince us of the realness of these events, but it also makes us very conscious of the commentator himself. When Arlott tells us that 'Close . . . oh! tried to cut outside the off stump' and then makes the mistaken reference to ants and pants followed by a correction (ll. 30–4) our awareness of what is happening on and around the pitch is indistinguishable from an awareness of the very human qualities of the speaker. This awareness is heightened by two other factors. The first is that the commentator's presence is an unmitigated one. As we have seen, he can never leave events to speak for themselves as his television counterpart can, but must fill the entire medium except for a few isolated and often unintelligible sounds which exist, as it were, round the edges. And the second factor which may increase our awareness of him is the inherent quality of his voice – its timbre and accent. We observed that in radio news the invariable delivery in RP further minimizes the reader's presence, but when we read the above extract we must imagine the words as being spoken not only as if impromptu but in the gruff Hampshire burr which made Arlott's presence quite unmistakable. Thus, as we saw in Chapter 3, radio language is a *binary* code in that *words* act as symbols of the objects they represent while *voice* is the index of the speaker. But we have seen in this chapter that it is also binary in the sense that words are also an index of the speaker, even when (as in our reproduction of John Arlott's) they cannot be heard: for his use of certain words in preference to others very much proclaims his personality – his level of awareness, command of language, emotional state, and so on. Anyone who doubts this indexical function of words may recall that when confronted with a piece of writing which we have not previously read we can often infer the identity of its author merely by discerning within it characteristics of style and vocabulary which we have noticed in his other writings. If such characteristics did not exist, we would never be able to enjoy literary parodies, such as Max Beerbohm's of Henry James. Linguisticians have a term for this characteristic mode of utterance, whether written or spoken – idiolect.

Let us sum up what we have suggested so far. No matter how accurately and objectively the radio commentator describes a particular event, his efforts will have two closely related and paradoxical effects: he will perforce create a 'fiction' from this event in the listener's mind and he will establish a strong sense of his own presence. Indeed we have noted that the radio OB differs radically from its television counterpart in giving us first-hand evidence of little else: through his voice and words the commentator is virtually the only thing we are directly aware of, so that he is quite literally a story-teller – the sole source and in that sense the 'creator' of the things he describes. Our interest in these things is therefore indistinguishable from an interest in the commentator himself – specifically, in his creative intelligence, the way he perceives the events and transmutes them into something 'perceivable' by us. This is confirmed by the popularity of radio commentary among those who are present at the event as well as those who have the option of watching on television, where the commentator's role is merely ancillary. Using our own example we might say that our interest in the test match is much the same as an enjoyment of John Arlott's company, so that the relationship between the commentator as mouthpiece and the listener as hearer which we described earlier leads to a third level with which it is inseparably connected yet in extreme contrast: the commentator as 'personality' and the listener as his companion.

This sense of companionship between broadcaster and listener is not, of course, peculiar to commentary. It is generated by all personal presentation on the radio, but is especially obvious in the field of light entertainment – programmes on Radios 1 and 2 with 'personality' presenters such as Simon Bates and Gloria Hunniford. These broadcasters exist ostensibly to play records but it has been observed that the playlist is limited and the presenters make more impression than the music, providing missing companionship for their predominantly female and housebound listeners (Hobson, 1980, 107). In the *Radio Times* such programmes are almost always billed in terms of their presenters rather than the type of music they contain. This sense of companionship is perhaps no more than one would expect of programmes whose material is relatively limited and whose presenters speak in language which Jakobson classifies as 'emotive' – that is intended to express them as personalities. But one is rather more surprised to find it in news and commentary, where the language is predominantly referential and the intention of the broadcaster is to be objective and self-effacing. And there can be no doubt that this *is* the intention. The idea of describing the OB of a test match as the 'John Arlott Show' would be repugnant and at odds with the BBC's tacit yet proud claim to veracity and objectivity in the reportage of all events, not simply the news.

But the final point of importance is that however strong our sense of his personality in comparison with the events he describes the commentator is, of course, a 'fiction', too. I have just asserted that he is almost the sole reality we are aware of since we can hear him continuously, whereas the events have scarcely any existence outside the words which symbolize them. But the sound of his voice requires us to 'complete' him within our imagination just as his commentary requires us to imagine the test match, and with little more likelihood of corresponding to the reality. The late William Hardcastle, euphonious presenter of *The World at One* and an individual of some corpulence, once received a letter from a female listener who had just seen a photograph of him and was outraged to discover that he was not the slim and handsome figure she had quite naturally assumed him to be. But from the sound of a broadcaster's voice the listener will infer not simply his appearance but an impression of his personality which transcends that appearance. Many years ago an experiment was conducted to discover how accurately listeners could infer a broadcaster's personality from the quality of his voice. The results varied enormously from listener to listener and were substantially inaccurate (Pear, 1931, 178–242). However in this experiment the subjects did not speak their own words but read a single passage from *The Pickwick Papers*, and we have been arguing that *words* quite as much as voice are an index of the speaker's personality: they suggest his educational level, intelligence, nature and mode of perception, and so on. But in the case of commentary at least, they are only obliquely self-revelatory, for the focus of attention is always upon the public event – the test match or the royal wedding – and the commentator's description thereof, delivered as it is in that blend of companionship and anonymity which characterizes the medium yet is quite untypical of most social interaction, may well give a positively misleading impression of his 'real' self. Nevertheless the important point is not how accurate the listener's impression is, but the fact that it is formed in a quite different way – and from much less information – than the impression he would form from direct experience of that person or even from being able to see him on television.

We can conclude by saying that for all its concern to portray events as realistically and impersonally as possible, listeners tune in to the radio OB for a version of them which is in the strict sense imaginary and for a concomitant sense of companionship with a commentator who is also very largely imagined. Since radio's attempts to deal directly with the outside world seem to lead inevitably to the creation of fictions it is time to take a closer look at its dealings with the realm of the imagination.

Suggestions for further work

Plan a commentary on some public event near you – a local soccer match, student rag procession, traction-engine rally, for example. Research in advance the background and context – what has led up to the event and what, precisely, it will consist of; the relevant personal details of the participants; the topography of the venue (including a quiet vantage-point from which you will be able to observe the action). Take a tape recorder along to the event and for about ten minutes conduct a running commentary, remembering to punctuate it with 'associative material' – relevant statistics, weather conditions, some description of the larger environment, and so on. You will find excellent guidance on all this in Evans (1977) and McLeish (1978). Finally, play your commentary back to any people who were not present at the event and see what sense they make of it.

PART THREE
THE IMAGINATION

7 RADIO DRAMA

> The best in this kind are but shadows; and the worst are
> no worse, if imagination amend them.
>> (Shakespeare, *A Midsummer Night's Dream*, V, i)

Since we have arrived in the realm of make-believe, we should
perhaps revert briefly to the more conventional distinction
between fact and fiction and hint at the semiotic complexity
which such a distinction entails. Although radio involves us in
acts of imagination, in making fictions even when its concerns
are factual, the conventional distinction between fact and fiction
is between sign-systems or codes which refer to things that exist
in the real world, such as Mrs Thatcher or the miners' strike of
1984–5, and those which refer to things that do not exist in the
real world, such as unicorns or Tess of the D'Urbervilles.
Though obvious enough in itself, this distinction creates
semiotic complications, for if the word-signs of a newspaper are
symbols of the real things which they signify and the word-signs
of a novel are symbols of the unreal things which they signify,
there is a further semiotic relationship between the unreal and
the real, between fiction or make-believe on the one hand and
fact on the other; and it is one which is essentially *iconic*.
Literature, as they say, is a mirror of life. In one way or another
works of fiction reflect the real world and are intelligible only
because they do so. The events of Thomas Hardy's *Tess*, though
conveyed in verbal symbols, in some sense resemble those
which occur in real life. This is true of drama as of novels. The
characters and events of Shakespeare's *Othello*, even if it is not
based on actual history as many of his plays are, have a broadly
iconic relationship to the people and events of real life.

Having established the nature of the relationship which exists between the make-believe world of novels and drama and the real world, I now want to concentrate on what constitutes the *difference* between novels and drama. If novels create their fictional worlds through words, how do plays create theirs? One thing which might seem essential to drama is dialogue, which radio is peculiarly good at; but not all drama is characterized by dialogue or even monologue. There is the drama of mime, which reinforces the basic conviction that drama is essentially a *spectacle*, that one of the main things which distinguishes it from the signifying modes of most other arts, particularly literature, is *ostension*, whereby its fictional world is *shown* to the audience rather than merely described, explained or defined (Elam, 1980, 29–30). The character of Othello is not merely conveyed in writing, as Tess is, but shown to us in the form of a dark-skinned man in Venetian costume. However this would seem to rule out the possibility of drama on the radio, for in its strict, literal sense ostension is impossible in such a medium. A radio producer put his finger on the difficulty many years ago:

> we are all accustomed, in everyday phraseology, to going 'to see' plays, as opposed to going 'to hear' them. In consequence the mere juxtaposition of the words 'radio' and 'play' must imply for many people a contradiction in terms.
>
> (Gielgud, 1957, 85)

On the radio there can be no scenery, lighting, properties, costumes or make-up. At the very least, the absence of vision imposes huge restrictions on the *kinds* of plays radio can do. Large cast dramas are next to impossible: in any one scene the listener can accommodate at best only four or five major speaking characters with distinctive voices. While one character is speaking it is not possible to show the reactions of the other characters to him, to counterpoint what is heard with what is seen. No character who is present in a scene can stay silent for long, for if not regularly heard or referred to he 'disappears'. Moreover no elaborate stage business is possible since its prerequisite is space, and our sense of space – of *proxemics*, or the physical position of the characters relative to one another, and *kinesics*, their moves and actions – is primarily visual. Stage business is shown or 'ostended' to us, so if ostension is a distinguishing characteristic of drama and radio is blind, we are again forced to ask how radio drama can be said to exist. Even judged on its own, purely acoustic, terms the genre is restricted. The technology of the medium compresses the vocal range available to the actors, making dramatic contrast harder to achieve because shouts must be distanced and/or muted and whispers slightly amplified. Moreover the sounds have to maintain a fairly unbroken flow to hold the listener's attention since there is no visual dimension to fill out prolonged silences. Nor do the apparent deficiencies of radio drama end there, for its audience is not only blind but absent. Its members are not where the play is being performed but surrounded by the distractions of their own separate environments. In the conventional theatre the spectator, as Elam points out (1980, 95–6), initiates the communication process in a number of ways. By buying a ticket she sponsors, or commissions, the performance, makes a contract whereby she delegates an initiative to the actors. On the other hand she comprises with the other spectators an audience whose most significant signal is its mere presence. Its reactions exert a double influence – on the performance itself and on its reception. The spectators can influence the actors' performance and also one another through stimulation (for instance, by laughter), through confirmation (the spectator can find her own responses reinforced by others') and through integration (the spectator is encouraged in consequence to surrender her individual function to the larger unit of which she is a part). But the role and circumstances of the radio drama audience are radically different, a point which was made many years ago (McWhinnie, 1959, 33–6). Its members have not paid for their seats, so are unlikely to have a highly developed sense of occasion. But they are exacting in that they need not sit the play out, they can simply switch it off. Moreover since they cannot use their reactions to influence or control the performance in any other way and are usually listening as isolated individuals they may feel that this is the only option left to them; for they not only lack the visual cues offered by actors on the stage, but also cannot be influenced by the reactions of others in the audience. The business of understanding and judgement thus falls solely and squarely upon the individual listener.

Yet despite all these disadvantages, radio drama appears to be in a flourishing state: its variety and sheer quantity can easily be underestimated. It occurs not merely in the form of 'straight' plays and soap operas, such as *The Archers*, but in an 'applied' form – as an element in commercials, trailers, comedy shows and features – and in 'characterized readings' – narratives or story-tellings. Thus it may appear in varied guises, as a comic or illustrative sketch, a monologue, a reading from a diary, journal or poem. On BBC network radio alone over a thousand dramatic productions are broadcast every year (Paulu, 1981, 290).

How, then, does radio set about surmounting its limitations and create something analogous to conventional drama? Partly by a process of 'transcodification' – the replacement of one code or set of codes, in this case visual ones, by another, in this case auditory, the code of speech. We have already seen in the case of news and education programmes that the spoken word is a relatively crude vehicle of communication. But in radio drama it has to carry extra freight, for as well as the dialogue itself it has to convey through dialogue, or at least through narration, almost all the other kinds of information that the theatregoer would be able to see for herself – that is, whatever the audience needs to know about setting, time of day, the stature, dress and actions of the characters, any physical objects they may make use of, and so on. Hence transcodifiers – pointers such as 'Look out, he's got a gun!', which sound so contrived and superfluous in the visual media – are essential on the radio. Anyone present in a scene has to be identified – given speech, addressed or referred to fairly regularly so that the listener remains aware of him. Of course it is important to remember that radio is not devoid of *all* the resources of theatrical drama: it has sound, including sound effects. But the role of sound is a complicated one: it seems to occupy a position intermediate between speech, the primary code of radio, and the purely visual codes of the theatre, which radio can convey only in a transcodified form. For present purposes I shall distinguish between *noises* – sounds which are extraneous to speech (the creak of a door, for

138

example), and *sound effects* (SFX) – acoustic treatments of speech or sounds such as the fading up or down of speech or noises, or the addition of echo to a voice. Here we can see that the line between SFX and ordinary speech is a fine one, for the addition of echo to a voice may convey very similar spatial information to the sound of a raised voice. Noises and SFX can be used as *environmental* indicators, acoustic means of depicting scenes or settings (birdsong can suggest the countryside, echoing voices and noises a dungeon, and so on) and scene changes (the fading up and down of voices is analogous to the rise and fall of curtains and/or the brightening and dimming of stage lights in the conventional theatre). They can also act as *spatial* indicators – ways of revealing proxemics, the physical distances between the various characters, and kinesics, their movements relative to one another and to the listener. Proxemic and kinesic information is most frequently and effectively conveyed by locating the actors at varying distances from the microphone and by moving the actors in and out of its sound-gathering areas. This means that a single sound effect, the fading out of a voice, is often used to convey both environmental and spatial information: it signifies either of two things which would be perceived to be quite different on a stage, the end of a scene or the exit of a character during a scene, but the radio listener would have no difficulty in distinguishing which of them was happening.

How does the listener know what these noises and SFX mean? John Drakakis describes them as 'really a kind of mediating system of "sound signs" which both [broadcasters and listeners] agree will conventionally represent particular kinds of experience' (1981, 30). This description is helpful if it implies that such sounds convey in radio drama what would primarily be conveyed by visual means in the theatre and that our awareness of what is in effect their extended signification depends on a process of cultural familiarization. As we saw in Chapter 3, the sound of hooting may represent not only an owl but also by frequent association a dark, sinister setting, such as a graveyard at night-time. But Drakakis's description is misleading if it suggests that the relationship between these sound signs and what they signify is arbitrary in the way that the relationship between *word* signs and what they signify is arbitrary. Both

Drakakis and Erving Goffman ('Sound substitutes become conventionalized for what would ordinarily be conveyed visually', 1980, 163) seem to overlook the fact that in our perception of the world sound is a natural property even of those things which present themselves to us by predominantly visual means: it is not something which we *substitute* for its properties, as words are. And this is equally true of the predominantly visual world of the theatre. We do not simply *see* what is presented to us, we hear it. Our awareness of a stage murder derives not simply from the sight of one character drawing his gun upon another, but from the sound of a shot and the victim's cry, and our awareness of the characters' moves on to, around and off the stage stems not only from our sight of them but in however small a measure from the variations in the level of the sounds they make. In this sense, then, the noises and SFX of radio are *not* what Goffman perceives as 'substitutes' or 'equivalents' of what happens in the visual world; they are a *part* of what happens. Their relationship to what they represent is indexical, not merely symbolic, and so to regard them as transcodifications is misleading. Hence the point I wish to make is that drama may be distinguished by ostension or showing, but ostension is partly a matter of *sound* as well as vision: we register the activities on the stage through what we can hear as well as what we can see. In certain cases, that of thunder perhaps, sound might even be the primary means of ostension in the conventional theatre, just as it would be in a radio play.

Radio dramatists and producers have, of course, long been aware of the ostensive possibilities of sound, as is demonstrated by the fact that there have been plays such as Andrew Sachs's *The Revenge* (1978) which have consisted only of sound effects – a term which, as SFX, I shall henceforth use to denote non-verbal and non-musical noises of any kind. Such plays might be regarded as a wordless but acoustic equivalent of theatrical mime. Nevertheless it has to be recognized that a substantial number of sounds are not easily identifiable in isolation, as we saw in the example of the rustled recording tape in Chapter 3. Such sounds are capable of 'existing' on the radio, but to the extent that they have no intrinsic identity their status is much the same as that of visual phenomena, they can be 'revealed' to the listener only through the transcodifying process of speech. The rustling recording tape is as 'unknowable' to her as are the dress of the characters, the time of day, the place in which the action is set, and so on, and only the words adjacent to that sound will enable her to know whether what she is hearing is someone walking through undergrowth, the swish of a woman's gown or the unwrapping of a package. Indeed we also noted in Chapter 3 that it seems doubtful whether any radio sound is ultimately meaningful without the help of speech – even conventional, instantly recognizable, sounds are seldom very precise in their signification. Does birdsong, for instance, signify 'a garden' or 'the open countryside'? Do seawash and the cry of gulls mean 'the shore' or 'the open sea'? If the question is important it is only the narrative or the dialogue which will finally give us the answer.

We might attempt to summarize what is semiotically significant in a comparison of radio drama and theatrical drama by splitting the signs of the former into their component parts of 'signifier' and 'signified'. Anything which would signify itself in the theatre primarily by being seen (for example a clock) cannot occur on the radio except as a signified which is identified by a non-visual signifier – either verbal ('That's a nice-looking clock') or acoustic (SFX: TICKING SOUND). Transcending their function as dialogue, words are the primary signifiers, identifying for the listener both the things which would be visible in the theatre and sounds, which even when not difficult to recognize in themselves generally have an uncertain function. And sounds occupy an intermediate position in that they 'signify' or identify many of those things which would primarily identify themselves by being seen (the clock): but because sounds are often ambiguous or insufficiently expressive in themselves they need to be given identity or significance by words (SFX: CLOCK CHIMES. 'My God, is that the time? I'm late', and so on). To put it yet another way, the most natural and obvious mode of ostension, and one which is possible in the theatre, is for an object to be *seen*. On radio this must be replaced by an equally natural if 'secondary' mode of ostension: the object must be *heard*. But if this is impossible or unhelpful the object must be rendered by means of an 'artificial' sign or signs – symbols

141

called *words*, and this process is known as transcodification.

But of course this distinction I have been making between words and sounds is a false one. Words may merely *describe* what they refer to but they also 'show' the speaker, for in drama words are sounds also – the normal sounds made by human beings which have the advantage of being both intelligible in themselves and able to explain other sounds. Hence these words are not extraneous to the drama, made use of to remedy its ostensive deficiencies. As indexes of the characters who speak them, they are part of its ostensive apparatus. Since ostension is not just a visual matter but a showing of any kind, many readers will by now be aware that it is much the same as our formulation of iconism at the beginning of the chapter, which implied a general resemblance to life and not merely a visual one. A brief recapitulation will be helpful here. We began by suggesting that the relationship between the fictional world of novels and plays and the real world is broadly iconic, but that whereas the fictional world of novels is created out of words – and there is therefore a *symbolic* relationship between these words and the world they describe – the fictional world of plays is *shown* to the audience. To be rather more precise, what the audience is shown on the stage is an image or icon of the fictional world of the play. Indeed the very notion of acting is iconic, since it is an attempt by one person to resemble or imitate another. The dark-skinned actor in Venetian dress is an icon of Othello, the wooden scenery an icon of the citadel of Cyprus, the handkerchief probably a real handkerchief but also an icon of Desdemona's handkerchief. But the iconism does not end there, for it is a natural and inherent property of the objects in this fictional world not only to be visible but to be *heard* (Othello, like all human beings, makes sounds 'spontaneously' in the form of words and most, perhaps all, inanimate objects are audible if treated in certain ways): consequently the theatrical icons or images which 'show' them will be heard, too. In this sense, then, the principle of iconism and ostension applies to plays on the radio as well as on the stage because their speech and sounds are not simply indexes of the people and things that make them, they are a part of drama's broad resemblance to the world it represents. Nevertheless, while everything that we hear in a radio play is an act of ostension in that even if the only fully intelligible code is speech, that speech 'shows' the person or persons uttering it; not everything in the world it portrays is ostended. Those things which cannot directly reveal themselves through their own speech or sounds are merely transcodified from the visual medium to the symbolic, descriptive medium of words. But at this point it is important to remember that ostension is not absolute in the conventional theatre either: we must not make the mistake of assuming that because radio plays are forced to describe what they cannot ostend drama is free from all such necessity in theatre, film and television. Words are needed not only to explain the purely visual phenomena and ambiguous sounds of the former but also the images of the latter, for in our discussion of television news and OBs in Chapters 4 and 6 we saw that images often mean little by themselves. They may establish a great deal of the reality they portray, but are in themselves an incomplete guide to the causes, motives, attitudes and relationships which make that reality what it is. 'There is more to this than meets the eye' runs the cliché, fossilizing, as all clichés unfortunately do, the important truth it is meant to express; and the only accurate way to convey these 'invisible', or at any rate largely diachronic, factors is through words. If this were not true, the mime and the silent movie would be more prolific and expressive genres than they are, and the latter would never need its captions. Thus, while I argued in Chapter 3 that words are the primary code of radio because they are needed to contextualize all its other codes, it could equally be argued that words are the primary code in *all* the media – in theatre, film and television as well as in the more obvious case of books and newspapers.

But even things which could be ostended in the conventional theatre are often merely described, largely because the main concerns of the playwright lie elsewhere. Battles, for instance, are frequently ostended in Shakespeare's plays, but in Act 1 of *Macbeth* the battles which gain the hero his rewards from King Duncan, and as it were provide a background to the play proper, are merely described, though this is not of course to deny that the descriptions ostend those characters, the Sergeant and Ross, who provide them. Once again it might be helpful to review our assertions. Whereas literature conveys its world through description, the symbolic power of words, drama is characterized by ostension, by icons of its world which embrace not only images but sounds (including the sound of words) and may even extend to smell. But ostension is seldom if ever absolute in drama. Some element of description is almost invariably present, and the difference between conventional drama and radio drama is merely one of degree: in the former there is likely to be a greater proportion of ostension and in the latter a greater proportion of description. For this reason some of the contrasts drawn between the achievements of the two strike me as exaggerated. It is suggested, for instance, that because radio drama shows less and involves the imagination more, it can 'stage' a whole range of situations which are quite beyond the scope of conventional drama. Some situations are certainly beyond it, but not as many as might be assumed by those who are used to a diet of naturalistic plays; for not only is theatrical ostension limited in extent, but it is highly variable in form. A bridge, for instance, might be represented on-stage by an actual bridge or by a picture or cardboard cut-out of a bridge or by an actor on all fours. If the bridge is represented by a cut-out, a character in a play (a giant, perhaps) could carry it about the stage in a surreal fashion; if it is represented by an actor on all fours it could complain about those who walked across it or could instantaneously change into something else, a chair or a human being, and perhaps become part of a quite different scene. And as well as its powers of ostension, the devices of mime and verbal description make conventional drama equal to almost anything – underwater scenes, aerial battles, and so on. Pub and street theatre thrives, despite a lack of elaborate ostensive apparatus such as scenery, lighting and properties. Two actors on a bare stage might, with the aid of recorded traffic noises, convey the atmosphere of a crowded street simply by verbal references to such a street, by boarding, dodging or pointing to imaginary vehicles, being jostled by imaginary pedestrians, and so on. Indeed, in the case of mime, wherein an actor adjusts himself to an object which is invisible, for instance when he pretends to pick up and carry a pane of glass, it can be almost impossible to tell where ostension ends and our imagination begins. But as with mime, so with theatre in general – the 'reality' of what is actually ostended vouches for the reality of what has to be imagined. In *Macbeth* it is not only the behaviour of the Sergeant and Ross but the strength of the entire dramatic illusion presented to us through images and sounds which helps us to believe in the reality of those rebellious 'kerns and galloglasses' whom we never actually see or hear. In this respect, then, the drama which is ostended to us is an *index* of that other part of the fictional world which exists around and beyond it.

Given this varying blend of ostension and description, of showing and telling, in both radio drama and drama in the visual media, what can radio 'convey' (a conveniently vague term which, along with 'present', I shall henceforth use to embrace both processes) which the conventional theatre cannot? Since it can ostend much less than conventional drama it invokes the audience's imagination to a much greater extent, and this ratio of ostension to description, which is a direct consequence of its blindness, gives radio a number of advantages.

From Chapters 1 and 6 we can already infer the most obvious of these – the fact that we can picture the visual phenomena of the play very largely as we would like them to be rather than having to accept them as they are. In the theatre the spectator may picture what is happening, or is referred to, off-stage but what is ostended to her on-stage allows little scope for her imagination to work. She may speculate about the personal background or inner being of the characters before her, but she is not free to imagine their actual appearance, to invent a moustache for one or change the build of another. Something of this difficulty attaches even to those minimalist forms of theatre we have just been considering, in which the actors wear neutral attire, occupy a bare stage and render through mime and/or description every other visual phenomenon the play encompasses. Here, as we have seen, ostension and imagination may often be almost indistinguishable. When a character marches about the stage with a walking-stick resting on his shoulder, the spectator may furnish him with a soldier's uniform and rifle even as she watches him. But while she may *add* to what she sees she will not be able to 'abolish' it, to change the basic physique of that

145

character. In radio, however, we are free – forced – to imagine everything, even the actual dramatis personae who ostend themselves to us in sounds and words. However often we hear them, and in however much detail they are described, we will be required to picture them in our own way, together with further details of them which are *not* described. This is because words can never be as exhaustive or specific as a visual image (Scholes, 1982, 66) – which is another way of saying that images are dogmatic, reductive. The relatively peripheral, or at any rate superficial, role which is afforded to the imagination by the visual media seems to be behind that variously attributed saying 'Television is chewing gum for the eyes' – that is, watching is an insipid, purely physical activity that does not engage the higher faculties.

But what is also of interest about the comprehensive role of the listener's imagination in radio is that it abolishes the conventional distinction between the actors (who perform) and the audience (who sit apart and watch) because the words, delivered by the actors who are a vast distance away yet through the paradox of technology 'closer' to us than they would be to a theatre audience, invade each of us alone and in our own surroundings and force us to take over some of the functions which would be performed on-stage. They make *us* 'construct' the appearance and movements of a character as much as or more than the actor who plays it, force *us* to build the scenery instead of the stage carpenter. Hence stage and auditorium become fused and are located inside each listener's head. But as we are already well aware, there are as many potential realizations of the play as there are listeners and this, together with the fact that radio can accompany the listener wherever she goes, renders the play not so much an external event as the private and unique creation of each person who hears it. Within the generalities of language she can visualize the play as she likes it and carry it around with her; and this isolation from the rest of the audience, which we earlier noted as a handicap, is in this sense part of the advantage.

But radio is at an advantage over the theatre not merely because it affords a greater scope to the audience's imagination and an easier 'access' to its plays; it can convey settings and situations which the theatre can stage only with a certain amount of difficulty and is in this respect more closely akin to film. Since the action is almost entirely in the listener's head radio can emulate the film camera in choosing settings which are virtually beyond the scope of the stage (the hero of Louis MacNeice's radio play, *He Had a Date*, 1944, was a man drowning at sea) and in switching between these settings with great speed and emphasis. I suggested earlier, however, that it is possible to exaggerate the theatre's difficulties in establishing certain settings and instanced the way in which two actors on a bare stage might convey the impression of being in a busy street. Nevertheless the existence of two visible, palpable characters within a context of invisible and imaginary properties and scenery conquers the difficulty only in a somewhat stylized, artificial way which is likely to strain the audience's credulity. In sparing us from the need to see *anything* (though some aspects of the setting may be audible) radio can convey these situations rather more plausibly: if the voices are naturalistic we can assume everything else is. Indeed the liberation of the listener from the need to see is useful even when what we would see in the play would be entirely naturalistic and 'believable'. The conventional theatre may be primarily a 'spectacle' in that it must first of all give us something to look at, but in its need to convey non-visual matters there are times when its visuality is if not exactly a disadvantage at any rate an embarrassment of riches. In contrast, it could be argued that radio has actually added to the potential of drama by being able to focus on certain aspects of the play which would normally be overwhelmed by the visual dimension. One can take a simple example of this from the radio production of Raymond Briggs's *When the Wind Blows* (Radio 4, 1983), in which an elderly couple have just survived a nuclear attack. The husband checks various domestic appliances, the fridge and the television, for example, to see if they are working. He reports, 'Nothing – all dead' and is echoed by his wife, 'All dead?' However vividly she may picture this scene, the listener is free from the need to *watch* it and therefore attends more closely to the words, to the possible nuances of the repeated 'dead' (as well as the appliances, those people who 'power' them – the engineers, broadcasters, and so on, and even the entire human

147

and animal worlds), than she would if she were seeing the play in the theatre or on television. In this respect, then, 'Words, isolated in the velvet of radio, [take] on a jewelled particularity. Television has quite the opposite effect: words are drowned in the visual soup in which they are obliged to be served' (Raphael, 1980, 305). But the particularity of these words is even greater than if they were served up in a purely literary medium:

> When you have written for the page, you do not see your readers reading you; which is just as well as you could never tell if in their heads they were 'hearing' you properly. But in [sound] broadcasting you can, given the right speakers, force your listeners at least to hear the words as they should.
>
> (MacNeice, 1964, 13)

For these reasons radio is good at creating drama out of situations in which there is literally nothing to see – the thoughts or conflicts which take place within a single character, for instance. These must also, of course, be conveyed in the conventional theatre, where dramatists tend to resort to mono- logue during which the character is seen on stage either talking to himself or staying silent while his recorded voice is heard. But neither convention is wholly satisfactory, for in the former the inner debate seems to be improbably externalized and in the latter there is an equally improbable dissociation of the character from his thoughts; so that in both cases the attempt to make the audience concentrate more on the words than on the spectacle seems self-defeating. In the blindness of radio, however, the monologue is much more effective. Since an individual can scarcely exist outside the sound he makes there can be no misleading separation of a silent character from the recorded 'sound' of his thoughts as there can be in the theatre. This means, of course, that in radio monologue the character seems to be actually talking to himself just as he often does in a stage monologue. But given that it is improbable that anyone would conduct his internal debates in this external way, the improbability is rather less obvious on radio. We may *hear* the character talking to himself, but at least we do not have to *see* him doing so, and such is the tyranny of vision that the convention of a visible man using invisible properties and furniture seems a good deal more obtrusive than that of an invisible man voicing unheard thoughts. If the latter is on radio no more than a voice, which we are able to accept as an index of his entire character as it would be revealed to us on a conventional stage; if this voice must not only convey his words but suggest all his other physical attributes – his height, dress, colour of hair; our belief is hardly strained if it also becomes the instrument of his unspoken thoughts. In any event the listener will regard the unnaturalness of the monologue as a small price to pay for the opportunity it gives her to inhabit without visual distraction the subjective world of a character, just as she can when reading a novel. Indeed it has been pointed out that a radio dramatist like Louis MacNeice can present a character's mind by the daring expedient of splitting it into *different* voices (Gray, 1981, 52–3). The problems such a device would pose for the conventional stage seem well-nigh insuperable: one character talking in two or more voices would be at best baffling and at worst ludicrous, and if the different voices were to be taken by different actors it would be difficult to convey the impression that these were meant to represent different facets of a single character rather than two or more separate characters. Only radio, it seems, can exploit this device without difficulties of staging, for 'It is in the nature of radio to establish connections that do not exist in space: such connections are entirely aural and not in the least visual, since they depend on a contiguity of voices, not of speakers' (Lewis, 1981b, 103). Thus, in a memorable phrase used by Ronald Hayman during a broadcast talk about radio drama entitled *The Invisible Performance* (Radio 3, 1983), what radio is particularly adept at is the 'dramatization of consciousness' – a fact which renders the question of how it deals with spatial relationships, with those matters of kinesics and proxemics that are rightly seen as being central to conventional drama (Elam, 1980, 56), as at once simple and inappropriate. In naturalistic drama the listener can visualize them with ease, and in non-naturalistic drama they simply do not exist. It is for this reason that certain technological advances can actually limit radio's unique potential by introducing irrelevant spatial considerations –

by locating the characters in an arc from left to right, stereo in radio drama also deprives it of its special advantage as an immaterial medium not definitely located in space, able to move between dream and reality, the inner world of the mind and the outer world of concrete objects.

(Esslin, 1980, 184)

– and as a result of this technological advance radio drama has been criticized for a damaging tendency to become feebly iconic – 'sound cinema' – rather than exploiting its descriptive, symbolic powers (Raban, 1981, 83).

But radio is at an advantage over the visual media in being able to convey not only what we do not want to see because it all takes place in the mind but also what we do not want to see because while it may exist in the material world it is literally invisible. On one of the BBC's long-playing SFX records (no. 21, 'Death and Horror') there is a track entitled 'Premature Burial' which depicts someone being buried alive. The listener's 'viewpoint' is evidently inside the coffin with the victim. She hears the superterranean sounds of the graveyard – the rooks cawing, the knell, the parson reading the obsequies – growing ever more muffled and distant as the gravedigger plies the shovel and earth rains down on the lid. At the same time the victim's heartbeat recommences and the track concludes with his panic-stricken groans and frantic attempts to claw his way out. This is an impossible perspective for a theatre audience and a difficult one for film spectators, but the real point is that radio can use sound to convey that which takes place in utter darkness. The slightest attempt by a film-maker to illuminate the situation would reduce the horror it is meant to impart, for however physical and 'external' the victim's predicament may be, the dramatic stage is really located *inside* his head. It is worth recalling that darkness was the shrewd choice of setting for the first play to be written especially for radio, *A Comedy of Danger* (1924) by Richard Hughes: its subject is miners trapped in a coal-mine and its very first line, 'The lights have gone out', places the characters on a par with the audience. There are, of course, symbolic and effective ways in which the conventional theatre has attempted to present situations which are invisible or which take place in darkness, a notable example being Peter Shaffer's hilarious *Black Comedy*. Most of the play's action takes place during a power failure in someone's flat – a failure which is conveyed by flooding the stage with light. Conversely during the brief periods when the flat lights are working, the stage – and the audience – are plunged into darkness! But for most of the play the audience can see what the characters are doing while they are 'blind'. This device is an important, indeed an integral, part of the overall comedy, but like many good jokes it depends for its effect on its *in*appropriateness, its tacit admission that the one spectacle which the theatre finds it difficult to stage is the spectacle of darkness. Difficult, but not actually impossible. In theory it is possible to sit an audience in a blacked-out theatre and play it a recording of 'Premature Burial'. But in the conventional theatre, the audience's need to have something to look at is so paramount, so imperative, that it could not be expected to sit for any length of time in total darkness (just as the television audience cannot be expected to hear the news without seeing pictures). In effect, such a measure would make the theatrical environment redundant: the audience would really be 'listening to the radio' and it is precisely because there is no such pressure on radio to provide something to look at that it would make a poor joke out of *Black Comedy*.

But the dramatic advantages of radio do not end even here. It can convey not merely what we do not want to see because it would distract us from what is being said, and not merely what we do not want to see because although it belongs to the material world it is invisible. It can also convey what we do not want to see because although a part of the material world in the play it does not exist as such in the world of our experience. It is an objectified fantasy of the dramatist and if reduced to a finite visual image would be unintentionally absurd. In this case it would not be the theatrical conventions which would strain the audience's credulity but the subject matter itself. This is well illustrated by the drama critic David Wade, who instances a play called *On a Day in a Garden in Summer* (1975) in which the main characters are not humans but dock plants in a garden. Its author Don Haworth perceives the medium's advantage in these terms:

Obviously if you really thought about talking dock plants . . .
it would be like a comic cartoon. The thing in radio is the
value of the ambiguity of existence in this way; one is not
always confronted with a picture of a plant, one doesn't think
'Well, where are their eyes, then?' One doesn't examine the
naturalistic background, there isn't the embarrassing presence
of something that is not a human being taking the human role.
(cit. Wade, 1981b, 230)

As Wade goes on to say (ibid., 231) futuristic worlds, fairy
stories, allegories, legends, myths and space odysseys are all
liable to reduction by sight and therefore worlds of drama in
which radio holds a virtual monopoly.

Finally, and perhaps most importantly, radio can convey what
we do not wish to see because as a matter of dramatic necessity
we must remain uncertain about the exact status of its existence.
Does a person or thing continue to exist after it has been named
or heard? Does a character exist in the material world or merely
in the mind – as the figment of another character's imagination?
In these forms of drama silence has an important role to play
since radio endows it with a peculiar potency. In what respect?
Sounds, the very essence of radio, exist in time and constantly
evaporate. If they are not renewed silence imposes itself. This
also occurs in the theatre and cinema but is not important since
these media provide images which exist in space and which
therefore endure through both sounds and silences. In radio,
however, silence is visually unfilled and therefore absolute.
Much more than in the theatre or cinema it is a quality which is
noticed, heard, *listened* to. The difference is, or used to be, well
illustrated by radio programmes which preview new films by
featuring unedited excerpts from their soundtracks. To the
unseeing listener the pauses in the dialogue seem pointless and
interminable. Indeed, so threatening is silence to the radio
medium that if it persists for more than a few seconds the
listener rightly concludes that the station transmitter or her own
receiver has either broken down or been switched off.

But silence on the radio does not simply consist of audible
breaks in the sound-flow: there are also 'unheard' silences – for
instance, the failure of a character to contribute to an unbroken

dialogue even though his presence has previously been indicated. To counter the impression that he has departed or simply evaporated he must therefore be heard, referred to or addressed anew. In various ways, then, radio is positively besieged by silence – a silence which portends non-existence, annihilation. These nihilistic tendencies also remind us that the relationship between word and thing in radio is rather more complex than we have assumed. We have so far assumed that however variously we may picture it, an object exists simply by being named; but we should note that its existence is unlike that of physical objects since there is a sense in which it ceases to exist as soon as the naming is concluded. Nevertheless, this has its advantages: since radio's reality requires constant renewal, since it is susceptible to change and even annihilation, the medium is much better suited than the conventional theatre to the presentation of fluid, indeterminate worlds, especially those of absurdist drama. As Frances Gray points out (1981, 61–2) its lack of a consistent reality is itself absurd – a fact which abounds not only in absurdist but downright comic possibilities, as we shall see in the next chapter.

But even when radio presents a world which is internally stable and consistent, there may be things within that world whose ontological status is left deliberately ambiguous – and such ambiguity may also be suggested by heard or unheard silences. In Harold Pinter's play *A Slight Ache* (1959), one of the characters is the mysterious match-seller whom Edward and Flora ask into their home and to whom they open their hearts. He never speaks. Does he really exist, or have they invented him? This question is part of the play's *raison d'être* but is immediately and damagingly resolved if the play is staged or televised. In this function silence again challenges our previous assumption that word and thing are much the same by demonstrating that a thing does not exist in radio simply because it is named; or rather, what is named may exist not as reality but as make-believe. We are unable to check that everything exists on the same plane and that is why, as Ronald Hayman pointed out in *The Invisible Performance*, radio is so much better than theatre at conveying confusions between subjective and objective reality. Moreover, and as will also be apparent in the next chapter, there is comic potential in the idea not only that an object may last for no longer than it takes to describe it, but that even when it does the description might be unhelpful and even misleading.

By now it should be clear that radio can combine ostension and description in various ways to produce drama which is at least as eclectic as theatrical drama. It is capable of presenting naturalistic plays, psychological dramas whose action is largely internal and invisible, fantasies, and those blends of realism and fantasy which make up absurdist and surreal drama. Such eclecticism is an effect of various characteristics of the medium which suggest that radio drama bears at least as close a resemblance to imaginative literature as to the conventional theatre – a resemblance which has frequently been stressed (Lewis, 1981a, 8; Drakakis, 1981, 28; Raban, 1981, 81). It is worth reviewing some of the characteristics they have in common:

1 Both must rely on words since neither has visual images. Both involve the audience in a creative act by providing it with a 'text' from which its members make a complementary effort of imagination. The illusion is not externally preconstructed for them as it so largely is in theatre, film and television but internally realized by them: and because they are 'blind' media, both literature and radio can inhabit not only visible but also invisible worlds, whether subjective or material, and make rapid switches of focus in time and space between speech and thought, consciousness and dreams. (It is also worth nothing that the first ever radio play was written not by an established dramatist but by a novelist, Richard Hughes, whose theme – darkness – enshrined the novelist's perception that the imagination can 'see' where in a literal sense there is nothing to see.)

2 Both literature and radio drama address mass audiences, but whereas attendance at the theatre or cinema is a public, social experience, listening and reading are generally private, solitary experiences. The realization of the illusion and the judgement passed upon it are not only internal but also individual matters and to that extent may take an indefinite number of forms.

154

3 Both literature and radio drama are 'portable'. Books and radios are not in a fixed location like the theatre or cinema but may be carried around by the individual members of their audiences and so their worlds can be more effectively 'entered into'.

Important as they are, the resemblances must not be pressed too far, for radio drama has non-linguistic codes, too, and is therefore more 'fleshed out' than imaginative literature. As in the theatre, we can 'hear' the presence of the characters (as well as that of other phenomena) and as in the theatre, the combination of text and voice can be much more evocative than text alone. Moreover radio drama can achieve its effects more concisely than literature – for instance in its presentation of stream-of-consciousness, since whatever the subject thereof the voice and accent of the character who delivers it can convey his likely social position and previous history within a matter of moments (Rodger, 1982, 136–7).

It seems most appropriate to locate radio drama somewhere *between* imaginative literature and the conventional theatre. In the theatre the characters are presented both audibly and visibly; in literature the characters are neither visible as such nor audible, but must be realized in the audience's head. In radio drama the characters are audible but the audience must picture them, so that what radio succeeds in doing is to combine the realism or 'concreteness' of the former with the imaginative flexibility of the latter. But it is also important to guard against the notion that radio drama is simply the aggregate of literature and drama or that it is the mere adjunct of either. Certain of its effects are not to be found in books or theatres. It not only combines concreteness with imaginative flexibility but enhances these qualities by not making even the visual demand upon its audience that is made by the printed word. As a secondary medium accompanying its members while they are engaged in 'primary' activities it can therefore infiltrate their view of the world in a way which is all the more powerful for being only half-conscious:

As soon as we hear a word in a radio play, we are close to the experience it signifies; in fact the sound is literally inside us.

To submit to this kind of invasion, to allow another's picture of the universe to enter and undermine our own, is to become vulnerable in a way we do not when we watch a film or a play, where the alien world is demonstrably outside.

(Gray, 1981, 51)

This is attested by the gross 'framing' errors which frequently occur on the radio, with listeners sending flowers and wreaths to the studio after the death of a character in a soap opera. One such death – that of Grace Fairbrother in *The Archers* – completely upstaged the opening of ITV in September 1955 (A. Briggs, 1979, 1013–14). In the theatre such errors occur much less frequently since the conventionalized markers are much clearer (Elam, 1980, 89–90); nor, for the same reasons, are they common among readers of literature.

Suggestions for further work

Obtain the script of a stage play and choose a scene which could be adapted for radio, but which contains much important information that would primarily be conveyed to the audience by *visual* means. Rewrite the scene using transcodifiers which will convey this information as naturalistically as possible. Get your fellow students to act and record it, then find out how successful you have been by listening critically (preferably with your eyes shut!) or better still, playing it to an uninitiated audience.

8 COMEDY AND LIGHT ENTERTAINMENT

Seagoon Thank yuckakabakkas, we're still in time – first I must get these bonds untied – have you got a knot?

Crun Yes.

Seagoon Quick, glue one onto my bonds and then untie them.

Bill Listeners, as knot-glueing and untying has no audible sound we suggest you make your own – within reason, that is.

(*Goon Show*, no. 141, 'The Hastings Flyer')

There are two factors which would appear to militate against comedy on the radio. The first is that comedy is often thought of as predominantly *visual*, a matter of facial expressions, gestures, postures and other physical business, and radio lacks this visual dimension. The nearest it comes to comic business or physical humour is in its use of SFX, and as we have seen even these are ambiguous without verbal identification. The second factor is that listening to the radio is often a solitary activity, yet laughter is not the *normal* response of a solitary person. It is mostly a collective, social activity, and as we saw in our discussion of radio drama the isolated listener cannot look to the rest of the audience for guidance in, or confirmation of, his responses. Yet although the medium would seem to be an inherently unrewarding one, comedy has not only been hugely successful on the radio but also achieved its success in a wide variety of forms.

Historically the problem of audience response was resolved almost before it was recognized. In the days of valve wireless sets listeners tended to listen in groups, and were thus in a position to influence one another's reactions. Moreover in the early days of broadcasting, radio comedy, like radio drama, was seen very largely in terms of the conventional theatre, as the transmission of pre-existing art-forms rather than as a potential art-form in its own right. The first radio comedy shows therefore consisted of live relays from music halls in which the reactions of the theatre audience were audible – sometimes excessively so (A. Briggs, 1965, 85) – and which inevitably influenced the listeners. It is significant that in 1930, when the BBC had all but exhausted the available material in the commercial theatres and created its own studio-based 'music hall', it retained a live audience (Black, 1972, 58–9) – and the live audience (or at any rate, an audience which could be heard) remained a feature of radio comedy and light entertainment throughout their heyday. The theory was evidently that since comedy sets out to achieve a response which is vocal, that of laughter, the programme producer must prompt – one might even say, appropriate – the response of the remote and often solitary listener by means of separately recorded ('canned') laughter or the laughter of a live audience. This studio audience really becomes a kind of broker in the transaction between performers and listeners. It is the agent of the former in exploiting the imitative effects of laughter, in encouraging the listeners to feel that they are part of a large assembly and may therefore give vent to a public emotion. And if live, it is also the agent of the listeners in being able to bring the best out of the performers by influencing the timing and delivery of their material.

But whatever the theoretical role of the studio audience, its actual effect on both performers and listeners has been somewhat variable. Some listeners have felt not so much that it is their agent or representative as that they are overhearing a show which is being addressed to someone else, that the audience is part of an event from which they are largely excluded. In this case, then, the presence of the studio audience is counter-productive, and the sound of its laughter, especially when prompted by something seen rather than heard, is likely to confirm the listeners' sense that their responses are being pre-empted. The attitudes of performers to the studio audience have also varied. Benny Hill sees it almost as superseding that other, absent audience it is meant to represent. Although referring to television shows Hill's remarks are relevant in illustrating the comedian's need for an audible response even when he is actually performing for millions of people who exist 'elsewhere':

To a great extent I'm guided by the studio audience. You say you are doing it for the people at home, but you are swayed a lot by the people in the studio. If you get coach parties who go 'who-hoo' when you say 'knickers' and who don't laugh at something a little more subtle, you find you are going that way.   (cit. Nathan, 1971, 166)

John Cleese, however, has come to regard the studio audience as more of a hindrance, an irrelevance. In *I'm Sorry I'll Read That Again*, which ran through 103 shows in 8 series between 1965 and 1975, Cleese was a member of a cast who initially encouraged the live audience to hiss, boo and groan at various jokes. But in the end the cast was thrown by its boisterous desire for mere catch-lines and suggestive bits (Wilmut, 1980, 126–7). This experience doubtless influenced Cleese's attitude towards the studio audience of the television series *Monty Python's Flying Circus*:

We had a studio audience and were polite to it, but it was ignored. The incredible thing about a lot of television shows is that the directors are more concerned about the three hundred people in the studio than the ten million people watching. It stems from a lack of confidence and a belief that if you can make the studio audience laugh it is a successful show, no matter if it looks absolute rubbish on the box.
                                                   (cit. Nathan, 1971, 186)

Hill's and Cleese's attitudes together illustrate an ambivalence in broadcasting's approach to light entertainment which has been neatly summarized in terms of television:

Previous live entertainments . . . have been seen in special places – theatres, bars, and so on, with an audience. What was going on was going on in the same place as the audience – the stage, the platform were there in the room with you. Television in contrast is watched at home, with a few people, even alone, and what is going on is going on somewhere else, is merely being transmitted to you. It is this last point that is important in any consideration of television, for producers seem seldom able to make up their minds whether television is simply a means of broadcasting other material or is an artistic medium in its own right. (Dyer, 1973, 13)

In radio, at least, there have been two broad genres of comedy, which enshrine the two attitudes to the audience that I have just outlined. First of all there is the older genre in which the comedy is conceived largely in terms of what might loosely be called 'the traditional theatre', if not actually adapted or relayed from it. Such theatre is recognizable by its picture-frame stage and its depiction of settings by means of fairly elaborate scenery and accessories rather than the suggestive powers of actors using a bare set and simple props. Naturally the rate at which it can change these settings is relatively slow. It is theatre which we might broadly categorize as naturalistic, although it also provides space in front of its proscenium curtain for various 'non-dramatic' entertainers to perform their acts, such as comedians, singers and impressionists. In radio the genre is almost invariably characterized by the presence of a studio audience and implicitly regards the blindness of the medium as a negative quality to be minimized by a choice of settings which are naturalistic, or at any rate not outside the conventions of the traditional theatre. In contrast the newer genre sees comedy in terms of radio itself, regarding the blindness of the medium as a positive quality in its ability to liberate the listener's imagination. This means that the speed with which such comedy is performed and its settings changed, and the nature and scope of these settings, are of an order which transcends the conventions of the traditional theatre. On-stage, such comedy could at best be presented only in a stylized, impressionistic sort of way and in some cases could not be presented at all. Since it does not originate in the conventional theatre, it may not always be characterized by the presence of a studio audience. Indeed not only its early history but the entire development of radio comedy resembles that of radio drama, for in both the medium was perceived as being a means, despite its blindness, of relaying

160

conventional shows and plays to a wider audience and only subsequently as capable of creating, *because* of its blindness, forms which transcend those of the conventional theatre. And in radio comedy as in radio drama, the two broad genres co-exist to make for a surprisingly rich and diverse output.

Let us look at the older, more 'theatrical' genre first. One of its manifestations has been the telling of jokes and funny stories, which are the stock-in-trade of the 'stand-up' comic in the music hall and have always been effective on the radio since they are essentially verbal and can often succeed without visual reinforcement. This means that they are ubiquitous on the medium – frequently heard in shows that one would not regard as primarily 'comic'. But for many years they were the mainstay of such programmes as *Workers' Playtime*, a music and comedy variety show. Another manifestation of this genre is situation comedy ('sitcom'), which seems to be based on the music hall sketch or on forms of comic drama which exist in the 'straight' theatre. In this type of show the jokes and facetious dialogue, though plentiful, are of less interest in themselves than the characters and situations which they illuminate. It is conceived in terms of the traditional theatre and transplants fairly easily to television, using naturalistic settings and without requiring special technical effects. The most famous BBC radio sitcom was *Hancock's Half Hour*, which was brilliantly successful throughout its run in the late 1950s. But such shows can commute so easily between radio and television that it is sometimes hard to remember which they were first written for: as well as *Hancock's Half Hour*, *Steptoe and Son*, *Dad's Army* and more recently *Yes, Minister* are examples of sitcoms which have been successfully presented in both media.

The first hint that radio might be capable of a form of comedy which transcends traditional stage presentation came as early as 1939 with Tommy Handley's show, *ITMA*, an acronym of 'It's That Man Again'. Although *ITMA* was conceived on the traditional formula of jokes and comic patter, Handley instinctively exploited radio's qualities of sound and speed to produce something which could not be matched by the traditional theatre. The show's main prop was a door which was fitted with various locks, bars and bolts. The sound of its handle being turned indicated a character's arrival, a slam his departure. This was the idea of scriptwriter Ted Kavanagh and was particularly suited to radio since, as Peter Black points out (1972, 113), it allowed the characters to come and go with the speed of imagination. It is significant that even though *ITMA* was one of the most popular comedy shows in radio history the stage version of it, which was made with the same cast, failed because 'Slowed down to the speed at which characters could move about a stage, its verbal acrobatics lost the key qualities of surprise and pace' (Black, 1972, 112).

There is some evidence that the production team of *ITMA* were aware of themselves as pioneers. In his book on Tommy Handley, Kavanagh wrote

> My own idea of radio writing was an obvious one – it was to use sound for all it was worth, the sound of different voices and accents, the use of catchphrases, the impact of funny sounds in words, of grotesque effects to give atmosphere – every device to create the illusion of rather crazy or inverted reality   (cit. Took, 1976, 30)

and producer Francis Worsley's experiments with the live audience included dispensing with it altogether (Took, 1976, 25).

The newer, radiogenic form of comedy begun by *ITMA* was especially sensitive to the fact that word and thing are much the same on the radio, that its worlds can be created with the speed of utterance. To appreciate how it differs from the older, more theatrical genre one has only to compare the leisurely progress of *Hancock's Half Hour* with the rapid pace of *The Goon Show* or *I'm Sorry I'll Read That Again*. But it also recognizes the important difference which exists between visual and sound signs. The former are governed by the principle of permanence: unless they are changed they will persist. Sound signs are governed by the principle of change: unless renewed they will vanish. There is a conventional understanding in radio that although the signs vanish the things they signify will remain unless the nature of the subsequent signs indicates the contrary. But the evanescence of its signs means that radio can achieve not only pace, but easy and rapid changes of scene, just as for different reasons a film can: and it is not surprising that the newer, radiogenic kind of comedy should seize upon this potential and, indeed, show structural affinities to film. Whereas Tony Hancock often remained for the entire programme in the sitting-room of his house in East Cheam, the colourful yarns of *The Goon Show* took place in settings which succeeded one another without regard to the problems of time and distance; *Round the Horne* included quickfire imitations of romantic and science fiction movies; the various sketches of *I'm Sorry I'll Read That Again* were simultaneously changed and linked by the use of puns (Wilmut, 1980, 133); and the satirical *Week Ending* consists of a sequence of comic episodes which follow one another like the items of a film newsreel. *Week Ending* is also notable for its lack of a studio audience – an affirmation, despite the fact that laughter is commonly a social activity, of belief in the comic possibilities of the 'solitary' nature of the medium, or more precisely, in the ability of the listener to appreciate jokes without the need for audible prompting, just as the reader of a humorous novel can.

One comedy series which is highly radiogenic yet in a category all of its own is *The Goon Show*, which was written by Spike Milligan and broadcast between 1951 and 1960, and is probably the most original and popular comedy show in the history of radio. It must be said at once that much of the *Goon Show* humour would have been funny in any medium – a fact which is suggested by the eclectic nature of its origins. *ITMA* was clearly an important influence, but the others were largely literary: Lewis Carroll, Stephen Leacock, S. J. Perelman and Beachcomber (Black, 1972, 193). Aristophanes' satire has also been discerned and from the visual media, Hollywood cartoons, the Marx Brothers, and the quickfire patter of English music hall comedy (Wilmut, 1976, 99). Nevertheless the Goon shows are of especial interest to students of radio because they are uniquely aware of the specifically *comic* potential of the medium's transient and uncertain reality:

Their world shifts and changes. Objects appear when needed for a quick laugh:
Dr Londongle Silence – don't move, any of you, or I'll shoot.

Seagoon   Fool – put down that tin of potted shrimps.
Dr Londongle   And starve to death? Never.

They disappear with equal speed, for in this world nothing is certain, not even the body itself. 'How dare you come in here when I'm changing me knees?' snaps a Colosseum gladiator.

(Gray, 1981, 59)

What therefore distinguishes *The Goon Show* from other radiogenic comedies is that it uses the blindness of radio and the evanescence of its signs not just as a structural principle but as *part of the joke.* Taking the proposition that 'in Sound Radio we may go where we wish when we wish – all we have to do is to say so' (McWhinnie, 1959, 38), the Goons pushed it with great gusto to its logical, and absurd, conclusion: for if we can go to East Cheam merely by saying so, then why not to the South Pole, the moon, or even up somebody's trouser-leg? And if the laws of time and space can be flouted then why can't other physical laws? In 'Tales of Old Dartmoor', for instance, Neddy Seagoon, the governor of Dartmoor Prison, is persuaded to take the prison to France – and does so simply by loading it on to a horse-drawn cart. A few words like 'Gee up' and SFX of hooves and creaking axles enable us to picture the achievement with speed and ease. In 'The Dreaded Batter Pudding Hurler' Bloodnok and Seagoon attempt to save their sinking ship by loading it into one of its own lifeboats and then board another lifeboat, at the end of which is a gas-stove. Inside its oven is an iron staircase which Moriarty descends, singing. Hence *The Goon Show* creates its worlds through the symbolism of words just as movies create theirs through the iconism of images: but as we saw in the last chapter its achievement is not the merely descriptive one of literature, nor is it simply the narration of jokes and comic fantasies in the timeless fashion of the stand-up comedian: a substantial element of ostension is present, for the continual accompaniment of SFX suggests that its words refer to something 'actual', they confirm that a reality of sorts lies behind the language. The achievement has been usefully summarized thus:

The Goon Show . . . developed a form that set it off from any comparable undertaking, in that it used radio not as a makeshift or surrogate for the live, visual performance but as the authentic medium for an entertainment and for a humour whose effect lay entirely in language and its sound accompaniment. Conceived from the start in purely acoustic terms, it made its mark as 'really pure radio'. Grotesque and surrealistic as it was, it achieved so perfect a blend of language with the innate possibilities of radio that the listener, left to himself, would never regard the restriction to a single, acoustic medium as in any sense an impoverishment.

(Priessnitz, 1981, 36)

It has often been claimed that the Goons' tricks with physical laws are a unique form of humour, one which cannot be reproduced outside the radio medium, and it is certainly true that such tricks are beyond the scope of the live performance-media, whether theatre or television. It is also a claim made by the Goons themselves. When Major Bloodnok commands 'Eccles, stand on my shoulders and pull me up', Eccles replies 'I'd like to see them do this on television' (cit. Gray, 1981, 58). The reference is clearly to *live* television − or at any rate to television as a substitute for live theatre, without special technical effects and to which radio sitcom transfers so comfortably. But certain advances in video technology pertaining not only to graphics but also to the filming of natural objects, notably a technique known as colour separation overlay (CSO) which allows tricks with scale, now mean that almost none of *The Goon Show*'s jokes with the physical world would be beyond film or video realization of some sort. Indeed such jokes regularly occur in *The Kenny Everett Television Show*, no doubt largely because Everett is a great admirer of Goon humour. But they were achievable long before the invention of video by means of the animated cartoon, versions of which actually formed, as we have seen, part of the inspiration for *The Goon Show*; Spike Milligan apparently took the term 'goon' not from the description of their German guards by British prisoners of war but from a creature in a Popeye film (Nathan, 1971, 49). In almost all respects, then, vision can match the evocativeness of words and achieve the jokes performed on the radio, but it does of course remain true that radio has its own, inimitable way of realizing these jokes, or more precisely, gives each listener his own way, whereas the visual media can offer only single, finite, pre-emptive versions of them.

There remains, however, one comic effect created by words which does seem to be beyond the visual media, or at any rate which the latter could achieve only by making almost impossible demands on their audiences. Radio allows the Goons to assume Protean form. Usually of normal size Moriarty can, as we have seen, become small enough to descend a staircase inside the oven of a stove. At one moment a 'hairless midget', Neddy Seagoon might at another be enormous enough to be wearing trousers which afford total concealment to Eccles. All this, of course, can be achieved on film if not on 'live' visual media, but might still make it hard for an audience to recognize any principle of consistency within such characters. More significant is the fact that the characters may vary not only in their physique but also, within broad limits, their roles. Roger Wilmut makes the interesting point (1976, 81) that all the Goon shows operate at three levels. At the first level there are the actors, Spike Milligan, Harry Secombe, Peter Sellers; at the second level there are the stock characters they play, Eccles, Seagoon, Moriarty, and so on; and at the third level there are the ad hoc roles these characters adopt in the individual shows. In most of the shows Neddy Seagoon is an adventurous single young man in the mould of the hero of a boys' adventure story, but in 'The Gold Plate Robbery', for instance, he becomes Lord Seagoon with a wife, Lady Lavinia, and in 'Call of the West' Harry Seagoon, a movie actor, playing the part of Double Captain Rapture, a sharp-shooting cowboy. Depending on the story-lines of the various shows these roles range in time and setting from the colonial wars of the past to the science fiction of the future. The comic significance of all this lies in the irony which is generated between the various levels of the action. The story-lines of some of the individual shows may require the characters to behave as if they are meeting for the first time and do not recognize one another, but as Wilmut points out they often make asides which show that they really 'know' one another and are therefore only acting. In fact, the ironies resonate through *all* the levels, the frequent references to Seagoon's physical bulk being enriched by the audience's knowledge of Secombe's.

This multi-levelled action is not peculiar to the Goon shows: it is also discernible in other shows, such as *Ray's a Laugh* (Took, 1976, 94–5), but it does seem to be peculiar to radio. What is interesting is that whereas the listener's imagination is perfectly equal to such action, which combines for him the delights of familiarity with those of novelty, it seems almost impossible in the visual media, where its first two levels, which comprise the basic irony of dramatic impersonation – an actor disguised as a character and pretending to have no identity outside it, are so blatant, so insistent, that further levels of action and irony are likely only to confuse the spectator. How can the imagination be equal to something which the visual sense cannot comprehend? Its workings are strange and difficult if not impossible to chart, but we might venture to suggest that although we often imagine more details than are actually described to us, in a normal state of consciousness we never imagine as vividly as we can see. We thus arrive at the paradox that with fewer materials to work with – its characters present only as voices and in other respects immaterial – radio is able to convey a reality both more complex in itself and richer in comic possibilities than the visual media can. The world we can imagine and the world we can see are not equal in scope or intensity, a fact which recalls us to the significance of radio's blindness. Not surprisingly, it is a significance which the Goons were fully alert to, as is shown by Spike Milligan's frequent adoption of film themes for his story-lines; for these were not mere *imitations* of films but parodies of them – and parody relies for its effect not only on a resemblance to the original but also on a fundamental, and therefore ludicrous, dissimilarity. This is made obvious in a Goon show entitled 'Call of the West', a 'wonder ear film' in the idiom of the cowboy movie. The show begins in the style of a Hollywood trailer, combining the extravagant language of the narrator, played by Peter Sellers, with western 'Gun Law' music and 'sound clips' of the stars as they will appear in the action.

Peter   (OVER MUSIC) See, hear and smell hairless-midget Harry Seagoon as Double Captain Rapture, hard-riding, hard-shooting, hard up cowboy.

Seagoon   (KENSINGTON ACCENT) Hello you 'orny critters.
Peter   This role calls for great audience imagination. See,
     feel and hit, Spike Milligna [sic] as the dying actor.

(Milligan, 1974, 75)

Hence the joke which is fundamental to all *The Goon Show*'s
'film' stories lies in pretending that the radio medium is visual
when it is not – that radio can provide a spectacle which is as
literal and vivid as a film's. Of course the narrator's command
'See' is capable of a figurative sense, 'Imagine' – something
which we can and inevitably do: but its repeated collocation
with other verbs describing the primary senses 'hear – smell –
feel' suggests that it is the literal meaning which is dominant
here. Our imagination is invoked, but we are reminded above all
that we are insuperably blind.

Let us explore the significance of this blindness a little more
fully. We might begin by summarizing in semiotic terms the
conclusions we have reached so far. Blindness forces radio to
rely ultimately on a code or system of signs which are symbolic
– do not resemble what they represent. And the lack of
resemblance between the words and the things they represent
has strangely contrasting implications. On the one hand it means
that we are obliged to take the relationship between symbol (or
signifier) and signified, word and thing, on trust: and as a result
they tend to become closely identified on the radio. This is the
basis of its expressive or 'pictorial' power – of Donald
McWhinnie's confidence that 'we may go where we wish . . . all
we have to do is to say so'. But the lack of resemblance between
words and the things they represent means that these things can
never be as vividly realized as if they were represented by an
image. Yet this, as we have just seen, can actually *enhance* the
expressive power of the signs. It is precisely because the words
evoking the multi-levelled characterization of the Goon Shows
do *not* resemble it, as images would, that it is much easier for us
to comprehend and appreciate such characterization on the radio
than it would be on stage or screen. Likewise, in the last chapter
we noted various kinds of radio drama whose effectiveness
depends upon our being spared from the need to *see*, however
vividly we may imagine. Yet on the other hand the lack of

168

resemblance also means that the relationship between verbal signs and things is inherently looser and therefore a potentially uncertain one: as we saw in our discussion of *A Slight Ache* the fact that something is named on the radio is no guarantee that it exists. Hence the blindness of the medium is significant not only as the precondition of its pictorial power but as the means of preventing it; not only because it promotes a close correspondence between words and things but because it can subvert it. Once again, it is the Goons who exploit this negative function of the medium. I have been discussing radio as though its messages consisted only of symbols – words; but of course it is not a purely verbal medium, as literature is, it includes the indexical code of noises or SFX. Nevertheless I have stressed that words are the 'ultimate' or primary code of radio because as we saw in Chapters 3 and 7 the indexical relationship between noises and things is also an uncertain one and the uncertainty can be dispelled only by verbal clues – words. In radio we therefore run the risk of having obscure sounds interpreted for us by unreliable words. And in *The Goon Show* this is exactly what happens. The sound of clucking may lead us to infer the presence of a chicken, and then we may be told that what we are hearing is in fact a horse. But since we are aware that the relationship between words and things is itself dubious, merely a symbolic and arbitrary one, it is clear that however expressive or eloquent verbal and non-verbal sound–signs may be, their only ultimate corroboration is vision. The inadequacy of the medium is exposed and the listener teased for his blindness:

Seagoon   . . . Taxi!
F.X.   BAGPIPES, RUNNING DOWN
Spike   Yes?
Seagoon   The Bexhill Gas Works, and step on it.
Spike   Yes.
F.X.   BAGPIPES FADE OFF
Bill   Listeners may be puzzled by a taxi sounding like bagpipes. The truth is – it is all part of the BBC new economy campaign. They have discovered that it is cheaper to travel by bagpipes – not only are they more musical, but they come in a wide variety of colours. See your local

Bagpipe Offices and ask for particulars – you won't be disappointed.

('The Dreaded Batter Pudding Hurler', Milligan, 1972, 29–30)

Of course, jokes which subvert the relationship between signs and objects are by no means peculiar to radio: simply watching a play or film does not mean that we can see everything its words refer to, nor that they (or the words of a book) refer to everything in the conventional way. But such jokes are bound to have a fuller impact in a medium where blindness is an absolute quality and we can *never* see what the signs refer to, yet where there is the sound of people and of other physical phenomena which is never present in literature. This particular joke is a form of double bluff. What the listener assumes to be a taxi turns out to be bagpipes; but then the bagpipes do, indeed, possess the properties of a taxi. In fact the two objects are conflated so that the sound of bagpipes represents not conventional bagpipes at all but ones you can travel by, nor are these adequately conveyed by the term 'taxi'. Thus both index and symbol turn out to be inaccurate: the thing they purport to signify is neither recognizable bagpipes nor recognizable taxi. Such exotic conflations can be achieved not only by juxtaposing words and sounds, but merely by counterpointing words which signify objects with disparate or incompatible qualities. In an exchange which I quoted earlier as an example of signs and things being much the same, what is described as if it were a gun turns out to be a tin of potted shrimps.

Spike Milligan's alertness to the comic possibilities of subverting the conventional correspondence between sound-signs and objects is suggested not only by the jokes played on the listener but by those which are generated among the characters themselves:

Seagoon   (WHISPERS) Blast, it's Grytpype-Thynne. Leave this to me, I'm a brilliant impressionist. (CHICKEN CLUCKING)
Grytpype-Thynne   A horse? There's no horses in this fort.
Seagoon   (WHISPERS) (DOG HOWLING)
Grytpype-Thynne   There's no chickens either.

('The Gold Plate Robbery', Milligan, 1974, 137)

Sometimes such jokes are occasioned by a pun – one sign which refers to two possible objects. The listener is encouraged to understand it as referring to one object, only to discover that the other object is being signified:

Grams   SPLASH. SEAL BARK. BAGPIPES.
Seagoon   You imposter [sic], that's a seal. But why
    the bagpipes?
Moriarty   It's the Great Seal of Scotland.
                ('The Gold Plate Robbery', Milligan, 1974, 130)

The barking sound followed by Seagoon's remark leads us to interpret 'seal' as an amphibious mammal, and then the sound of bagpipes – here more a symbol of Scottishness than an index either of the mammal or of the imprinted wax disc – cues Moriarty's revelation about the true nature of the object. But the real point is that none of these sound–signs correspond to the 'reality' they represent, imprinted wax discs conventionally manifesting themselves neither through splashes, barks nor bagpipes.

Occasionally too, there are sounds which do not merely purport to signify things that do not normally manifest themselves in sound (like the Great Seal of Scotland); they are unrecognizable as sounds made by anything else.

Bill   It was the year 1907 and here is the orchestra
    to play it.
Orchestra   NEW MAD LINK ALL OVER THE SHOP. SINGING
    IN THE MIDDLE. SOUND F.X. IN MUSIC. FINISHES ON A CHORD.
                ('Battle of Spion Kop', Milligan, 1974, 21)

In all the Goon shows there is an absurd confidence that the acoustic medium is equal to everything.

The inevitable effect of this dissociation of the signs from the things they signify or represent is to *blot out* those things, to draw the listener's attention to the fact that the signs are *only* signs, that all is mere artifice. Applause cuts in and then ends abruptly instead of being faded up and down naturalistically. Often, SFX are shamelessly 'milked' – or speeded up and slowed down to remind us that they originate not in the world but on a gramophone turntable. Moreover the characters themselves often confuse signs with that which they represent.

> *Seagoon*   Bluebottle, you keep me covered with this photo-
> graph of a gun. Right – let's go in –
> *F.X.*   DOOR KICKED
> *Seagoon*   Hands up!
>
> ('The Hastings Flyer', Milligan, 1972, 169)

Their artificial nature is further emphasized by certain exaggerated claims which the characters make for them, for instance by alluding to SFX as if they were not only auditory but visual:

> *Bloodnok*   Wait! Great galloping crabs, look in the sky.
> *Grams*   HELICOPTER
> *Bloodnok*   It's a recording of a helicopter – saved!
>
> ('Napoleon's Piano', Milligan, 1972, 110)

Thus, although as we have seen elsewhere the SFX often confirm through their indexical role the 'reality' that words can only convey symbolically, they can also be used to confirm that the whole show is an invention – a bag of tricks. And this is true not only of sounds and photographs but of words. In purely verbal terms Bluebottle frequently makes the same mistake as Seagoon and Bloodnok by confusing his stage-instructions with the actions they describe:

> moves right – puts dreaded dynamite under signal box for safety – does not notice dreaded wires leading to plunger up in signal cabin. Thinks. I'm for the dreaded deading alright this week.
>
> ('The Hastings Flyer', Milligan, 1972, 169)

This is in the best tradition of clowning in its paradoxical impression of painful effort and insouciant ease. In an attempt to overcome the limitations of the medium and convey to us what we cannot see, Bluebottle involves himself in the most improbable dramatic irony, for he 'does not notice' the dreaded wires (comical enough since it is he who tells us he doesn't) and yet recognizes without doing anything to prevent it that he is in for the 'dreaded deading'. Yet there is a sense too of Bluebottle cutting straight through the Gordian knot: the limitations of the medium are magnificently ignored, and thus emphasized even as they are overcome. His achievement is at once fatuous and shrewd – fatuous because the actions he must perform require the visual ostension of the conventional theatre and this is not the conventional theatre but radio, which is blind; and shrewd because if Bluebottle *had* performed these soundless actions instead of describing them we would have remained utterly ignorant of them. Hence on the radio words assume a greater reality than the things they describe. There is a sense in which reality shrinks to the dimensions of the signs, not just because we can never see what the signs refer to (which is also the case in literature) but because the signs themselves are temporary, short-lived. We noted earlier that in their power to make rapid changes of scene the evanescence of words on the radio helped to evoke a dynamic and ever-changing world: but in another way it is a world which dwindles to the ephemeral nature of words and which has no existence outside them.

As we would expect, the Goons take this tendency to its logical, and ridiculous, conclusion. Not only are the signifieds reduced to the dimensions of the signifiers, but the artificial nature of the latter is further demonstrated by using signifiers which have no signifieds at all. *The Goon Show* is permeated with nonsense words – meaningless exclamations and strange noises. Though gibberish, many of them occur in sentences whose structure is conventional enough to remind us that they are still to be recognized as signifiers – ciphers to which, so arbitrary and artificial are signs in general, the listener may care to attach his own meanings:

> *Bill*   I'm sorry I'm late but the flinn of the flonn sclunned the nib of the Ploon.
>
>   ('The Scarlet Capsule', Milligan, 1974, 94)

The world has been reduced to symbols and these are nothing but noises – opaque and meaningless.

Thus we might summarize the achievement of the *Goon Show* by saying that whatever the themes of the individual shows (and they are many and various) it is fundamentally a joke about the possibilities and limitations of radio itself. It exploits our assumption that the correspondence of words (and sounds) to things will be a conventional one: and it does this partly by confirming it and partly by denying it; partly by activating the listener's imagination and partly by bumping him up against the blindness of the medium; partly by conceding that words are, indeed, things and partly by reminding us that they are sometimes mere signs. It uses the referential power of words and sounds to create full-blooded fantasies and further, to present levels of characterization and action which would be beyond our ability to assimilate visually: and it also uses the precondition of blindness to frustrate the imagination and reduce everything to noises and tricks. It could therefore be seen as combining the implicit recognition of radiogenic comedy that the medium can liberate the imagination with the older, more theatrical genre's awareness that since the listener is blind his imagination may be misled and ought therefore to be tied closely to his familiarity with the naturalistic conventions of the stage. In a word *The Goon Show* uses its jokes to explore and illustrate the nature of radio, and on the analogy of the literary critics' term 'metafiction' to describe novels which use the novel form itself to discuss or illustrate the nature of fiction (Waugh, 1984, 1–7), we might coin for it the term 'metaradio' – though with the caution that it is not strictly analogous to Jakobson's term 'metalingual'. It will be recalled from Chapter 3 that Jakobson defines as 'metalingual' statements or communications which pertain to *code* rather than to contact or medium, though these are, as we have seen, largely determined by the nature of the contact.

But however we define in terms of radio the self-consciousness of such as *The Goon Show*, it seems true to say that the success of any kind of comedy is bound up with the audience's sense of itself, and I would like to round off this discussion by returning to the listener's role in relation first to comedy and then to other forms of light entertainment. In realizing or 'registering' the joke the listener acquires some of the creative insight of its perpetrator, and this flatters him. It gives him a sense of who he is – of his abilities and values. Hence in making him laugh the comedy show invites the listener to see himself in a certain way and to identify with people of like mind. It has been pointed out that one technique of *The Goon Show* was to include just the punch-lines of lewd jokes (Wilmut, 1976, 78). Evidently the

174

purpose of this was not only to give the worldlier listeners a pleasurable reminder of the whole joke but also to imbue them with the sense of belonging to an exclusive group. Another comedy technique with a similar purpose, though by no means peculiar to the Goon shows or even to radio, was the regular inclusion of catchphrases: 'their power to fix a person in the mind's eye quickly made them an invaluable recognition signal, the aural equivalent of George Robey's eyebrows' (Black, 1972, 116). But they have a further significance for the audience:

> In a sketch in the first series [of *The Goon Show*] Milligan had propounded the theory that a catchphrase was simply a meaningless remark repeated until the audience was brainwashed into laughing at it. He illustrated this with a character opening a door, shouting 'More Coal!' and exiting again. It was demonstrated that on the first hearing, this was followed by dead silence; on the thousandth it was greeted by rapturous . . . applause. (Wilmut, 1976, 94)

The main function of such phrases is partly expressed by Peter Black: 'the secret of the catchphrase's appeal . . . remains, simply its easy availability. It put within everyone's reach, on a very simple level, the national vice of using quotations' (1972, 117). More precisely, the listener can use it as a kind of cultural badge or password – a means of establishing an identity of taste between himself and other listeners. Since, as Spike Milligan pointed out, the catchphrase is often intrinsically unfunny (Little Jim's exclamation 'He's fallen in the water!' is another which springs to mind) the studio audience's rapturous response to it must be particularly infuriating to the uninitiated listener; but it is not surprising that so many producers of comedy shows – even those in the newer, radiogenic style – should think it worth running the risk of alienating him by retaining the studio audience. In so narrowly conative a genre – where the object is to persuade the remote and isolated listener to laugh – there is a pressing need to represent him in the medium, to make his putative laughter audible within it. But even in comedy shows without a studio audience, the jokes imply a highly developed sense of who the listener is and thus give him a kind of presence on the medium which seems much more insistent than in other types of programme.

A similar effect is striven for in radio quiz games, which are almost invariably characterized by the inclusion of a studio audience. If the listener and the audience are given the answers to the questions, as they were in the long-running series *Twenty Questions*, they can then savour the panel's wit or stupidity as it tries to guess them. The pleasure here seems very similar, if not identical, to the voyeuristic pleasure of dramatic irony in the theatre, where the audience experiences a corporate sense of superiority or self-satisfaction through knowing what those involved in the action do not know. But in most quiz games, such as *My Word*, *My Music*, *The News Quiz*, *Top of the Form* and *Brain of Britain*, the answers are withheld from the listener and the studio audience, just as they are from the panel of contestants. This means that the sympathy between listener and audience is if anything greater than it is in comedy shows since the latter is never, as it sometimes is in comedy, in a privileged position: the contestants' efforts that the audience applauds are much more exclusively a matter of sound than the efforts of comedians to get laughs, and therefore more readily endorsed by the listener at home. But the listener's role is much less passive than in comedy because the challenge which the questions pose to his knowledge or intelligence seems much more insistent than that posed to his sense of humour by jokes. It is usually easier to understand jokes than to answer questions, but even more important to one's self-esteem to attempt the latter, though the satisfaction at having answered a question correctly seems analogous to that of 'getting' the joke. The difference, however, is that the 'star' performers of quiz games, the contestants, are not the perpetrators of the questions as the star performers of comedy shows are the perpetrators of the jokes; they are the *recipients*. This means that the listener identifies not with the studio audience but only with the panellists – which moves him vicariously to the centre of the action. And not only does he identify with them, he competes against them – which means that when he matches any of their performances he is logically if not actually as much the object of the studio applause as they are. All this gives him not just a heightened sense of his identity and abilities *vis-à-vis* the studio audience and performers, as it does in comedy shows, but a greater involvement in the action – a sense of himself as *participant*, performer.

Certain other forms of light entertainment on the radio, such as music request programmes and 'meet the people' shows, give the listener even more of a presence on the medium by taking him, or at any rate the 'common people' of whom he is one, as part of their actual theme. The titles of such programmes, which date from the height of radio's popularity, reflect their concern with a homely, workaday world outside the rarefied atmosphere of the radio station – *FAMILY Favourites*, *HOUSEWIVES' Choice*, *Down YOUR Way*, and so on. In music request programmes the object is not simply to play music which the requester/dedicatee likes (most such listeners can play their own on a domestic gramophone or cassette player), but to *associate* him with it by naming him on the air. By this means he and all the other listeners who are potential requesters/dedicatees can feel a personal stake in the station's output, a sense that it is not the preserve of professional broadcasters. Gaining a similar effect by different means are the inexhaustible *Down Your Way*, in which Brian Johnston visits small communities, interviews their members about their lives and jobs, and plays their favourite music; and Wilfred Pickles' famous *Have a Go*, which in 1947 commanded an audience of 12 million and travelled around the country ostensibly as a quiz game involving local people but really as a way of capturing the vitality of ordinary folk (Black, 1972, 179–81). The show's epigraph, as announced every week by Pickles, was 'to bring the people to the people' – and before the advent of the instantaneous phone-in it was probably the most effective way in which radio could give the impression of being a two-way medium – accessible to, and vitalized by, its audiences. It is time to look at these audiences in more detail – their requirements and the potentially active and passive nature of their roles.

Suggestions for further work

1 Write a short comedy sketch, or two or three pages of

177

dialogue consisting of not only jokes but also a humorous situation and characters, in order to see if it is possible to be funny without benefit of visual cues or of comic business other than that which is audible. (One useful approach might be to parody a radio advert or well-known programme.) Can you use the medium itself as part of the joke? Be warned that dialogue often 'feels' hilarious when you are recording it but may sound less funny when played back: so play your recording to an objective audience and pay even closer attention to their reactions *while* they are listening than to the comments they make afterwards.

2 Write a critical commentary on, or analysis of, a radio quiz game such as *The News Quiz* or *My Music*. The absence of a distracting visual dimension may enable you to concentrate on the following questions: What assumptions do these games make about the knowledge and intelligence of the panellists? Even more important, what assumptions do they make about the knowledge and intelligence of the listener? How far do they reflect and foster the widespread belief that knowledge has no value other than as a commodity or status symbol? How far does the entertainment that the listener derives from these games depend on his own ability to answer the questions, how far on other factors? Finally, and more broadly, is there such a thing as 'pure' entertainment – or in order to entertain must the entertainers always be doing something else, too?

PART FOUR
THE LISTENER

9 PHONE-INS

> That the man in the street should have anything vital to
> contribute to broadcasting was an idea slow to gain
> acceptance. That he should actually use broadcasting to
> express his own opinions in his own unvarnished
> words, was regarded as almost the end of all good social
> order.
>
> (D. G. Bridson, *Prospero and Ariel*)

It was suggested at the end of Chapter 3 that the purpose of the
phone-in is to attempt the ultimately impossible feat of
providing feedback for the audience, and that its dominant
function is therefore phatic and metalingual. It creates the
illusion of radio as a two-way medium and is concerned to
verify that the station or channel has an audience and that this
audience is capable of understanding and responding to the
message which the station transmits. Nevertheless it has to be
added that this function may not always be self-evident. Let us
imagine a phone-in which includes a call from a mother who is
tempted to batter her baby. Her call produces an immediate
response from a social worker who may be a studio guest or the
next telephone caller and an on-air discussion ensues during
which the mother's problem is solved. In this case the station has
been acting as a switchboard. For the mother it provided a way
of getting something done, and as a result she and the other
callers and listeners may regard the station as a genuine welfare
agency. But however happy it may be to be regarded in this
light, the station's prior concern is that when it has a phone-in
on this or on no particular topic its audience will declare its
presence and understanding by, in a corporate sense, making
itself heard on the medium. If the solution of the mother's
problem maintains or increases audience responsiveness, well
and good: but it is only the means to what is purely a radiogenic
end.

Broadcasters have always been at pains to give themselves and their listeners a sense of the latter's presence on the medium, and we saw in the last chapter that this is an important function of much radio light entertainment. A considerable amount of language on the radio is phatic in its intention and, generally speaking, the less formal the style of presentation the more openly that intention can be declared: 'We can't go over to Roker Park now, but we'll bring you that report later in the programme, OK?' Since this language involves an element of pretence or make-believe – that the listener is capable of direct and audible feedback – it is particularly appropriate to light entertainment. Disc-jockeys presenting programmes for an audience consisting largely of isolated housewives use a flirtatious direct address which implies that they are talking only to a single listener and that she is visible and making an audible response. 'How are you? You're looking nice today.' The Radio 1 disc-jockey, Steve Wright, takes the process a stage further in his afternoon programme: when he reads out sensational items from the newspapers he plays in the reactions of recorded voices, 'Ooh! Wow!', which are evidently meant to represent those of his listeners. But this is merely a comic illustration of a need which is imperative in all broadcasting – to remind the broadcaster that he has an audience, even though he cannot see or hear it, and to encourage that audience to keep listening. Even the announcer's or presenter's initial greeting 'Good morning' is an expression of this need. As Erving Goffman points out, the broadcaster must talk *as if* responsive people were before his eyes and ears. He must be 'response-constructive', which might extend to inventing dialogue in which he either pauses for the listener's putative reply or conducts both sides of the conversation, one side in a disguised voice to represent that of the listener. But 'In both cases the timing characteristics of dialogue are simulated' (Goffman, 1981, 241).

The phone-in was regarded as such a major development in broadcasting because for the first time it gave the viewer or listener a presence on the medium which was *audible* – not as the result of his having a letter read out on the air or going into a studio or attending an outside broadcast in his neighbourhood, but spontaneously and away from broadcasting equipment, in his own home or local telephone box or at his place of work. Paulu (1981, 219) implies that its origins are American, but in this country it was the brain-child of a BBC staff member named Walter Wallich and first heard in 1970 on a Radio 4 programme which was presented by Robin Day and entitled *It's Your Line*. It was also taken up by television, but the phone-in has been especially important to radio because as we are well aware the radio message differs from that of television in being entirely invisible and thus more easily disattended or misunderstood. This means that its phatic and metalingual needs are particularly pressing. Phone-ins on television are fairly infrequent, partly no doubt because there is nothing to fill the eye while the caller is speaking; but they are ubiquitous on the radio – not uncommonly as programmes in their own right and even more often as an element in other programmes – 'chat' or record shows, for example. It therefore seems no exaggeration to say that the phone-in is highly radiogenic – peculiarly suited to the medium.

We began by looking at the function which the phone-in has for the broadcaster, a function which we have regarded as the dominant one in view of the fact that it is the broadcaster who *initiates* the communication act; but it is also important to consider its function for the caller. It is complementary to that of the broadcaster, an opportunity to influence the radio 'text' or message by making an actual contribution to it. The caller may avail himself of the phone-in to make suggestions about the station's output or to voice criticisms of it: but even when he wishes to discuss something quite unrelated to the radio station or merely phones in to advertise or bid for goods in a 'swap shop', he modifies its output merely by his presence on the medium. As far as the caller is concerned, then, we might broadly define the function of the phone-in as being 'emotive' in Jakobson's sense of the term – concerned to reveal one's own personality and interests – and perhaps conative too, a means of influencing others; and this overall function seems to assume one or other of three main forms which shade into one another but which I shall nevertheless distinguish as the *expressive*, the *exhibitionist* and the *confessional*.

In the expressive phone-in the caller's purpose is to air his views on some issue or topic, and if the caller so wishes it gives him 'for the first time some chance of challenging the power of the media men and interested parties to impose their view of events on the community at large' (Evans, 1977, 56). Using the graphic Australian term 'talk-back' Higgins and Moss describe the significance of this type of phone-in in rather more formidable terms: it is 'a counter-hegemonic discourse phenomenon – as it is one of the few ways people can find to give public expression to private and perhaps dissonant viewpoints in a culture otherwise saturated with approved meanings' (1982, 1). Other media analysts take a similar view: such phone-ins 'represent an attempt to accommodate the mounting pressure from excluded and under-represented groups for greater access to scarce communications facilities' (Murdock and Golding, 1977, 38). In the terms of our own discussion of radio we might describe this type of phone-in as an opportunity for the listener to counter, if he wishes, the 'bardic' tendencies of the medium. As was pointed out in Chapters 3 and 4, radio language has to be relatively simple because of the nature of the medium: but of course the use of relatively simple language does not always imply an inability to extend ideas and knowledge – a fact confirmed by much spoken output on Radios 3 and 4 and in educational broadcasting. Nevertheless, as a mass medium with audiences which are highly heterogeneous in terms of background, education and taste, radio frequently succumbs to a tendency to rehearse the conventional or collective wisdom. The expressive phone-in gives the listener of minority or unorthodox views a chance to challenge or modify that wisdom in language which is spontaneously oral, and therefore likely to be fairly intelligible to the other listeners.

Two further points are worth making with respect to the expressive phone-in. The first is that since the arrival of television, politicians have largely abandoned the hustings and availed themselves of its influence to address the people in such a way that they cannot be questioned or criticized. Television, then, has enhanced their rhetorical powers and, which is much the same thing, protected them from direct and immediate feedback. But it could be said that the phone-in has partly rectified this situation: it is a challenge which no electioneering politician can afford to ignore – and yet it is a way of putting him back on the hustings by forcing him to face objections to his own arguments. The second point is that although the phone-in originated on network radio it is most prevalent in local radio, an important reason for which seems to be that the caller regards himself as having to compete with fewer other callers to gain access to the medium and as having a better chance in his neighbourhood than nationally of influencing opinion to get things done. In this sense the phone-in would seem to be a happy adjunct to local radio because it has been suggested that the latter was in the first place a general institutional attempt to make the medium two-way (Smith, 1974, 151).

The exhibitionist phone-in is one in which the caller's aim is not so much to vent his opinions on a particular topic as to project his personality, to become a performer. The programme presenter – on this occasion less a chairperson than a controller of ceremonies – encourages the caller to tell jokes, sing songs, or simply talk about himself and his interests. In a phone-in quiz the caller is invited to answer questions, perhaps in competition with other callers, and for the audience at large the object is simply entertainment, sometimes of an unscheduled sort where the caller behaves in an exhibitionist fashion even when there is nothing in the manner of the presenter or the nature of the programme to encourage him to do so.

The third type of phone-in might be described as confessional, in which the caller's primary aim is to express his individual needs or problems. He 'confides' – tells his troubles or behaves like a patient, and the role of the presenter and/or her studio guest(s) is correspondingly that of therapist, confessor, confidante or counsellor. The mixture of invisibility and companionship which radio provides (see Chapters 1 and 6) – a mixture which is even more potent than in television, where the presenter, at least, can be seen – is of particular significance to the phone-in, and one should not be surprised that it is so often confessional in nature. The caller can regard the presenter as an invisible friend, someone whom he can hear and talk to without the embarrassment of visual confrontation, and it is possible to regard not only confessional but also all types of phone-in as therapeutic in their effects. When the caller wishes to air his views or to reveal his personality even more directly the presenter, heard but not seen, facilitates this act of self-exposure before an audience which is (happily) both *un*heard and *un*seen. Indeed it is possible to discern a therapeutic function not only in phone-ins but in all kinds of sound broadcasting. Invisible herself, the broadcaster must in some respects find it easier to communicate with an unseen and unheard audience than with those whom she knows personally – and it might not be too far-fetched to evolve a pathological theory of the effective broadcaster as the innocuous, socially acceptable version of the anonymous phone-caller. What is certainly true is that many popular broadcasters are shy introverts whose personalities seem to be transformed by the presence of a live microphone. But to return to the phone-in: while it is true that its basic function is phatic and therefore that the callers are members of the audience in the broadest sense of that term (for even a caller who is not a regular listener to the station must, at however many removes, be a recipient of its message to know that the phone-in exists), there are many other members of the audience who are 'present' at the phone-in but only in the silent, passive role of listeners, and it is important to examine its function for them.

The listeners' attitude to the caller would appear to be a profoundly ambivalent one. In the first place there is a strong sense of identification. The telephone acoustic proclaims that he is 'one of them', a member of the audience challenging the monopoly of the professional broadcasters. The 'voices' elsewhere in radio are there because in some way *accredited* – the eyewitness, the celebrity, the expert, the person in the news. In the phone-in the caller is on the air as a result of nothing more than picking up a handset and dialling a number and he is in this sense representative of the listener, irrespective of whether the latter sympathizes with him or with his views. Thus in a curious way the medium is inverted – turned inside out. The audience members become the broadcasters: they are, as it were, enabled to reflect themselves. For the individual who is merely listening to the phone-in there is not only the likely and conventional pleasure of hearing a discussion – what Higgins and Moss describe as 'argument as theatre' (1982, 117) – but an impression, however misleading, created by those phoning in of innumerable *other* listeners who approximate to the community at large. The title of the BBC's phone-in, *Voice of the People* (Radio 4), was evidently meant to confirm this impression of breadth and representativeness. More recently the network has gone even further and joined with the World Service to present an international phone-in entitled *It's Your World*: but as we have just seen the phone-in is particularly popular in local radio, where audiences often have a more tangible sense of communal values and are enabled to respond to and influence developments in their immediate neighbourhood.

But the radio phone-in also exerts a contrary effect upon the listener – one which distinguishes it from its television counterpart. On television the distinction between callers and 'official' broadcasters remains clear-cut and the continued ascendancy of the latter is proclaimed by the fact that they can be seen while the callers can not. In the radio phone-in there is, despite the difference in acoustic between telephonic and studio voices, a substantially greater sense of parity between callers and broadcasters. Noting in a *Sunday Times* article that 'radio has many strengths beyond the power of television' Alan Brien instanced the phone-in as providing 'a direct, intimate, practical kind of "access" which . . . camera-dominated studio confrontations can never match. A discussion between public and pundits gains when both are equally invisible' (cit. Evans, 1977, 57). Hence, because *all* the parties in the phone-in are invisible there is the paradox that however 'unaccredited' the caller may be, he acquires a kind of authoritativeness merely by being on the air, he becomes a broadcaster, a performer, on a par with those in the studio. But this inevitably creates a feeling of detachment in the listener, the apartness that he normally feels when listening to a discussion between 'professional' broadcasters. In this respect his role is like that of the eavesdropper, and his sense of this is sharpened by the telephone acoustic, which, combined with the frequently confessional nature of the discussion, gives him the powerful impression of listening in on a crossed line, of overhearing words which are being addressed to someone else. Indeed an indication of how near the phone-in comes to being a private medium is the fact that if it encounters a crossed line the radio station must immediately ring off, since under the terms of the Wireless and Post Office Telegraphy Act it is illegal to listen in to a private telephone conversation. Something else which often occurs in a phone-in is that a caller who reveals a problem is immediately followed by another caller who can help him – a social worker or clergyman, perhaps – and the station will then connect them on the air. The listener thus finds himself listening in to a discussion which is *entirely* conducted in a telephone acoustic. All this makes him a bit like the aural equivalent of the voyeur, and we are again reminded of the effect of dramatic irony in the theatre except that the caller is a performer with even less sense of his audience than he would have on a stage or before a microphone; for he is not in a studio but on a private medium, the telephone, and the listener complements his pretence of talking to just one person but in fact wishing to reveal himself to a mass audience, by a kind of pretended absence – by giving no hint of his awareness of the discussion but by listening in all the same. Thus the phone-in is capable of unique effects within radio, for it is a half-private, half-public medium in which one element of the audience becomes part of the performance and involved in a complex and unusual relationship with the remaining element.

The presence of two 'audiences' makes the role of the third party in the phone-in, the presenter, an equally complex and shifting one, and it is not altogether surprising that some presenters concentrate on one at the expense of the other, for practical purposes regarding either the callers or the listeners as their 'target' audience. Phone-ins which concentrate on the caller are often virtually unmediated by the presenter and without an agenda: the callers simply phone in to discuss almost any subject they wish and within broad limits the presenter allows them to say what they like. The listeners to such phone-ins are important to the extent that they are able to hear what is being said, but as far as the presenter and the station are concerned whatever interest it may have for them is incidental, or at any rate secondary, to the purpose of publicizing the phone-in facility to would-be callers. Nevertheless, relatively few stations will conduct phone-ins which are so completely indifferent to their listeners' needs, if only because it is from the ranks of these listeners that their future callers must come. At the other extreme, phone-ins which concentrate on the listener are usually based on a firm theme or agenda and highly mediated by the presenter. The caller is still, of course, their *raison d'être*, but once he is on the line and the station has demonstrated to itself and to the outside world the physical fact that it has an audience, the presenter will concentrate on fulfilling the needs of that unheard but larger and therefore more important section of the audience who are listening. The presenter of this type of phone-in is normally distinguished by presence of mind, wit, articulacy and a readiness to 'squash' the caller as soon as he ceases to be interesting, and the calculation is that the listener will be satisfied wherever his sympathies lie. If they lie with the presenter and /or if he is primarily interested in the theme under discussion he will be pleased by the 'extinction' of the caller, and if they lie with the caller he will 'love to hate' the presenter and continue to listen in the hope that a subsequent caller will get the better of her. But phone-ins of this sort do run some risk of deterring callers and even alienating the listeners.

As we might expect, the great majority of phone-ins are conducted by a presenter who provides at least 'the semblance of personal interaction with the caller, yet at the same time uses the medium to entertain the wider listening audience' (Higgins and Moss, 1982, 19). She tries to balance her duty to the individual caller, who needs to have his say, with her duty to the listeners at large, who need to hear something of interest. The task is a difficult one, especially in phone-ins of a confessional nature. As McLeish puts it (1978, 142–3), how far are private and individual problems of general interest? And in what circum-stances do they transcend that interest? Conversely is it proper, even with the implied assent of the caller, to exploit private problems for public entertainment? Sometimes the presenter may be required to silence not only the boring or offensive caller for the sake of the listeners, but also the rashly self-revealing caller for his *own* sake – even when what he says may be of immense fascination to the listeners. Such questions properly belong to the realm of professional ethics rather than media analysis, but it is worth repeating that if we discount any studio guests, who are in any case somewhat peripheral to the phone-in itself, the interests that the presenter must balance lie entirely within the audience and not partly with the audience and partly with a separate category of 'official' broadcasters.

We can conclude by suggesting that the phone-in is of importance to the student of radio in three main respects. First it represents a synthesis of private and public media since it is an individual 'point to point' mode of communication which is overheard by a mass audience of indeterminate size. Indeed it could be seen as an advance towards that elusive goal, 'access' radio, since it makes the medium at once a private channel of expression and a public forum. Secondly the phone-in represents a kind of inversion of the radio medium. The programme is *about* its audience, which in a way and to an extent otherwise unknown in the medium gains a sense of itself as a varied yet corporate entity, the 'consumers' of the radio message who are both separate from, yet on a par with, the 'professionals' – the broadcasters, pundits and personalities. And thirdly the phone-in demonstrates that the radio audience can use the medium in many different ways, some active and some passive, and that the relationship between callers and listeners is a complex and varying one. We must now look at one or two of the ways in which this audience and its uses of the medium may be more closely analysed, and at some of the problems which such analysis faces.

Suggestions for further work

Listen to several callers from as wide a range of network and LR phone-ins as you can. Are the phone-ins 'free-for-alls'? If not, can you detect the principles according to which the callers are selected? Are they chosen to provide a balance of opinions, genders, social backgrounds, and so on? What can you infer about the callers' motives in phoning in? Make a preliminary grouping of the callers according to the expressive /exhibitionist / confessional classification I have offered above. You may soon find it too narrow for the range of callers you hear, or too broad for the finer distinctions you perceive between them. Can you therefore classify them in more useful ways?

10 AUDIENCES

> Oh! Oh! You radio!
> Oh! what I owe to you my radio:
> I listen in and you dispel the gloom,
> For you bring all the stars into my room;
> Oh! Oh! You radio!
> You're the most entertaining friend I know,
> You give me music, dancing, joys I never knew
> Oh! radio I'm radiating thanks to you.
>
> (Theme song of Radiolympia Exhibition, 1936)

'Audience studies' is a subject rich in questions and well-nigh barren of answers. Its methodological difficulties are huge, and as I hope to show later on, they are in some respects greater in the case of radio than television. This fact makes the subject demoralizing for many of its students and even, for some of its critics, somewhat disreputable.

Let us take a look at its difficulties. Those of definition and relevance seem truly overwhelming. When we discuss the question of the influences which the media exert, what do we mean by an 'influence' and how can we measure it scientifically? In considering the viewer or listener who may or may not be affected by the influence, what factors in her character and background (psychological, economic, environmental, and so on) are relevant and to what extent? How far can the audience researcher take for granted her powers of self-knowledge and/or self-expression? If two listeners approve of a programme, one because she 'enjoyed' it, the other because it was 'interesting', are they expressing different reactions or merely the same reaction in two different ways? And if the latter, is that reaction felt in equal measure by both?

An inevitable consequence of these difficulties is that researchers' findings often contradict one another. Rosengren (1974, 282)

191

cites two investigations of soap operas – one blaming them for reducing the listener's social and environmental awareness, the other commending them for increasing it. Another consequence is that many are inconclusive. Researchers cannot, apparently, show a clear correlation between the amount of exposure to the media and the extent of their influence (Golding, 1974, 11), or demonstrate whether the media have effects upon society or are themselves social products or effects (McQuail, 1983, 176–8). And a third consequence is that many findings would seem to be perverse – at odds with the promptings of what we loosely term 'instinct' or 'common sense'. For instance the fact that all societies impose at least some restrictions on the showing of violence on television suggests that for most of us there is a self-evident connection between violence on television and violence performed in real life. Yet audience research has failed to demonstrate such a connection and in some instances even impugned it. On the other hand when research findings do conform to common sense they seem to be redundant – little more than statements of the obvious. When the Yale Communication Research Program found that 'Low-credibility sources were seen as more biased and more unfair than were high-credibility sources' (Lowery and De Fleur, 1983, 172), scientific observation was no longer distinguishable from banality and tautology. Whether it reaches or fails to reach conclusions, then, audience research gives the impression of applying scientific methods to a subject which is not suitable to them and has therefore been attacked for its use of 'scientism' and its naïvely quantitative approach (Smythe, 1972, 20–1; Burgelin, 1972, 324). The broad effect of these difficulties has been described thus:

> Research findings have too often seemed negative or slight in importance, there has been little development of theory, and the accumulation of general findings has seemed slow and inadequate. The initial excitement of trying to discover the 'effects' of the new communications media gave way to a growing realization of the conceptual and methodological complexity of such an enterprise. The process was educative, but to some, depressing. (McQuail, 1972, 11)

What have been the main areas of audience study? These have been usefully summarized by McQuail (1983, 149):

1 To what extent is the audience a social group?
2 How much and what sort of activity do audiences indulge in?
3 What forces contribute to the formation of audiences?
4 How far do the media manipulate, and how far respond to, their audiences?

But its initial concern must be to *analyse* the audience: in radio terms, to discover how many are listening and what their social identity is. Yet even so simple and numerical an objective as the first one hides another complex question: what constitutes a listener?

Someone who owns, or has access to, a radio set?
Someone who listens to a whole programme?
Someone who listens to a minimum proportion of a programme (say, 50 per cent)?
Someone who listens for a minimum amount of time in the day (say, half an hour)?
Someone who listens for several hours a day but whose listening span corresponds to no complete programme, possibly because she switches between stations?

The question of audience size is further complicated by the practice of off-air recording – cassetting or 'time-shift' listening – which means that the number listening at the time of transmission will not amount to the total audience, not only because some members of that audience may listen at another time but also because some of them may listen to the transmission *several times over*. This must be particularly true of the many who illegally record pop music from the radio in order to listen repeatedly to the hit records they would otherwise have to buy.

To meet some of these difficulties the BBC's Broadcasting Research Department has found it useful to adopt more than one concept of the audience: there is the 'average' audience for a programme's duration; 'reach', the number of people who listen to at least a part of, for instance, a sequence programme such as *Today*; and the 'core' audience which stays with the entire programme (*BBC Annual Report and Handbook 1984*, 1983, 42).

Once it has been decided which concept of the audience to adopt and the number of listeners to any given programme computed, the question of their social identity may seem easier to determine. But this social identity may also be defined in several different ways – by age, gender, racial or political composition – according to the purposes of those with a professional interest in audiences, and the more useful ways are outlined by McQuail (1983, 150–5), among them the following:

1 The audience as a mass (cf. also Freidson, 1971, 199). This focuses on its overall size, its heterogeneity, anonymity, lack of social cohesion and geographical dispersion. Foremost among those in radio and television who think in terms of 'mass audiences' are the network controllers and station managers, even though the expression is sometimes used to imply 'low taste'.
2 The audience as a cohesive class or professional group – pre-existent to the media, not created by them, and so while served by them not dependent on them. This audience is alert, self-aware and largely autonomous. It might be characterized as part or all of 'the informed public' – a perspective which can be of particular use to programme planners and producers.
3 The audience as a market – the actual or potential consumers of a product or service. It is not a self-conscious or interactive group but could be a population area (e.g. Greater London) or a social category (e.g. housewives).

It is important to stress that these views of the audience are merely abstractions for particular purposes and are not mutually exclusive: many – most – of its members could be classified in several different ways. But knowing how big an audience is and even what percentage of it consists of owner-occupiers or potential purchasers of double glazing is not enough, if only because it gives broadcasters and advertisers no clue as to how such an audience may be retained, or preferably enlarged, in the future. As R. J. Silvey puts it of his early days in BBC listener research:

> however useful as a substitute for the box office, there were functions quantitative data could not fulfil. Knowing the size

of a programme's audience told one nothing about that audience's listening experience, what it was about the programme they had liked or not liked or why they felt about it as they did. (1974, 113)

One might even argue as Silvey does elsewhere (1974, 185) that there is no virtue in audience size for its own sake, what matters is the measure of the audience's appreciation: a small audience might have been delighted by what it heard, a large audience disappointed.

One way to discover what listeners think of the programmes is simply to rely on their unsolicited correspondence, as the BBC did during the first fourteen years of its existence. But this is an atypical reflection of audience attitudes because correspondents are atypically literate people and even more so, because they are people with atypically strong feelings ('Disgusted of Cheltenham'). Correspondence thus tends to reflect not the audience as a whole but only its more literate members, or rather only those more literate members with unusually strong feelings about the programmes (Silvey, 1974, 29–31).

A more scientific approach to audience research is to question a small sample of a station's total potential audience, since sampling, as Silvey points out, 'is based on the predicate that conclusions about large populations can be inferred from data about a limited number of them' (1974, 44). It enables researchers not only to learn about the attitudes of those listeners who are not in the habit of writing to the station but to discover who has *not* been listening, which is a kind of 'attitude' too, and with equally important implications for the broadcasters. If the reason for it is ignorance, then the solution may be better programme publicity; if the reason is apathy or aversion the answer may be better programmes; and if the reason is lack of access to a radio then the remedy may be to reschedule the programmes.

By now it will be apparent that we have moved on to the second, and major, concern of audience studies – with *effects* analysis, the consideration of what the media, specifically radio, do to their listeners and what they make them think. It is a subject laden with theories, all of them plausible, most of them conflicting, and none of them proven. When the question 'What effect do the media have upon their audiences?' was first put during the inter-war years it was assumed to be a simple one with an obvious answer: they exerted a persuasive and pervasive effect, transmitting simple and deliberate messages to which their audiences reacted in direct, predictable, uniform, and often dramatic ways (Lowery and De Fleur, 1983, 23, 366–7). Since media messages were thought of in almost ballistic terms – fired off as if from a gun and with almost equally inevitable results – this has sometimes been termed the 'magic bullet' or *stimulus–response* theory of audience behaviour. Lest such a theory seem laughably naïve to the modern reader, I must hasten to add that there were good reasons for adopting it during the 1930s. First of all, the media were newer and fewer than they are today: scepticism about their messages was not natural in an age less inured than ours is to the clamorous and conflicting voices not only of newspapers and radio but also of multi-channel television. And there were other reasons:

> There was the seeming ease with which World War I war-mongers and Fascist regimes in Europe of the 1930s had manipulated people's attitudes and bases of allegiance and behaviour. That impression was compatible with theories of mass society, current at the time the study of media effects began to take shape, which postulated that the dissolution of traditional forms of social organization under the impact of industrialization and urbanization had resulted in a social order in which individuals were atomized, cut off from traditional networks of social relationships, isolated from sources of social support, and consequently vulnerable to direct manipulation by remote and powerful élites in control of the mass media.
>
> (Blumler and Gurevitch, 1982, 242–3)

A dramatic vindication of stimulus–response theory seemed to occur in the USA in 1938 with Orson Welles's radio adaptation of H. G. Wells's *The War of the Worlds*. The mock news bulletin with which it began announced an invasion by creatures from Mars and caused widespread panic. According to some accounts, over a quarter of the estimated 6 million listeners believed what they heard, and a number of those living near the supposed invasion site got into their cars and fled. As Schramm points out (1971, 45), the affair dramatically illustrated three points: first, since persuasion seems to work better when it is hidden rather than overt, the importance of the broadcast *not* being perceived as manipulative; second, the effect of a threat against which listeners could think of no defence; and third, the use of a 'contractual cultural norm' – of a medium, radio, which was normally trusted as a reliable news source. But it has been pointed out that one limitation of stimulus–response theory is that 'we are limited to inferring that a message has had an influence only when we are able to observe a *change* or *difference* in the response chosen as the indicator of effects' (Roberts, 1971a, 359). Since a number of effects analyses made between 1946 and 1961 by the Yale Program of Research on Communication and Attitude Change seemed to suggest that media messages did *not* appreciably change audiences' views, or at least that there were no simple ways of achieving or predicting attitude-change through the media (Lowery and De Fleur, 1983, 148–75, 367–70), stimulus–response theory gave way to new and often overlapping schools of thought. The first held that media effects are negligible (as we shall see, a more fruitful hypothesis than it might at first appear); the second that the media are more effective in *confirming* the beliefs and attitudes of their audiences than in changing them.

Many of the findings on which this second line of thought, known as *reinforcement* theory, is based are summarized in the revised edition of *The Processes and Effects of Mass Communication* (1971), edited by Schramm and Roberts. From two major studies of voting behaviour in US elections Berelson, Lazarsfeld and McPhee concluded that the media strengthened rather than challenged the political opinions of their audiences (655–77). Lazarsfeld and Merton suggest (560–77) that while the media confer 'status' on certain issues and social movements by publicizing them, these originate within society itself, whose various elements the media help to cement. Their general finding is that the media change opinions only if their audiences are predisposed to change – otherwise the effect is one of reinforcement (cf. also Silvey, 1970, 312). It is at least noticeable

197

that while the media seem generally unable to change political and religious beliefs, their influence on the ephemeral fashions of pop music and clothes is considerable (cf. McQuail, 1977, 87). And Roberts argues (1971b, 519–20) that the media are only one element in a highly complex social system and that their fundamental effect is to maintain the status quo.

Reinforcement theory has been adopted and adapted by modern Marxist thinkers, who argue that those who control the media, and who therefore have an interest in maintaining the status quo, preclude any changes of attitude in their audiences by what is known as an 'agenda-setting' function, by transmitting messages which reinforce the 'dominant ideology' and limit the audiences' ability to see issues in any other terms, or indeed to see any other *issues*, than those 'on the agenda' they prescribe (Lowery and De Fleur, 1983, 380–1). Put simply, the media may not succeed in telling us what to think, but they do succeed in telling us what to think *about*: one of their roles is to act as 'gate-keeper', to debar from public scrutiny those issues or stories which may be inimical to the political establishment. This seems to have led Raymond Williams (1974, 122–6) to dismiss most effects studies as misplaced, since they are insufficiently concerned with social, political and cultural *causes*. But in his discussion of the audiences of radio soap-operas, Murdock uses the reinforcement and agenda-setting theories to suggest that in a deeper and subtler way than was at first envisaged, there is perhaps some truth in the old stimulus–response theory after all. At the conscious level listeners may not be crudely vulnerable to media messages in the sense that they will think whatever they are told to think; they may be

active rather than passive, participants rather than dupes. Even so, it is activity that remains confined by the limits set by the imaginative and ideological world presented by the serials. . . . [They] do indeed appear as vehicles for dominant and largely conservative values. Although the audiences were mainly working-class, the serials concentrated on the doings and attitudes of the upper class and the better-off sectors of the middle class. They therefore provided a powerful conduit for the downward transmission of dominant views and assumptions.   (Murdock, 1981, 156)

As Blumler and Gurevitch point out (1982, 249) it then becomes important to see whether the conservative views and values which the media foreground as suitable for public consumption are similarly foregrounded in the minds of their audiences. Moreover, if it is true that audiences are seldom consciously persuaded, either because they have already been prejudiced at a deeper, ideological level or because they are instinctively resistant to overt attempts to influence them, a logical development in audience research is from theories of reinforcement to those of *cognition*, to an examination of how much information audiences glean from the media (Blumler and Gurevitch, 1982, 248).

The other line of thought which succeeded stimulus–response theory – one which runs parallel to reinforcement theory, from which it is in some respects indistinguishable – is the *uses and gratifications* approach (Chaney, 1972, 22–34; Carey and Kreiling, 1974, 226–7). Since the effects of the media upon audiences seemed to be minimal yet 'consumption' of the media remained vast, this approach switched the focus of research from what the media do to people to what people do with the media, the *uses* to which they put them and the satisfactions or *gratifications* they obtain from them. We might note in passing that the notion of an active audience which uses and gratifications theory presupposes seems vindicated by the popularity of the phone-in; for the phone-in, as we saw in the previous chapter, depends upon an audience which is prepared to impose itself upon media output to the extent of originating it.

There are many useful summaries of uses and gratifications theory (e.g. McQuail, 1983, 82–3; Fiske, 1982, 135–40; Lowery and De Fleur, 1983, 374–5), but its basic assumption is that the message is much more a matter of what the audience makes of it than what the broadcaster intends and that for the former there are four main kinds of gratification:

1 Diversion – the need for escape from life's routine and problems, for emotional release.
2 Social integration – the need for companionship, to form relationships with others.
3 Self-awareness – the need to compare personalities to oneself, programme content to one's own situation.

4 Surveillance – the need for information about the world.

The classic uses and gratifications study was conducted by Katz, Gurevitch and Haas (1973, 164–81), a summary of which may be found in Fiske (1982, 18–21). They drew attention to the fact that the potential media 'consumer' consciously discriminates among the media and their characteristic forms of content according to her psychological and social needs and her physical circumstances, all of which vary in time. For instance, it was discovered that the need to establish rapport with one's family was best served by television, and with friends by television or the cinema. But since newspaper *content* was an important basis of conversation with friends, it was clear that the choice was not simply between media, but sometimes between media and messages. Since the print media are generally more conducive than the electronic media to the transmission and retention of abstract and complex material, it is not surprising that the researchers found that the former were preferred by the more educated, the latter by the less educated. Of the main needs listed – for knowledge, 'escape', aesthetic pleasure, improving self-confidence and strengthening social ties – not one was best served by radio, despite the almost universal ownership of sets.

In exploring the ways in which the five main media catered to audience needs the researchers perceived an interrelationship or 'circumplex' between them, in which the position of one medium *vis-à-vis* the others depends on the closeness of the needs which they gratify. If we begin, arbitrarily, with the book then the interrelationship runs to its 'next of kin', the newspaper, thence to radio, television, cinema and so full-circle back to the book. Thus if we lack books we are likely to seek gratification either from newspapers or the cinema, whose functions most nearly match their own: we are less likely to switch on the radio or television.

These findings need to be treated with some reserve. They seem to involve a degree of confusion between media and messages, sometimes regarding as part of the inherent nature of the medium what is quite arbitrarily a part of its content. It is said, for instance, that in order to relate more closely to social reality people select television, radio or newspapers rather than the cinema, but this has nothing to do with the *inherent* characteristics of any of these media. It is simply an accident of history not a part of the nature of the cinema medium that it has concerned itself more with fictional themes than with social reality, and in the case of books there is surely a distinction between the gratifications afforded by fact and those afforded by fiction. Similarly, while the connection the researchers perceive between media use and educational level seems plausible, radio would almost certainly be more popular with the better-educated classes in Britain than with those in the USA or Israel (where the study was conducted), since with networks such as Radio 3 Britain has a much stronger tradition of catering to the needs of the educated. Finally, the conclusion that not one need was best served by radio seems to rely on what is in both senses a partial definition of audience 'needs', particularly since (as we have seen) the medium has certain unique potentialities.

Nevertheless the study was important because it was the first attempt to understand audience needs in terms not simply of abstract 'content' but of the distinctive attributes of the various media which purvey it and the social circumstances in which they can be resorted to. It reminds us that listeners and viewers are not separate and rival species but that the listener at 9 am is a viewer at 9 pm – that audiences are capable of discriminating quite consciously between the different media. Indeed it has since been pointed out that during major political crises such as the Kennedy assassination, the variety of the media and the public's attitude towards them are a force for calm rather than panic since the public tends to seek verification from more than one medium, whereas panic is the natural consequence of rumour and ambiguity (McQuail, 1977, 86). The study also enabled important distinctions to be drawn (Katz, Blumler and Gurevitch, 1974, 24) between the gratifications to be derived from the *content* of a medium ('I enjoy listening to *Desert Island Discs*'); from *exposure* to the medium *per se*, which might consist as much of 'dial twiddling' as listening to individual programmes ('I enjoy listening to the radio'); and from the social *context* which typifies the exposure to the medium ('I enjoy listening to the radio while I'm shaving'). Furthermore the 'horses for courses' emphasis of the Katz, Gurevitch and Haas study gave theoretical justification to attempts, some of which had already been made, to study the effects of one medium in isolation from all the others. In 'Listening to radio' (1964, 239–49) Mendelsohn had already pointed out that listeners do not greatly distinguish between different kinds of content, whether informative or entertaining, but use radio to 'structure' their day and as a 'companion'. It provides material for conversation, and its importance lies less in the amount of time people listen to it than in the psychological needs which it gratifies. In this and a more recent study of housewives and radio (Hobson, 1980, 105–14) it is stressed that radio gives the isolated listener a feeling of community not simply with the broadcasters but with the *other* isolated listeners, two different needs for social contact which do not seem to have been distinguished by Katz, Gurevitch and Haas. The experience of many listeners would, I suspect, confirm Mendelsohn's and Hobson's findings, which suggest that our attitude to radio is 'utilitarian' in a way that our attitude to television cannot be. It is true that we also use television to fulfil our psychological and social needs: followers of soap opera, for example, respond to the medium in an active and critical way, closely relating its content to the preoccupations of their everyday lives (Hobson, 1982, 119–36). But it also requires them to 'suspend' their lives during the time that they watch it. Since we do not sit and watch the radio but live our lives *while* we are listening, its content is, as it were, transplanted into our own existence and adapted to our own purposes, and with the reader's indulgence I would like to illustrate this point a little more fully through my own use of the medium.

The period from 8.45 to 9.15 am is a clearly demarcated stage of the weekday when I am in my car – or, to change the emphasis, when there is a hiatus between home and work which is partly filled by listening to the radio. I leave home with my daughter, drive her to school and deposit her there at just before nine o'clock, and during the drive we listen to Mike Read on Radio 1. After she has got out I switch to Radio 4 for the nine o'clock News summary and at five past nine I switch to Radio 3 to listen to as much as I can of *This Week's Composer* before arriving at work. There seem to be two notable features about this pattern of listening: despite the fact that unless I am lucky enough to encounter heavy traffic it is seldom as much as half an hour, it spans no fewer than three channels or networks and three programme boundaries.

Why the span of networks? Radio 1 starts the sequence because two of us are in the car and it is a better compromise of our tastes than any other network. Its output is lively and wakes us up. My daughter, being young, enjoys the music with a clear conscience and I, being less young, listen to it with an equally pleasurable sense of guilt. We are also impressed by Mike Read's imitations of all the other Radio 1 disc-jockeys. After I have dropped my daughter I feel less entitled to listen to Radio 1, and in any case stronger reasons call me to the nine o'clock news summary on Radio 4. First I wish to check my watch against the time-signal and secondly, although I have heard the eight o'clock news and scanned the headlines in the paper I was too sleepy to digest the former and the latter are already likely to be out of date. At five past nine I turn to Radio 3, having been made sufficiently wakeful by the sounds of Radio 1 and the catalogue of the day's crises on Radio 4. Radio 3's nine o'clock news summary was also a possibility but I find its delivery a little too sedate for the time of day. Now, however, I feel the need to face work in a calmer, more thoughtful mood and *This Week's Composer* often helps to create this, especially if he is a favourite. All this 'channel hopping' , indisputably an 'active' attitude to the medium, serves a number of needs and gratifications, most of which are recognizable in terms of the studies we have looked at. There are the self-directed needs – for self-confidence and aesthetic pleasure – and the more 'outward' needs – to find out what time it is and what is happening in the world. But the importance of *situation* must also be noted, not simply that of being about to 'face the day' but of listening to a *car* radio rather than a portable set: for the simple fact that like most car radios mine has push-button tuning, whereas tuning on a portable requires rather more dexterity, means that I hop between channels much more than I otherwise would, and I am therefore able to extend the range of gratifications open to me.

But the fact that my listening spans programme boundaries is even more significant than the spanning of networks. I begin by hearing the last fifteen minutes of Mike Read, who has in fact been broadcasting for *two hours*, beginning at seven o'clock. I then listen to a complete news bulletin of five minutes' duration and conclude with the first five or ten minutes of *This Week's Composer*, which will continue for another forty-five minutes or so until ten o'clock. If my listening span had been confined to a single network it would still not have embraced any complete programme other than the News. Had I stayed with Radio 1 I would have heard in addition to Mike Read's show the first ten or fifteen minutes of Simon Bates, who continues for another two and three-quarter hours until midday. Radio 4 would have been even bittier: I would have switched on ten minutes after the beginning of *Yesterday in Parliament*, heard a complete news summary, and then a mere ten minutes of some such highly structured and self-contained programme as *The Living World* or *Tuesday Call*, which would have continued until ten o'clock. And on Radio 3, apart from the first few bars of *This Week's Composer*, I should have heard only the news headlines and the last fifteen minutes of *Morning Concert*, which had begun at seven o'clock. My point, then, is that radio is 'appropriated' by the individual much more than is any other medium because the span of attention she is able to give it is dictated not so much by the programmes it offers her as by the highly variable yet often rigid circumstances of her own life. I should not have inflicted an account of my own use of the radio on the reader if I had thought that it was particularly idiosyncratic: or perhaps it is truer to say that *everybody*'s is. My own demand on the medium is an arbitrary half-hour or so, at the end of which I am forced to switch off. The demands made by the housewife, the student and the company representative will differ in time and in lengths of time from mine and from each other's. Yet they will all be alike in being determined largely by the exigencies of their lives and only in the second place by what the networks and stations provide. Nor can these exigencies necessarily be foreseen or altered by the listener herself. Let us take the case of the company representative who in a typical working day travels a hundred miles from his base to visit three or four of his customers in a single town. For the two hours or so of his initial journey he can listen to his car radio without interruption, perhaps hearing two complete programmes. But then he arrives at his first call and irrespective of the point which the present programme has reached, he must switch off: the day is short, there are several customers to visit, and the length of his visits will vary. Thenceforward his use of the radio will be in short snatches and at unforeseeable intervals between visits. In terms of the programmes that radio has traditionally provided this use of the medium is almost nonsensical: the programme planners would have a headache in providing for our company 'rep' alone, quite apart from all the other people listening at times and for spells which are equally arbitrary. Yet in an age of transistor portables and car radios, such casual and desultory listening is also inevitable. Naturally, Radios 1 and 2 can cope with this better than the 'quality' networks, since unlike 'developing' forms – the drama, the documentary and the classical concert – the pop song, which is the basis of their output, is seldom more than five minutes in length. (Do music producers make pop songs not with record-buyers' but with radio-listeners' habits in mind?) It is an interesting thought that the greater popularity of Radios 1 and 2 may be due entirely to the fact that unlike that of Radios 3 and 4 their output can be cut up into intelligible five-minute segments: perhaps if Tom Stoppard wrote a continuous sequence of five-minute plays for Radio 3 the ratings would be reversed!

But listeners are active not only in the fact that they use the radio for varying lengths of time which often have little to do with programme span, but in the ways they interpret programme content. It has been pointed out, for example, that different listeners will use a single media message to gratify their differing psychological needs (Johnstone, 1974, 36). These uses might be termed 'variant decodings' of an intentional nature: the solitary person might use a soap-opera to reinforce her private fantasies, the gregarious person might use it as a topic of conversation, but they are 'intentional' in the sense that the scriptwriter provides for both uses within the content. On the other hand there may be variant decodings of an unintentional nature – unintended by the broadcaster or the listener or both (McLeod and Becker, 1974, 141–2). A broadcaster's programme categories may be at variance with the psychological categorizations of the listener: the former may, for instance, conceive of

The Archers as a drama series while the latter perceives it as a features programme about farming made on behalf of the Department of Agriculture. Sometimes the message may not correspond to the *listener*'s intentions, as when she switches on a programme entitled *Animal Farm* in the expectation of an agricultural documentary but instead hears, and enjoys, a dramatization of George Orwell's political allegory. Finally there may be 'errant decodings' in which listeners misunderstand media messages or consciously distort them to make them more palatable (Cooper and Jahoda, 1971, 287–93). Such decodings could, of course, be used to support the 'magic bullet' theory of audience effects, for the *War of the Worlds* broadcast was one such decoding. But the 'uses and gratifications' theorist would probably argue from the fact that listeners misinterpret so many more messages to their advantage than to their disadvantage that their role is a good deal less passive than magic bullet theory would imply. Still, errant decodings do indicate the respect in which uses and gratifications theory and reinforcement theory are at one: regardless of the intentions of broadcasters listeners will hear what they want to hear:

> Occasionally . . . a broadcaster may aim at a pigeon and shoot a crow; he may fail completely to meet the need he intended to gratify, while in fact gratifying a need of an entirely different kind. A notorious case in point is the broadcaster who intended, by a word-picture, to satisfy the homebound listener's desire to visualize a Naval Review but who, instead, succeeded triumphantly in satisfying the need to be entertained.
> (Silvey, 1970, 303)

For these reasons it is important for audience researchers to distinguish media *effects* – any of the consequences of programme output – from *effectiveness*, a programme's ability to achieve a given objective (McQuail, 1977, 70).

Much uses and gratifications theory suggests, then, that broadcasters have little influence over their audiences – or to put it another way, that audiences are busy and alert but that among their more predictable responses is the ability to *resist* media effects. Robert Silvey is one of its most eloquent exponents since he was the first Head of BBC Audience Research and studied listener behaviour for over thirty years. His descriptions of the ordinary listener, naturally wary and critical, mostly active but proof against persuasion even when she is not, make reassuring reading (1970, 305–8; 1974, 166–7). Silvey points out that the listener is not a mere receptacle. She *becomes* a listener through an act of choice: she selects certain programmes rather than others. She is not obliged to switch on, and once her radio is on she can switch it off. She can reject or disagree with what she hears, and her natural human inertia will make it easier for her to resist the pressures to change her views than succumb to them. Challenge is stimulating but also discomforting: she is more likely to want to relax and be entertained than think. Consequently she can simply reduce the amount of attention she gives to the broadcast, to the point of ignoring it altogether. Or she may practise selective perception by listening to some parts and ignoring others. Or she may consciously or unconsciously distort its message to fit her own preconceptions. And if all else fails, she can simply forget what she has heard.

Nevertheless, uses and gratifications theory remains open to certain criticisms: not everyone agrees on the nature of the uses to which the listener puts the media, nor on the amount of gratification she seeks from them, nor on the extent to which she is proof against their effects. What precisely is meant by 'uses' and 'gratifications'?

> A host of studies has attempted to set forth lists of the needs satisfied by media content, or typologies of motivation and functions involved in attention to mass communication. Unfortunately, such lists and typologies vary greatly from one investigator to another. No agreement exists, at least up to now, why people select particular content, what needs a given form of content satisfies, or how such gratification leads to behavioral consequences.
>
> (Lowery and De Fleur, 1983, 375)

Mendelsohn adopts a similar argument (1974, 306), pointing out that the listener's 'needs' in relation to the media are not always self-evident but reflected in a variety of ways. The criterion of 'need' does not adequately explain the different use patterns to which the media are put, nor the presumable difference in the gratifications afforded by these different kinds of media experience. Why, for instance, does one listener in search of diversion turn to a Samuel Beckett play on Radio 3 and another to *The Archers* on Radio 4 – what is the difference in these two forms of gratification which the single word 'diversion' hides?

Elliott discerns even more radical problems in the concept of 'needs' (1974, 255), alleging that unlike 'deficiency' needs such as hunger, they are merely 'growth' needs which have been learned through social experience, including experience of the media. We must then talk of the media gratifying needs they have helped to create. In any case, as Golding avers (1974, 10–11), these needs and gratifications may be extremely hard to articulate even for the listener herself, a point developed by Lowery and De Fleur (1983, 375):

> One might raise the objection that such [listeners] may not be aware of the underlying motivations that draw them to particular kinds of content. What they claim in lay terms may have little to do with their 'true' motivations because these motivations may not be understood at the conscious level. One can also ask whether age, sex, socioeconomic status, and other such common variables of social research are the ones that should be given priority in gratifications research. The answers to these issues are not at all clear.

But it is not even beyond dispute that audiences are as active in their uses of the media or as resistant to their messages as researchers like Silvey suggest, and it is in this respect that radio is a medium of peculiar significance to effects analysis. We have already seen that radio is unique in being a secondary medium and that this is what enables it to be used in a casual, desultory way that television cannot: we can slip into and out of its content as our circumstances dictate and with little or no reference to programme structure. Nevertheless we have assumed that while the radio is on, the listener's attention to it is both uniform and close even though she is likely to be doing something else. I have painted a self-portrait of someone who even while he is driving is constantly monitoring radio content to the extent of changing channels every few minutes, and I have suggested that such listening behaviour is not atypical. But I have not sufficiently stressed that radio is variable not only in the odd and arbitrary times we can make use of it but also in the amount of attention we pay to it *while it is on,* and it must also be typical listening behaviour to disregard it almost entirely and treat it as 'background'. Of course, television may be treated as background too, and is in a surprisingly large number of households, but since a large part of its message is visual we can say that in such circumstances it is being ignored. This means that unlike television's, there is some doubt as to who radio's actual audience *is,* and we have returned to the question we posed at the outset: in respect not only of duration but of attentiveness, what constitutes a listener?

> Having taken over the word ['audience'] from the theatre, cinema, or concert hall, where it has a generally agreed meaning, we have overlooked the fact that it cannot be applied to broadcasting in a similarly precise way. The audience for a performance of a play is the people who were present in the theatre when it was performed. They are in a sense a 'captive' audience. But the people who are exposed to a broadcast are not similarly captive. Some of them, it is true, may remain in their chairs throughout, enthralled from start to finish by what they hear . . . ; some, though present in the room, may virtually ignore the broadcast their set is receiving. . . . Is the listener who reads a newspaper to the accompaniment of a radio discussion part of its audience or is he not? . . .

> The answers to such questions as [this] depend, of course, on how you choose to define the term 'audience'. You may choose to define it conservatively, confining it to those who have given the broadcast their full attention throughout, or you can define it generously, including all within earshot, or indeed you can choose any point along this continuum. But whatever your decision, be assured that it is highly relevant to the question of audience size, for if a broadcast's audience is deemed to include all within earshot it may be many times larger than if it is deemed to exclude all but the fully attentive.
> (Silvey, 1974, 179)

At first sight this would appear to vindicate uses and gratifications

209

theory in its suggestion of 'mind over medium', of many – perhaps most – listeners exercising even more than viewers their freedom to pay scant attention to radio's messages or even to ignore them altogether. But to describe such listeners as 'conscious' or 'active' in their use of the medium seems misleading, to say the least. It has long been known, for instance, that the time at which they listen is far more important to most listeners than the nature of the programmes they are listening to:

Without any change in the content of a programme, the size of its audience could be radically altered simply by transmitting it at a different time or by changing its placing; put it immediately after, or even immediately before, a programme which had a large following and its audience went up. Even a mere change of title could make a difference. No series of Chamber Music programmes ever attracted a substantial following until someone thought of leaving those fatal words out of the billing and calling it simply *Music in Miniature*.

(Silvey, 1974, 113; cf. also Emmett, 1972, 206–7)

Of course the times at which people listen are not always a matter of pure choice, but when the choice is between their usual network and their favourite programme the facts are more telling. In 1966 *The Archers* lost a million listeners simply by moving from the Light Programme to the Home Service (Wade, 1981a, 101), and programmes originating on Radio 3 invariably attract bigger audiences when repeated on Radio 4 (*Broadcasting in the Seventies*, 1969, 4). All this paints a disturbing picture of an inert majority of listeners who switch on at a fixed time and to a fixed station irrespective of programme content, and who in so far as they exercise any preferences are easily duped out of them by mere changes of title. Nevertheless, as we have seen, some uses and gratifications theorists such as Silvey would regard this inertia as itself part of the weaponry with which the listener resists media effects: it is not so much that she is duped as detached – not greatly affected by what she hears, provided that it does not take up too much of her attention or try too hard to change her views, and as long as it affords her some general sense of routine and companionship. But the evidence is profoundly ambivalent. She may hardly be listening, but unlike the television, which she experiences while disengaged from most other activities and which she is therefore much more likely to recognize as extraneous to her personal situation, her radio is on simultaneously with her primary activity. This means that whatever their proportions relative to each other it is often hard to separate first-hand experience from vicarious, 'radio' experience: 'Where did I hear that story? Was it someone at work or Simon Bates on Radio 1?'. It may be that precisely because it is ignored radio is capable of strong effects, that its content can infiltrate the listener just because her conscious faculties are primarily engaged elsewhere and her mental defences therefore down. This is a plausible challenge to the conventional view that the most influential media are the visual ones: there seem good reasons for arguing the opposite, that they are the more resistible for being perceived consciously and being perceived 'out there', as separate from the events of our own lives. The existence of unconscious media effects is, of course, almost impossible to prove by their very nature: as soon as we assert their existence we are open to the objection that if we are sufficiently aware of them to discuss them they cannot be 'unconscious' at all. Perhaps the best we can do is to appeal to personal experience. How often do we find ourselves humming a song which we detest and do not remember having heard, yet which we could only have got from the radio? How often are we aware of knowing something as a result of listening to the radio, but which we remember hearing only by reference to the *primary* activity we were engaged in at the time, for example shaving or cleaning the car? Speaking for myself, there are certain songs I always vividly associate with particular streets because it was while driving along those streets that I first heard them on the radio. Of course it is a moot point whether I was paying much less attention to the music than to the driving: I can only assert that I was hardly aware of the music at the time.

But if we grant that radio has discernible effects even upon the inattentive listener, how much more, or less, influenced is our active, channel-hopping listener? If the former is open to strong but unperceived effects the latter is surely highly resistant to them, ready to change stations to get what *she* wants rather than what the broadcasters may wish to foist upon her. Against her, the programme planners may be virtually impotent. On the other hand it could be argued that since she is listening harder she is more open to influences than the less attentive listener. They are likely to be the influences or effects she desires. She will probably, as the reinforcement theorists suggest, be seeking confirmation of her prejudices. But in so doing she will be more susceptible than the listener whose prejudices wither away because she never listens hard enough to content which would strengthen them.

It could be argued, however, that I have set up a misleading contrast between these two kinds of listener, for one factor which is common to both of them and which sets them at the opposite extreme from another kind of listener is that in different ways – the inattentive listener by using whatever she hears as mere background, the selective listener by paying close attention but not at sufficient length to do it justice – they treat radio content not on its own terms but as subordinate to their *own* needs or activities. One could argue that the real contrast is between these listeners and the truly attentive listeners, perhaps the company rep on his long drive or the housewife cooking in the kitchen, who hear *Afternoon Theatre* or *Woman's Hour* in its entirety and who, moreover, listen to it *on its own terms*. Surely it is to such listeners as these that we should look for media effects, that what *they* think of programme content or what it does to *them* will be of much more significance than in the case of the listener who is mostly ignoring what she hears or who is using it merely to 'structure' her existence in some way and will require a change of mood and channel before it ends. It may be that because they are much less concerned with moulding content to their own uses and gratifications but let it 'speak for itself', our rep and our housewife are much more open to its effects; or conversely, because they neither impose themselves upon content nor simply allow it to seep into their subconscious they are much less open to its effects. But whichever is nearer to the truth, I would suggest that the distinction between these and our previous categories of listener is only one of degree rather than kind: for to the eternal exasperation of radio broadcasters, for whom in one sense it makes programme standards always more exacting than those of television, our two model listeners will resemble the vast majority of other listeners in doing something else *while* they listen – something which will, however occasionally and briefly, dominate over radio content to the extent of its being ignored. The housewife may leave the kitchen (and the radio) to fetch the peas from the freezer in the garage, the rep may stop listening in order to brake hard and avoid the slow lorry. Why have they both switched on? For an aesthetic experience or for information, certainly, but also for reasons which are extraneous to content and have everything to do with their personal circumstances – company, the need to relieve the tedium of cooking and driving – and in this respect they are unlike the reader of the women's magazine or the spectator at the theatre, for whom what is before them is the sole object of attention. This means that the principles governing the effects of radio upon these listeners will be much the same as those governing its effects upon our previous kinds of listener: the nature and extent of the effects will certainly be no clearer!

Perhaps I exaggerate the 'secondariness' of radio, in which case some light can be thrown on listening habits by the programming of the different BBC networks. It is certainly true that the varied and self-contained programmes of Radio 4 and the 'highbrow' talks and concerts of Radio 3 seem to imply a different span of listening and order of attentiveness from the chat-and-pop-music sequences of Radios 1 and 2. Indeed Radio 3 was especially conceived for audiences who would discriminate among its programmes, listen to them rather than just 'hear' them, and then switch off after they had finished (A. Briggs, 1979, 66). None the less, there are signs that such audience behaviour has succumbed before the portability of the transistor set on the one hand and the vision of television on the other: despite superficial differences the programme formats of all four networks are growing ever more alike. Continuous pop music on Radio 1 is balanced by two-hour programmes of continuous classical music on Radio 3, where music is now 76 per cent of output and drama a mere 1.8 per cent (*BBC Annual Report and Handbook 1985*, 1984, 145). The two- and three-hour 'sequences' of Radios 1 and 2 and local radio (magazine-like programmes consisting of brief items of music and talk whose main unifying principle is the presenter) are complemented by similar sequences on Radio 4: the *Today* programme in the early morning, and recently the experimental *Rollercoaster*, whose style of presentation was, as the title implies, a good deal more 'populist' than previous Radio 4 output. On a recent computation music alone comprised 61.3 per cent of total network output (*BBC Annual Report and Handbook 1985*, 1984, 145), compared with less than 50 per cent of network output in 1954–5 (Paulu, 1956, 223); when added to news and current affairs output, those other staples of sequence programming, the figure was 85 per cent (*BBC Annual Report and Handbook 1985*, 1984, 145).

The general tendency is therefore towards 'flow', the principle of programming noticed by Raymond Williams (1974, 86–94; Higgins and Moss, 1982, 34) as characteristic of television. Williams very shrewdly points out that the programme boundaries on television are constantly being obscured by adverts and / or trailers, the purpose of which is to keep the viewer fixed to her set for as long as possible. It is true that John Ellis (1982, 116–26) has identified a contrary principle of programming which he calls 'segmentation' – the fact that television material is divided into units, each 'a coherent group of sounds and images' (p. 116) which never lasts more than a few minutes and is discernible in the forms of a single advert within a commercial break, a single item within a news bulletin, a scene in a film or serial, and so on, and is indeed the basis of almost the entire output. Nevertheless the difference between Williams and Ellis is, as the latter implies (p. 117), more apparent than real, for each is concerned to stress a different aspect of the same fact – that the *actual* principle according to which output is organized is something other than the declared principle. For all their internal coherence and mutual independence, the segments are so brief and thus so numerous as to create an agglomerative effect which transcends programme boundaries and for which we can therefore use Williams's description, flow. But I would suggest that flow is even more characteristic of radio and with rather different connotations. There is a need to obscure programme boundaries on television because on the whole they still exist: there are relatively few sequences, most of them (breakfast television, sports programmes, election specials) dealing with current affairs, a subject which requires constant updating. But on radio, with its largely inattentive and intermittent audience, programmes have much less rationale. They are seldom conterminous with the listening habits of the audience and so it is much better that the listeners should be offered something continuous which they can dip in and out of at will. This is why continuity announcers no longer speak of 'The evening's *programmes* on Radio 1' but 'Night-time *listening* on Radio 1'. Nevertheless an analysis of flow on the radio will also reveal that it consists of the segments which form the basis of flow on the television: indeed, in the more popular networks and stations, whether BBC or ILR, the segmentation is much more obvious – snatches of disc-jockey's /presenter's patter, songs or records, jingles, trailers, adverts, newsflashes, all succeeding one another so rapidly as to blur into a single stream devoid of any overall structural principle which might determine the length of the programme in the way that it might be determined by the plot of a play. Hence whereas on television what Williams describes as flow and Ellis as segmentation is intended to sustain or *prolong* viewing, its primary function on radio is to allow *sporadic* listening – to enable us whether in our heads or with our fingers to switch on and off without feeling that we have missed anything of major importance.

It might be helpful to conclude with a summary of our findings. Radio is almost invariably a *secondary* medium: we listen to it while doing something else, and this has certain important implications for audience studies. Before looking at those implications let us briefly remind ourselves what 'secondary medium' means. It means that radio is imported into the ordinary life of the audience to a much greater extent than television is. We cannot watch while we work but we can often listen. The listener's use of the radio is therefore determined not so much by the programme routines it offers as by her own daily routines, the times when her personal circumstances allow her to listen or prevent her from listening. She is therefore likely to use radio for spans of time which do not correspond to the programme spans. Furthermore, since listening is a secondary activity she may vary the amount of attention she gives to the radio even while it is switched on. She may be almost completely engrossed by what she hears, or she may ignore it altogether.

This seems to have implications for both audience and effects analysis and for uses and gratifications theory. It means first of all that the very *identity* of the radio audience is much more problematical than that of the television audience: or to put it another way, because other media make a more absolute claim on our attention the distinctions between media consumption and our other activities are much sharper. When we watch television we can do very little else. Of course television may also be treated as mere 'background', but since a large part of its message is visual we can say that in these circumstances the audience is not strictly an 'audience' at all. We cannot make such confident assumptions about the radio audience. Nor can we attempt to identify our audience as those who are most affected or influenced by its messages, for we have also seen that there is no simple correlation between the amount of exposure to the medium or the measure of attention the listener gives to it and the extent of its effects upon her. Indeed there is some, albeit subjective, evidence that because it is more integrated into everyday life than are the other media its effects are greater, that the medium is the more influential for being less perceived. Hence effects analysis is an even more complex matter in radio than in the other media, for whatever else may be said about television, we can say that its direct effects will be found only within the ranks of those who have been paying attention. We cannot say the same about radio, for its effects may be found among the inattentive, too.

All this is at once a vindication of uses and gratifications theory and a demonstration of its limitations. It is a vindication because radio's secondariness means that it is self-evidently 'used'. We switch it on because it can accompany and enhance our ordinary activities in a way that television or newspapers cannot. If radio were attended to for its own sake we would not be able to perform these activities at the same time, and it is surprising that uses and gratifications theorists have not more frequently sought to justify themselves by citing the way in which most people listen to the radio. On the other hand, if we can describe all those who treat radio as secondary as 'using' the

216

medium, from those who listen closely to those who are virtually ignoring it, the concept of use has become over-elastic and tighter definitions are required. Moreover uses and gratifications theory obscures but does not dispose of the old problem of effects and influences, for the fact that even the most inattentive listener is in some sense using the medium does not preclude the possibility that it might be 'using' her, too – that she might be subject to its influence in almost subliminal ways. It would appear that radio's distinctive role in the field of audience studies is simply to add to the complexity of its problems!

Suggestions for further work

Devise a questionnaire to find out about your fellow students' use of the radio (or that of any other section of the community). This might include versions of some or all of the following questions. Do you possess a radio of your own? Do you normally listen alone? Are you normally doing something else while you are listening? If so, what main activities does your listening accompany? At what times of the day do you listen and for how long? Do you listen primarily to a station or to a particular kind of output? What sort of gratifications does the station/output provide? Are there any kinds of output which radio does not currently provide but which you feel it could and should provide? And when you have an equal choice between watching television and listening to the radio, do you ever choose the latter? If so, why? The questionnaire might include further questions which enable you to compare the subjects' consumption of radio with their consumption of other media – television, newspapers, cinema; also questions which enable you to discover how far this consumption has been affected by such recent technological and organizational developments as audio-cassettes, breakfast and cable television, video recorders, and so on. When the questionnaire has been completed, examine the overall profile of listener identity/use that it gives you. You might then imagine that you are the controller of a network or a local or a community radio station. Draw up a programming policy in order to attract a particular group of listeners.

CONCLUSION

Throughout the previous chapters we have attempted to identify the distinctive characteristics of radio by discussing the different kinds of programme – and audience uses – which would appear to illuminate them. It seems fitting to conclude our discussion by addressing two further questions: of what use or significance are the findings we have reached, and what, briefly, is the medium's future?

The significance of our findings would seem to range from the theoretical to the practical, but it must also be said that part of this significance pertains to things *outside* radio – that in some ways the medium is not so much of interest in itself as for the light it throws upon the ordinary means by which we perceive the world or upon the more 'conventional' ways in which its messages are conveyed. It may not, for instance, be too pretentious to suggest that radio's broadest theoretical significance is philosophical – that the faculties which it deploys and denies tell us something about *epistemology*, or the way in which we normally know of the existence of things and are able to make sense of them. We discovered that radio is a blind medium whose codes consist only of noise and silence, and that among these codes only that of words is ultimately intelligible and able to make meaningful those of music, sounds and silence. The epistemological significance of this lies in the fact that our discovery included the perception that the faculty through which we make sense of the world is primarily visual, that of sight; whereas since discrete images are seldom self-explanatory the faculty through which we *communicate* about it is primarily verbal, that of words. Similarly, our comparison of radio with the other mass media in order to identify the advantages and limitations of the former is also of significance for the insight it afforded us into some of the special characteristics of the latter. The comparison showed that the blindness of radio distinguishes it not only from film and television since the contexts to which its messages refer are invisible, but also from the print media since even the *signs* of which its messages consist cannot be seen. Nevertheless since the comparison involved looking in some detail at the different forms which certain kinds of content assume in the different media, we could assert that it threw almost as much light on the distinctive features of newspaper and television news, televised outside broadcasts, theatrical drama and certain narrative modes of literature as it threw upon their corresponding forms in radio.

Since neither context nor message is visible in radio and its primary code is that of words, it follows that this code must be a *spoken* one; but since speech exists in time and is therefore always evanescent we also discovered that radio is of limited efficiency in conveying highly complex ideas and information: it is a somewhat crude teaching medium. Nevertheless Ong (1982) has pointed out the artificiality of the distinction between speech and writing, orality and literacy, and therefore by implication the worthiness of speech as an object of study. However, in the past speech could be fixed only by 'de-personalizing' it – and hence by excluding various important communicative elements – in the form of literature. Through tapes, records and cassettes, technology has now made speech a much more manageable object of study and in so doing has enhanced the academic status of such study. But for the student of radio the more practical significance of this is, as we noted in Chapter 5, that off-air recording may have substantial long-term effects on programme production. As the listener shows more interest in the preservation and retrieval of certain kinds of programmes, the producers of these programmes may become less concerned with what makes an immediate impact and more prepared to explore more complex and substantial themes. (An interesting if minor speculation in this context is whether the commercially produced cassettes and records which are listened to in large numbers constitute a kind of 'time-shift radio' or whether they should be considered as a different kind of medium.)

Another consequence of the fact that radio's primary code is oral is that its words can never be distinguished from the presence of a speaker: it is therefore a *binary* code. We noted, then, that however limited their ability to convey abstract ideas words in their descriptive function can exert a powerful effect on the listener's imagination, in some respects more so than literary words can because they are enhanced by the inflections of the human voice – and what they describe may also be partly realized through SFX. Nevertheless the imaginary world which is evoked is not the simple counterpart of the one we can see. It is both less and more than the visible world: less in the sense that it is generally less vivid, more in that this relative lack of vividness renders the listener capable of grasping a more complex reality than could be assimilated visually. The listener is therefore grateful for the opportunity to picture what is being described, but for not having to *see* it when he wishes to concentrate on the non-visual aspects of the message. Moreover the lack of vision not only stimulates the imagination, but may mislead it in the sense that it allows the arbitrary relationship between words and things to be undermined. As we saw in the chapters on drama and light entertainment, radio is thus well equipped to pose ontological questions, present fantasies and indulge in comic deceptions. We are now, of course, discussing those things we have learned about radio which are of a more practical significance – and among these is the fact that as a binary code speech evokes the *speaker* in addition to the subject of her speech, and to a much greater extent than writing evokes the writer. Hence the imagination is powerfully involved on radio not just in respect of what is being described but of who is describing it, and as I suggested in Chapters 1 and 6 this evocation of the speaker is the basis of radio's pervasive though partly 'fictional' sense of personal companionship.

The last important consequence of radio's blindness is one which we have extensively discussed: it is very largely a secondary medium in that the great majority of its audience are likely to be doing something else while they are listening. This means that the circumstances of radio's reception are curious and even unique. For the (usually solitary) listener the companionship of the presenter, the 'reality' of the world of a play, or the emotional power of a piece of music are strangely superimposed upon, and variously 'colour', his primary activity, whether he is driving, cooking or eating: they do not *replace* it as they do when he watches the television or reads. But the term 'secondary' disguises a *range* of listening postures: his role is even more complex and variable than that of the 'consumers' of the other media. He can listen closely or treat the radio as mere background (an attitude which can be seen as both more and less active than that of the television viewer) – nor is there any clear correlation between the degree of his attentiveness and the extent of the medium's influence upon him. The secondariness of the medium is at once its great advantage and disadvantage, for the evidence suggests that radio is used more than ever before, but listened to less. For such a medium we might conclude that there are two kinds of content which seem ideal. The first is news, since as we noted from our investigations in Chapter 4 news in any medium appears to be primarily verbal and so the very latest events can be conveyed to the listener without requiring him to take his eyes from what is his primary activity. Secondly we can infer from our discussion in Chapter 3 that music is highly suitable for a medium which receives fluctuating attention, for since it does not 'refer to' things in the way that words do it does not force, though it may encourage, the exercise of the listener's imagination. It is not surprising, then, that that hybrid creature 'newsic' contributes the lion's share to modern radio output. So, despite its inherent disadvantages and despite continuing technological developments in other media, radio's secondariness gives it certain unconquerable advantages and thus an assured future – which is a partial answer to the second question we posed at the beginning of this chapter. Furthermore the technological developments within the medium itself point to a healthy and exciting future. As was suggested in Chapter 2 the prospect of a new tier of CR stations brings with it that of a greater editorial freedom for broadcasters and a wider choice for the listeners. Radio may well approximate more closely to the press in offering a broader range of specialized products and for its listeners a greater opportunity to 'shop around'. Moreover the very distinction between broadcasters and audience may be blurred by the greater opportunities for access and do-it-yourself broadcasting which CR will provide. The whole process of radio production and presentation may well become 'de-professionalized', bringing with it new styles of address and concepts of programming. When we notice the small box in our car or kitchen, whose appearance is so unassuming yet whose present and future power seems so formidable even in this televisual age, the exuberance of Lord Reith's description seems more than ever apposite: it is, indeed, a miraculous toy.

BIBLIOGRAPHY

Appleyard, B. (1983) 'Is Neil Diamond Land still a shining success?', *The Times*, 21 November.

Bailey, K. V. (1957) *The Listening Schools*, London: British Broadcasting Corporation.

Barnes, J. (1983) 'Interviewer with the judo touch', *Observer*, 31 July.

Baron, M. (1975) *Independent Radio*, Lavenham: Dalton.

Barthes, R. (1977) *Image – Music – Text*, (trans.) S. Heath, Glasgow: Fontana.

Bates, A. W. (1976) 'The effectiveness of educational broadcasting in western Europe', *IET Papers on Broadcasting, No. 68*, Milton Keynes: Open University.

Bates, A. W. (1984) *Broadcasting in Education*, London: Constable.

BBC Annual Report and Handbook 1984 (1983) London: British Broadcasting Corporation.

BBC Annual Report and Handbook 1985 (1984) London: British Broadcasting Corporation.

BBC Handbook 1978 (1977) London: British Broadcasting Corporation.

Berelson, B. R., Lazarsfeld, P. F. and McPhee, W. N. (1971) 'Political processes: the role of the mass media', in Schramm, W. and Roberts, D. (eds) *The Process and Effects of Mass Communication*, Urbana, Ill: University of Illinois, revised edn.

Bernstein, B. (ed.) (1971) *Class, Codes and Control*, vol. 1, London: Routledge & Kegan Paul.

Black, P. (1972) *The Biggest Aspidistra in the World*, London: British Broadcasting Corporation.

Blumler, J. G. and Gurevitch, M. (1982) 'The political effects of mass communication', in Gurevitch, M., Bennett, T., Curran, J. and Woollacott, J. (eds) *Culture, Society and the Media*, London: Methuen.

Bridson, D. G. (1971) *Prospero and Ariel*, London: Gollancz.

Briggs, A. (1961) *The History of Broadcasting in the United Kingdom:*

Volume I – The Birth of Broadcasting, London: Oxford University Press.

Briggs, A. (1965) *The History of Broadcasting in the United Kingdom: Volume II – The Golden Age of Wireless*, London: Oxford University Press.

Briggs, A. (1970) *The History of Broadcasting in the United Kingdom: Volume III – The War of Words*, London: Oxford University Press.

Briggs, A. (1979) *The History of Broadcasting in the United Kingdom: Volume IV – Sound and Vision*, Oxford: Oxford University Press.

Briggs, A. (1985) *The BBC: The First Fifty Years*, Oxford: Oxford University Press.

Briggs, S. (1981a) *Those Radio Times*, London: Weidenfeld & Nicolson.

Briggs, S. (1981b) 'From cats' whiskers to cathode rays', *Sunday Times Magazine*, 16 August.

Broadcasting in the Seventies (1969) London: British Broadcasting Corporation.

Brooks, R. (1984a) 'French new wave', *Sunday Times*, 23 September.

Brooks, R. (1984b) 'The IBA loosens its grip on local radio', *Sunday Times*, 11 November.

Burgelin, O. (1972) 'Structural analysis and mass communication', in McQuail, D. (ed.) *The Sociology of Mass Communications*, Harmondsworth: Penguin.

Cardiff, D. (1980) 'The serious and the popular: aspects of the evolution of style in the radio talk, 1928–1939', *Media, Culture and Society*, 2.

Carey, J. W. and Kreiling, A. L. (1974) 'Popular culture and uses and gratifications', in Blumler, J. and Katz, E. (eds) *The Uses of Mass Communications*, London: Sage Publications.

Chaney, D. (1972) *Processes of Mass Communication*, London: Macmillan.

Cooper, E. and Jahoda, M. (1971) 'The evasion of propaganda: how prejudiced people respond to anti-prejudice propaganda', in Schramm, W. and Roberts, D. (eds) *The Process and Effects of Mass Communication*, Urbana, Ill: University of Illinois Press, revised edn.

Drakakis, J. (1981) Introduction to Drakakis, J. (ed.) *British Radio Drama*, Cambridge: Cambridge University Press.

Dyer, R. (1973) *Light Entertainment*, London: BFI Television Monograph, no. 2.

Elam, K. (1980) *The Semiotics of Theatre and Drama*, London: Methuen.

Elliott, P. (1974) 'Uses and gratifications research: a critique and a sociological alternative', in Blumler, J. and Katz, E. (eds) *The Uses of Mass Communications*, London: Sage Publications.

Ellis, J. (1982) *Visible Fictions*, London: Routledge & Kegan Paul.

Emmett, B. P. (1972) 'The television and radio audience in Britain', in McQuail, D. (ed.) *The Sociology of Mass Communications*, Harmondsworth: Penguin.

Esslin, M. (1980) *Mediations: Essays on Brecht, Beckett and the Media*, London:Eyre–Methuen.

Evans, E. (1977) *Radio: A Guide to Broadcasting Techniques*, London: Barrie & Jenkins.

Fink, H. (1981) 'The sponsor's v. the nation's choice: North American radio drama', in Lewis, P. (ed.) *Radio Drama*, London and New York: Longman.

Fiske, J. (1982) *An Introduction to Communication Studies*, London: Methuen.

Fiske, J. and Hartley, J. (1978) *Reading Television*, London: Methuen.

Freidson, E. (1971) 'Communications research and the concept of the mass', in Schramm, W. and Roberts, D. (eds) *The Process and Effects of Mass Communication*, Urbana, Ill: University of Illinois Press, revised edn.

Gielgud, V. (1957) *British Radio Drama, 1922–1956*, London: Harrap.

Gillard, F. (1964) *Sound Radio in the Television Age*, BBC Lunch-time Lectures, second series, no. 6.

Goffman, E. (1980) 'The radio drama frame', in Corner, J. and Hawthorn, J. (eds) *Communication Studies*, London: Edward Arnold.

Goffman, E. (1981) *Forms of Talk*, Oxford: Basil Blackwell.

Goldhamer, H. (1971) 'The social effects of communication technology', in Schramm, W. and Roberts, D. (eds) *The Process and Effects of Mass Communication*, Urbana, Ill: University of Illinois Press, revised edn.

Golding, P. (1974) *The Mass Media*, London: Longman.

Gray, F. (1981) 'The nature of radio drama', in Lewis, P. (ed.) *Radio Drama*, London and New York: Longman.

Gregory, M. and Carroll, S. (1978) *Language and Situation*, London: Routledge & Kegan Paul.

Harris, P. (1970) *When Pirates Ruled the Waves*, London and Aberdeen: Impulse Books, fourth edn.

Hartley, J. (1982) *Understanding News*, London: Methuen.

Hawkes, T. (1977) *Structuralism and Semiotics*, London: Methuen.

Herbert, J. (1976) *The Techniques of Radio Journalism*, London: Adam & Charles Black.

Hewson, D. (1984) 'Breaks we don't want', *The Times*, 3 November.

Higgins, C. S. and Moss, P. D. (1982) *Sounds Real: Radio in Everyday Life*, St Lucia: University of Queensland Press.

Hobson, D. (1980) 'Housewives and the mass media', in Hall. S., Hobson, D., Lowe, A. and Willis, P. (eds) *Culture, Media, Language*, London: Hutchinson.

Hobson, D. (1982) *Crossroads: The Drama of a Soap Opera*, London: Methuen.

Hood, S. (1975) *Radio and Television*, Newton Abbot: David & Charles.

Introduction to Further Education Broadcasts (1977) London: British Broadcasting Corporation.

Introduction to School Broadcasts (1978) London: British Broadcasting Corporation.

Jakobson, R. (1960) 'Closing statement: linguistics and poetics', in

Sebeok, T. A. (ed.) *Style in Language*, Cambridge, Mass: Massachusetts Institute of Technology Press.

Johnstone, J. W. C. (1974) 'Social integration and mass media use among adolescents: a case study', in Blumler, J. and Katz, E. (eds) *The Uses of Mass Communications*, London: Sage Publications.

Katz, E., Gurevitch, M. and Haas, H. (1973) 'On the use of mass media for important things', *American Sociological Review*, 38.

Katz, E., Blumler, J. and Gurevitch, M. (1974) 'Utilization of mass communication by the individual', in Blumler, J. and Katz, E. (eds) *The Uses of Mass Communications*, London: Sage Publications.

Kumar, K. (1977) 'Holding the middle ground: the BBC, the public and the professional broadcaster', in Curran, J., Gurevitch, M. and Woollacott, J. (eds) *Mass Communication and Society*, London: Edward Arnold.

Lazarsfeld, P. F. and Merton, R. K. (1971) 'Mass communication, popular taste and organized social action', in Schramm, W. and Roberts, D. (eds) *The Process and Effects of Mass Communication*, Urbana, Ill: University of Illinois Press, revised edn.

Lewis, P. (1981a) Introduction to Lewis, P. (ed.) *Radio Drama*, London and New York: Longman.

Lewis, P. (1981b) 'The radio road to Llareggub', in Drakakis, J. (ed.) *British Radio Drama*, Cambridge: Cambridge University Press.

Lowery, S. and De Fleur, M. L. (1983) *Milestones in Mass Communication Research: Media Effects*, New York and London: Longman.

McLeish, R. (1978) *The Technique of Radio Production*, London: Focal Press.

McLeod, J. M. and Becker, L. B. (1974) 'Testing the validity of gratification measures through political effects analysis', in Blumler, J. and Katz, E. (eds) *The Uses of Mass Communications*, London: Sage Publications.

McLuhan, M. (1967) *Understanding Media*, London: Sphere.

MacNeice, L. (1964) Introduction to *The Dark Tower*, London: Faber & Faber.

McQuail, D. (1972) Introduction to McQuail, D. (ed.) *The Sociology of Mass Communications*, Harmondsworth: Penguin.

McQuail, D. (1977) 'The influence and effects of mass media', in Curran, J., Gurevitch, M. and Woollacott, J. (eds) *Mass Communication and Society*, London: Edward Arnold.

McQuail, D. (1983) *Mass Communication Theory*, London: Sage Publications.

McQuail, D. and Windahl, S. (1981) *Communication Models for the Study of Mass Communications*, London and New York: Longman.

McWhinnie, D. (1959) *The Art of Radio*, London: Faber & Faber.

Mendelsohn, H. (1964) 'Listening to radio', in Dexter, L. A. and White, D. M. (eds) *People, Society, and Mass Communications*, Glencoe: Free Press.

Mendelsohn, H. (1974) 'Some policy implications of the uses and gratifications paradigm', in Blumler, J. and Katz, E. (eds) *The Uses of Mass Communication*, London: Sage Publications.

Milligan, S. (1972) *The Goon Show Scripts*, London: Woburn Press.

Milligan, S. (1974) *More Goon Show Scripts*, London: Sphere.

Moorehead, C. (1983) 'The popular sound of intellect', *The Times*, 13 October.

Murdock, G. (1981) 'Organising the imagination: sociological perspectives on radio drama', in Lewis, P. (ed.) *Radio Drama*, London and New York: Longman.

Murdock, G. and Golding, P. (1977) 'Capitalism, communication and class relations', in Curran, J., Gurevitch, M. and Woollacott, J. (eds) *Mass Communication and Society*, London: Edward Arnold.

Nathan, D. (1971) *The Laughtermakers*, London: Peter Owen.

O'Donnell, W. and Todd, L. (1980) *Variety in Contemporary English*, London: George Allen & Unwin.

Ong. W. (1982) *Orality and Literacy*, London and New York: Methuen.

Open University Broadcast and Assignment Calendar 1983 (1982) Milton Keynes: Open University.

Palmer, R. (1947) *School Broadcasting in Britain*, London: British Broadcasting Corporation.

Paulu, B. (1956) *British Broadcasting: Radio and Television in the United Kingdom*, Minneapolis, Minn: University of Minnesota Press.

Paulu, B. (1961) *British Broadcasting in Transition*, Minneapolis, Minn: University of Minnesota Press.

Paulu, B. (1981) *Television and Radio in the United Kingdom*, London: Macmillan.

Pear, T. H. (1931) *Voice and Personality*, London: Chapman & Hall.

Pegg, M. (1983) *Broadcasting and Society, 1918–1939*, London and Canberra: Croom Helm.

Peirce, C. S. (1960) *Collected Papers*, vols I and II, (eds) Hartshorne, C. and Weiss, P., Cambridge, Mass: Harvard University Press.

Priessnitz, H. (1981) 'British radio drama: a survey', in Lewis, P. (ed.) *Radio Drama*, London and New York: Longman.

Raban, J. (1981) 'Icon or symbol: the writer and the "medium"', in Lewis, P. (ed.) *Radio Drama*, London and New York: Longman.

Raphael, F. (1980) 'The language of television', in Michaels, L. and Ricks, C. (eds) *The State of the Language*, London: University of California Press.

Roberts, D. F. (1971a) 'The nature of communication effects', in Schramm, W. and Roberts, D. (eds) *The Process and Effects of Mass Communication*, Urbana, Ill: University of Illinois Press, revised edn.

Roberts, D. F. (1971b) 'Social consequences of mass communications', in Schramm, W. and Roberts, D. (eds) *The Process and Effects of Mass Communication*, Urbana, Ill: University of Illinois Press, revised edn.

Rodger, I. (1982) *Radio Drama*, London: Macmillan.

227

Rosengren, K. E. (1974) 'Uses and gratifications: a paradigm outlined' in Blumler, J. and Katz, E. (eds) *The Uses of Mass Communications*, London: Sage Publications.

Scannell, P. and Cardiff, D. (1982) 'Serving the nation: public service broadcasting before the war', in Waites, B., Bennett, T. and Martin, G. (eds) *Popular Culture: Past and Present*, London: Croom Helm.

Scholes, R. (1982) *Semiotics and Interpretation*, New Haven, Conn. and London: Yale University Press.

Schramm, W. (1971) 'The nature of communication between humans', in Schramm, W. and Roberts, D. (eds) *The Process and Effects of Mass Communication*, Urbana, Ill: University of Illinois Press, revised edn.

Scupham, J. (1967) *Broadcasting and the Community*, London: C. A. Watts.

Sieveking, L. (1934) *The Stuff of Radio*, London: Cassell.

Silvey, R. (1970) 'Reflections on the impact of broadcasting', in Tunstall, J. (ed.) *Media Sociology*, London: Constable.

Silvey, R. (1974) *Who's Listening?*, London: George Allen & Unwin.

Silvey, R. (1978) 'The intelligibility of broadcast talks', in Davison, P., Meyersohn, R. and Shils, E. (eds) *Literary Taste, Culture and Mass Communication: Volume IX – Uses of Literacy; Media*, Cambridge: Chadwyck-Healey.

Smith, A. (ed.) (1974) *British Broadcasting*, Newton Abbot: David & Charles.

Smith, A. (1976) *The Shadow in the Cave*, London: Quartet Books, revised edn.

Smythe, D. W. (1972) 'Some observations on communications theory', in McQuail, D. (ed.) *The Sociology of Mass Communications*, Harmondsworth: Penguin.

Snagge, J. and Barsley, M. (1972) *Those Vintage Years of Radio*, London: Pitman.

Took, B. (1976) *Laughter in the Air*, London: Robson Books/British Broadcasting Corporation.

Trethowan, I. (1970) *Radio in the Seventies*, BBC Lunch-time Lectures, eighth series, no. 4.

Wade, D. (1981a) 'Popular radio drama', in Lewis, P. (ed.) *Radio Drama*, London and New York: Longman.

Wade, D. (1981b) 'British radio drama since 1960' in Drakakis, J. (ed.) *British Radio Drama*, Cambridge: Cambridge University Press.

Wade, D. (1983a) 'Chat is going up the charts', *The Times*, 8 January.

Wade, D. (1983b) 'Topical sense', *The Times*, 8 October.

Wade, D. (1984a) 'Can something different save Radio 4?', *The Times*, 6 April.

Wade, D. (1984b) 'All in the mind', *The Times*, 17 November.

Waugh, P. (1984) *Metafiction*, London: Methuen.

Webster, P. (1984) 'Radio concessions to beat pirates', *The Times*, 9 August.

Williams, R. (1974) *Television: Technology and Cultural Form*, Glasgow: Fontana.

Wilmut, R. (1976) *The Goon Show Companion*, London: Robson Books.

Wilmut, R. (1980) *From Fringe to Flying Circus*, London: Book Club Associates.

INDEX